THE JOTUNN WAR

IAN STUART
SHARPE

DEVMALYA
PRAMANIK

GER
CURTI

PAUL
LITTLE

ED
DUKESHIRE

VIKINGVERSE
GRAPHIC NOVEL

THE JOTUNN WAR

CREATED & WRITTEN BY: IAN STUART **SHARPE**

PENCILS & INKS BY: DEVMALYA **PRAMANIK** (ISSUES 01-03)

GER **CURTI** (ISSUE 04)

COLORS BY: PAUL **LITTLE**

LETTERS BY: ED **DUKESHIRE**

EDITED BY: ALANA JOLI **ABBOTT**

BOOK DESIGN BY: JEREMY D. **MOHLER**

LOGO DESIGN BY: SHAWN T. **KING**

COVER BY: JEREMY D. **MOHLER**

WWW.VIKINGVERSE.COM

OUTLAND ENTERTAINMENT

Jeremy D. Mohler
Publisher & Creative Director
Alana Joli Abbot
Editor in Chief

3119 Gillham Road
Kansas City, MO 64109 USA
Phone. 785.640.4324
Email. jeremy@outlandentertainment.com

WWW.OUTLANDENTERTAINMENT.COM

THE JÖTUNN WAR: A VIKINGVERSE GRAPHIC NOVEL
First Printing. Published by Outland Entertainment LLC, 3119 Gillham Road, Kansas City, MO 64109, USA.

INTRODUCTION

Standið upp, jötnar

When Thrym, the þursa dróttinn or lord of thurses addresses his people, he roars, "Stand up, giants!". If you are reading this, you are a jötunn among men (or a skessa among women!). So, stand up. Take a bow. Give yourself a round of applause. We Kickstarted four issues of this comic!

The first Kickstarter campaign launched in March 2019 at a local Comic Con in British Columbia. I sat opposite Jordan Stratford, the author of the "Wollstonecraft Detective Agency" books (and, since then, *Winter by Winter*, a novel about legendary Viking shield maiden Hladgertha). Jordan describes our hometown as "rumbling colonial capital on a windswept Pacific island, populated predominantly by octogenarians and carnivorous gulls." Suffice it to say, not many of the early birds were comic fans, but the raven banner carried the day, and *Jötunn War* Issue 1 was funded!

The actual scripts were all written well in advance, and so at first, there was an orderly procession to each release. The second campaign began in the October of the same year, and the third in February 2020.

And then COVID struck. I remember being at the Jorvík Viking Festival for the launch of the third comic (something Jordan and I billed as the Vinland Invasion—a kind of reverse Leif Erikson voyage, mixed with a little Beatles). It was just as news of the first wave of Italian cases hit the news and flying back to Canada felt like surfing a tsunami. Shipping the comic to backers became quite difficult—postal services either shut down or only delivered after massive delays.

Everyone had more important things to worry about than the Vikingverse—and rightly so. But the world turned, nonetheless. Our original artist, Dev Pramanik moved on to the staggeringly successful *Dune: House Atreides*, and we lost a second to pandemic pandemonium. Luckily, at the start of 2021, the talented Ger Curti unfurled his Sky Blossom and leapt into the fray, helping us conclude our saga.

Our protagonist's game of köttur and mús actually begins in the novel, the *All Father Paradox*. That story touches on the Jötunn War but can't really do it justice. The comics were designed to sit alongside the book andtell a new chapter in a more vivid and visceral way. I'm fascinated to hear from those who have read both as to whether you put all the pieces of the puzzle together!

So, a big, giant-sized thanks to all who supported this project and unleashed the jötnar on an unsuspecting public. It was a titanic struggle, but it wasn't quite the end of the world. We're saving that for the next project...

Who are the Jötnar?

"In the beginning God created the heaven and the earth."

See, that's where the Christianity has it all wrong. All good Vikings knew the real story of how it all really began. The same way it will all end.

With giants.

Ginnungagap was the great emptiness before there was the world, flanked by two inhospitable realms. There was Muspelheim, crossed by endless rivers of boiling poison and vast lakes of fire; and Niflheim, where icy volcanoes spewed forth frozen mists and arctic waters. Sparks and smoke met layers of rime and frost in the yawning void and from them came the first being.

A Jötunn, Ymir, appeared in the melting ice. From his sweat, the first Jötnar were born. Ymir fed on the milk of the primeval cow Auðumbla, also born of the melt-water. She licked the blocks of salty ice, releasing Búri, who was large, powerful, and beautiful to behold.

In time, Búri's son Borr had three sons: the gods Óðinn, Vili, and Vé. The three sons of Borr had no use for Ymir and his growing family of cruel and brutish giants, so they attacked and killed him. So much blood flowed from the body that it drowned all the other giants except for two—Bergelmir and his wife escaped. They stole away in a hollowed-out tree trunk, a makeshift boat floating on the sea of gore to safety, to a land they named Jötunheim, home of the giants.

From Ymir's body, the brothers made the world of humans: his blood, the seas and lakes; his flesh, the earth; his bones, the mountains; and his teeth, the rocks. From his skull, they made the dome of the sky, setting a dwarf at each of the four corners to hold it high above the earth. They protected the world from the Jötnar with a wall made from Ymir's eyebrows. Next, they caused time to exist and placed the orbs of the sun and moon in chariots, which were to circle around the sky.

Finally, the three brothers built their own realm: Ásgarð, a mighty stronghold, with green plains and shining palaces high over Miðgarð. They built the rainbow bridge Bifröst to link the realms. The Æsir, the guardians of men, crossed over the bridge and settled in Ásgarð.

There the gods would dwell, ever vigilant, until Ragnarok, the long-heralded last battle, when the monstrous Jötnar set about destroying the entire cosmos. Fenrir, the great wolf, consumes the world so swiftly that even the sun is dragged from its zenith and into the beast's stomach.

The Jötnar have a pivotal role in Norse mythology. To the men of the North, the Jötnar had the power of oncoming storms, roaring volcanoes, and the clamorous oceans—in some sense, they were the personification of the merciless and indifferent power of Nature. They were the sires of the gods, their spouses and lovers, their constant foes, and their inevitable doom.

And while the Jötnar are described as a race of beings distinct from the gods—as well as other creatures such as humans, elves, and dwarves—they are somewhat ambiguously described, both in their physique and their character. Some jötnar, such as Skrymir (who is known also as Útgarða-Loki), are depicted as being of an immense size, thus giving rise to the translation of the word "jötunn" into English as "giant."

Some jötnar, such as Skaði, were said to be extremely beautiful—in the Poetic Edda poem Grímnismál, Odin mentions the "ancient courts" of Þrymheimr, noting that the jötunn Þjazi once lived there, and that now his daughter Skaði does. Odin refers to Skaði as "the shining bride of the gods" and in some tales, the pair go on to marry and give birth to nations of kings. Some scholars go so far as to suggest that Scandinavia may be related to the name Skaði (potentially meaning "Skaði's island").

Other Jötnar were hideous. It is told in Snorri Sturluson's Gylfaginning that at Baldr's funeral his wife Nanna died of grief and was placed alongside him on his pyre. Hringhorni, Baldr's ship, was the largest of all such vessels and was to serve as the god's funeral ship. No one, however, could seem to launch the boat out to sea. The gods then enlisted the help of Hyrrokkin ("fire-withered"), who came from Jötunheimr, arriving on a giant wolf with vipers as reins. When she dismounted, Odin summoned four berserks to look after the animal, but they were unable to control it without first rendering it unconscious. With her seismic strength, the giantess rolled the boat into the water.

In the Vikingverse, these stories and characters are more than just ancient myth. In the way that the Bible forms the daily bread of manydevout Christians, the Jötnar are part of the fabric of society and its belief system.

Let me give you an example:

We were all horrified by the 2019 fire at Notre Dame. Social media was full of people's personal memories, their own connection with the great stone cathedral and all and relics. We felt all felt a sense of profound loss. Suddenly, the Gargoyles on the roof were leering out of memory, all across the internet. Not bad for a beast used by the Catholic Church to illustrate evil.

French legend tells of St. Romanus, bishop of Rouen, who delivered the country from a monster called Gargouille. La Gargouille is said to have been the typical dragon with bat-like wings, a long neck, and the ability to breathe fire from its mouth. Multiple versions of the story are given, either that St.

Romanus subdued the creature with a crucifix, or he captured the creature with the help of the only volunteer, a condemned man. In each, the monster is led back to Rouen and burned, but its head and neck would not burn due to being tempered by its own fire breath. The head was then mounted on the walls of the newly built church to scare off evil spirits and used for protection.

The parallels with the Jötnar are clear. Primeval, indefatigable titans who tread heavily in our nightmares, the bane of Christianity. Demons to be defeated and cast into the Abyss. Trophies to be mounted on the wall of our proud monuments.

Now imagine a world where Christianity had been put to the Viking sword, where there was no Mother Church left to determine who was a saint and who was a sinner, no Catholic priests to stem the pagan tide and contain the wild, untrammelled beliefs of the Northerners. Forget Armageddon, Hellfire, and the Antichrist. The world doesn't end with a bang, or a whimper. It ends with a horde of unstoppable Jötnar.

If you want a truly terrifying End of Days, embrace your inner Viking and read the *Jötunn War*.

--Ian Stuart Sharpe
May, 2021

AIDED BY KITH AND KIN

ACROSS THE WIDE LANDS WHICH REST BENEATH OUR SHIELD,
WE HAVE ADVANCED TO RESCUE NOT ONLY THE NÍU HEIMAR BUT
MANKIND FROM THE FOULEST AND MOST HAMR-TWISTING TYRANNY
WHICH HAS EVER STAINED THE PAGES OF HISTORY.

BE YE MEN OF DRENGR,
AND BE IN READINESS FOR THE CONFLICT;

FOR IT IS BETTER FOR
US TO PERISH IN BATTLE THAN
TO LOOK UPON THE OUTRAGE
TO OUR EMPIRE AND
OUR HÖRGAR.

ARM YOURSELVES

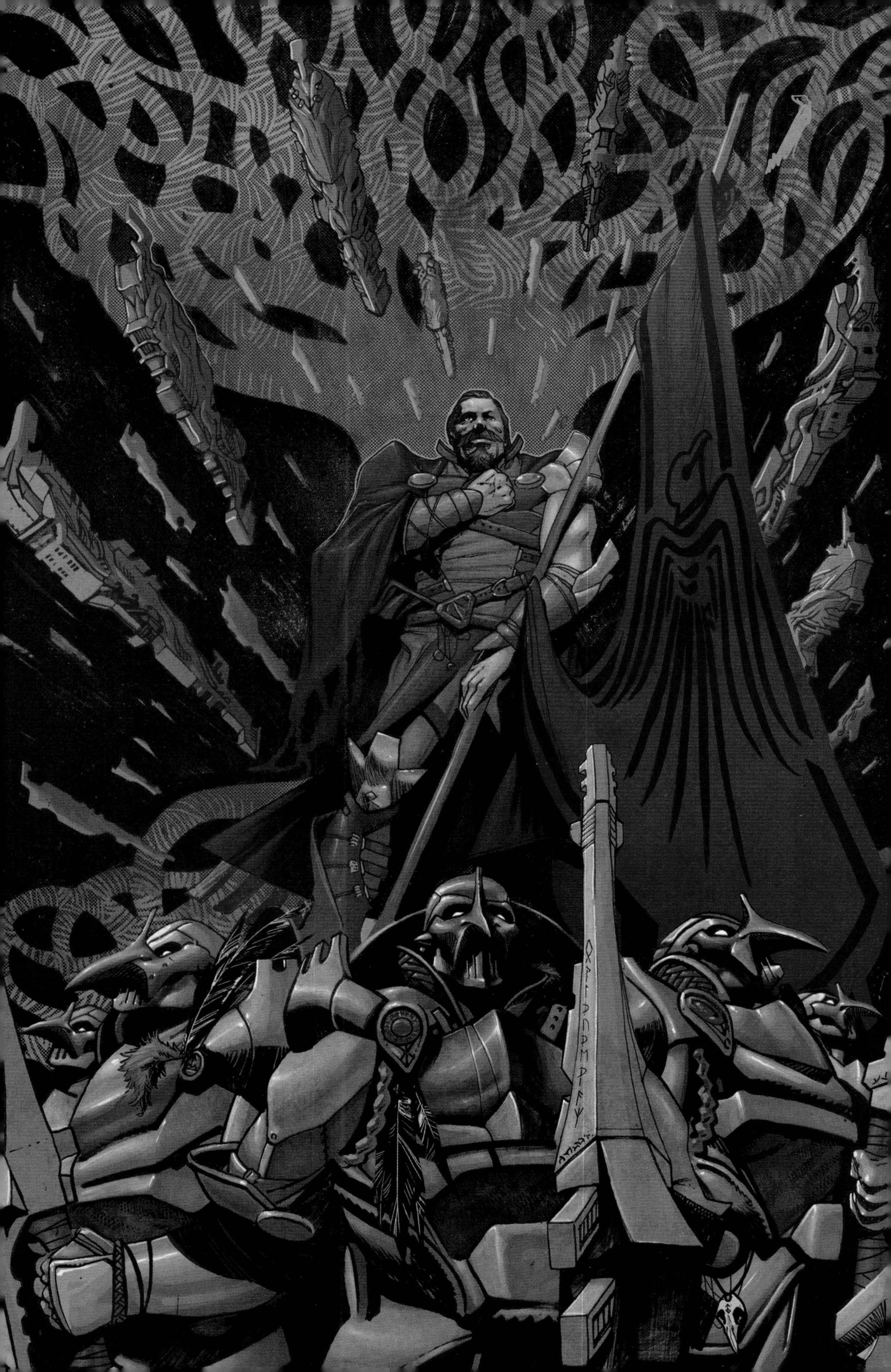

THIS TAKES ME BACK.

I USED TO LIE UNDER THE CONSTELLATIONS, AS A BOY. I'D WATCH THE LEIDANG AND DREAM OF RAIDING FOREIGN SHORES.

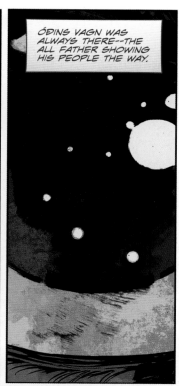

ÓÐINS VAGN WAS ALWAYS THERE--THE ALL FATHER SHOWING HIS PEOPLE THE WAY.

BUT I'M GETTING OLD.

AS OLD AS THE HILLS.

NOW I ONLY DREAM OF DEATH.

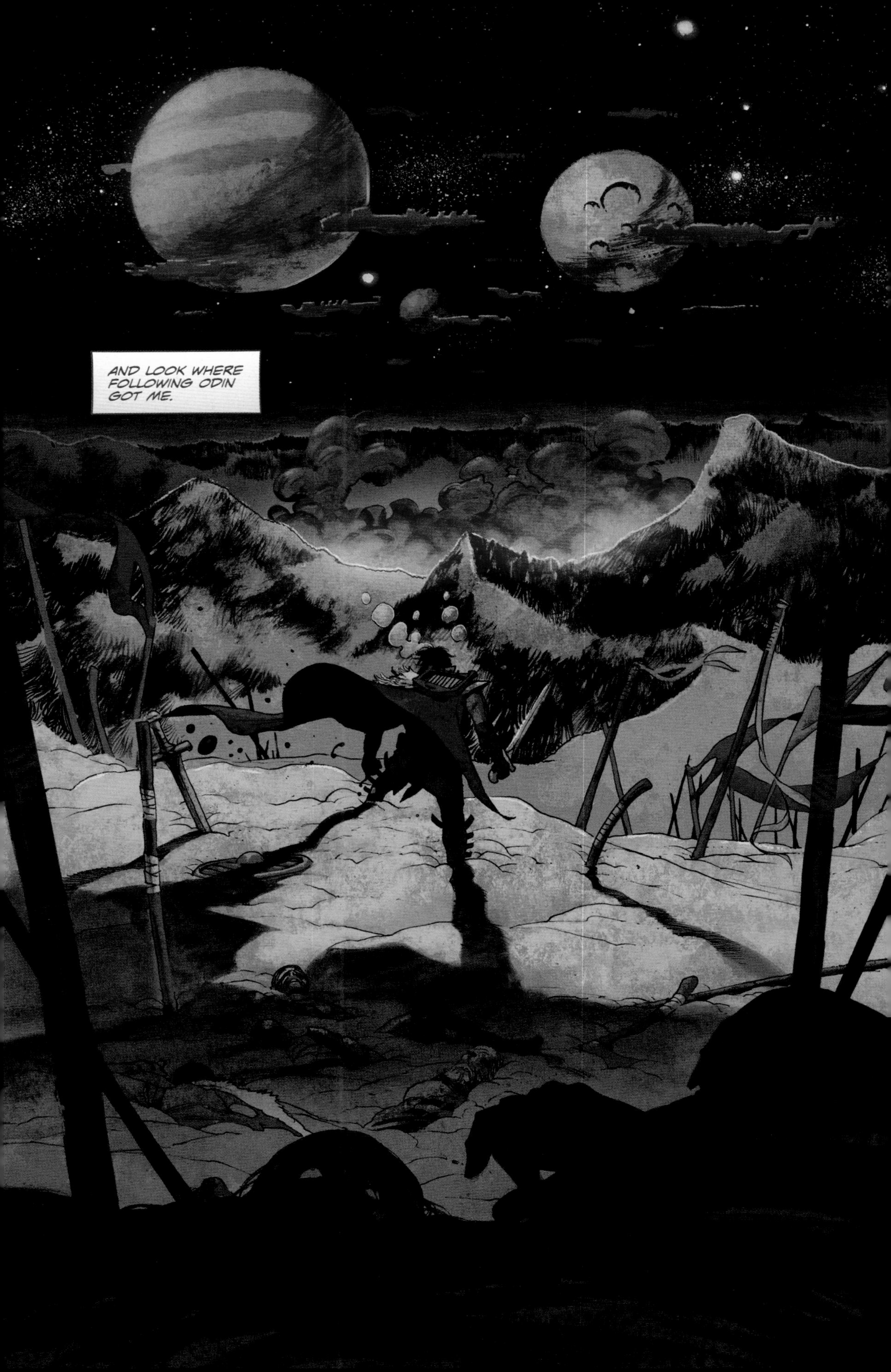
AND LOOK WHERE FOLLOWING ODIN GOT ME.

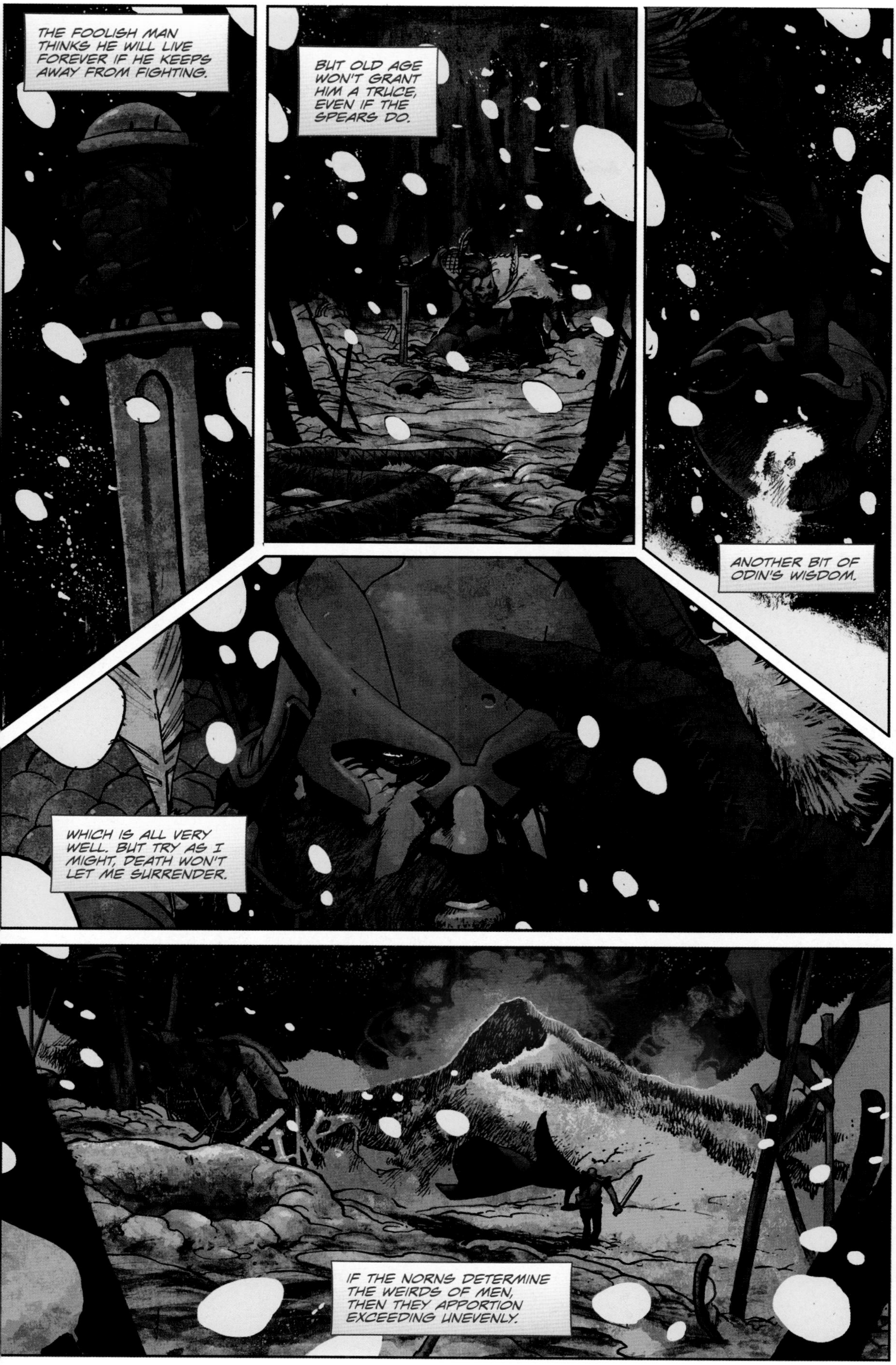
THE FOOLISH MAN THINKS HE WILL LIVE FOREVER IF HE KEEPS AWAY FROM FIGHTING.
BUT OLD AGE WON'T GRANT HIM A TRUCE, EVEN IF THE SPEARS DO.
ANOTHER BIT OF ODIN'S WISDOM.
WHICH IS ALL VERY WELL. BUT TRY AS I MIGHT, DEATH WON'T LET ME SURRENDER.
IF THE NORNS DETERMINE THE WEIRDS OF MEN, THEN THEY APPORTION EXCEEDING UNEVENLY.

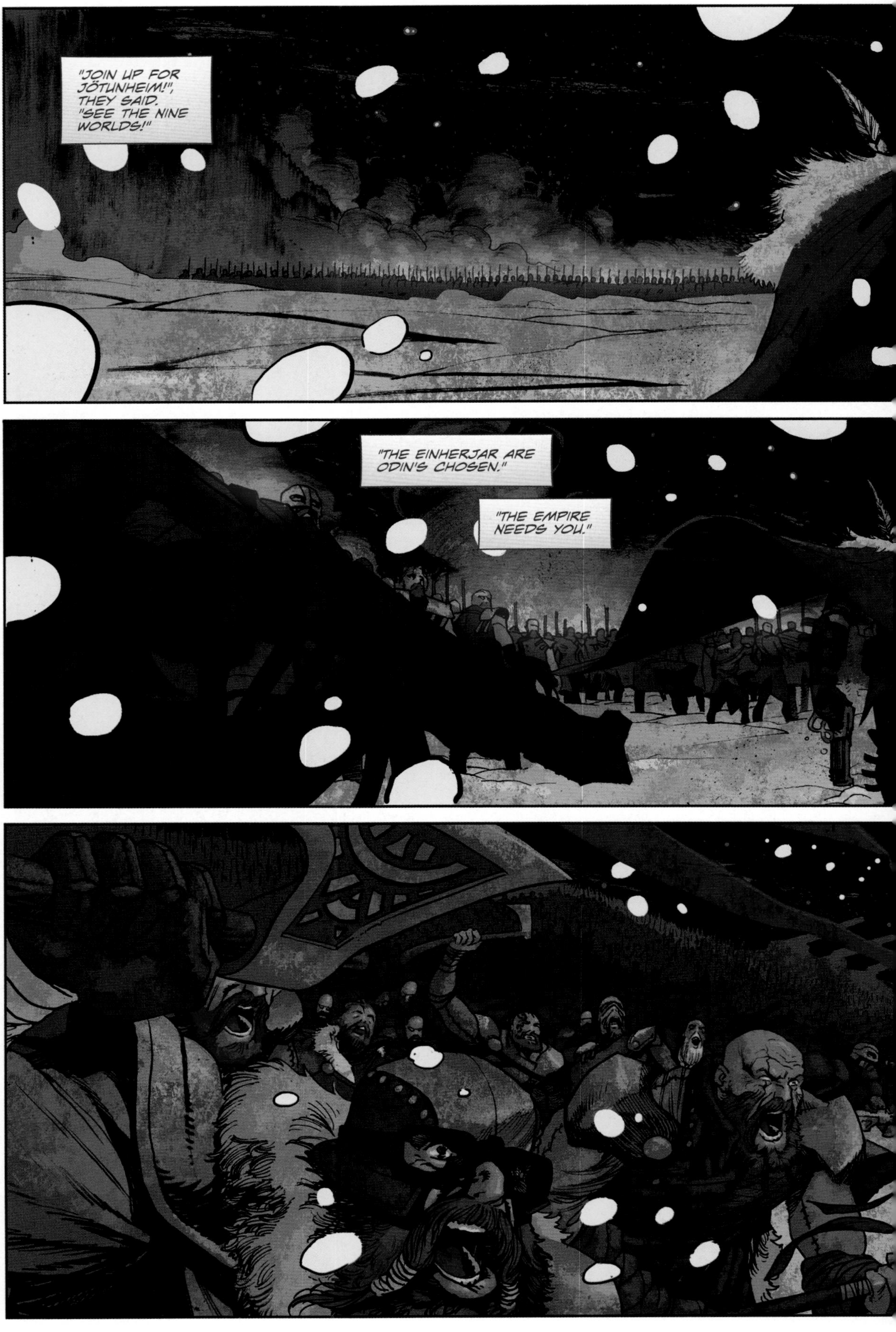
"JOIN UP FOR JÖTUNHEIM!", THEY SAID. "SEE THE NINE WORLDS!"
"THE EINHERJAR ARE ODIN'S CHOSEN."
"THE EMPIRE NEEDS YOU."

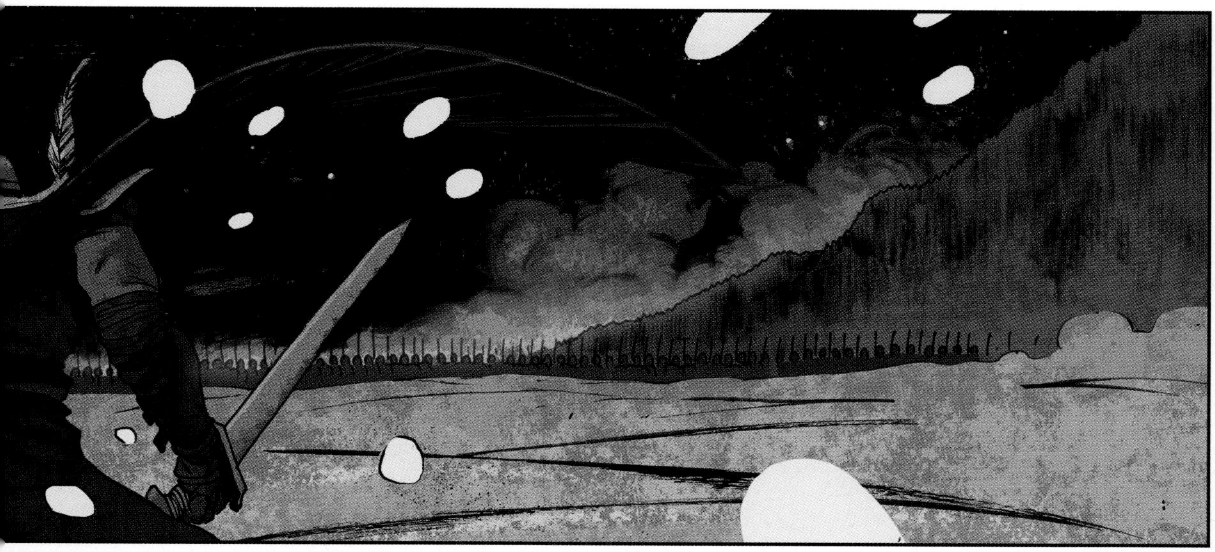

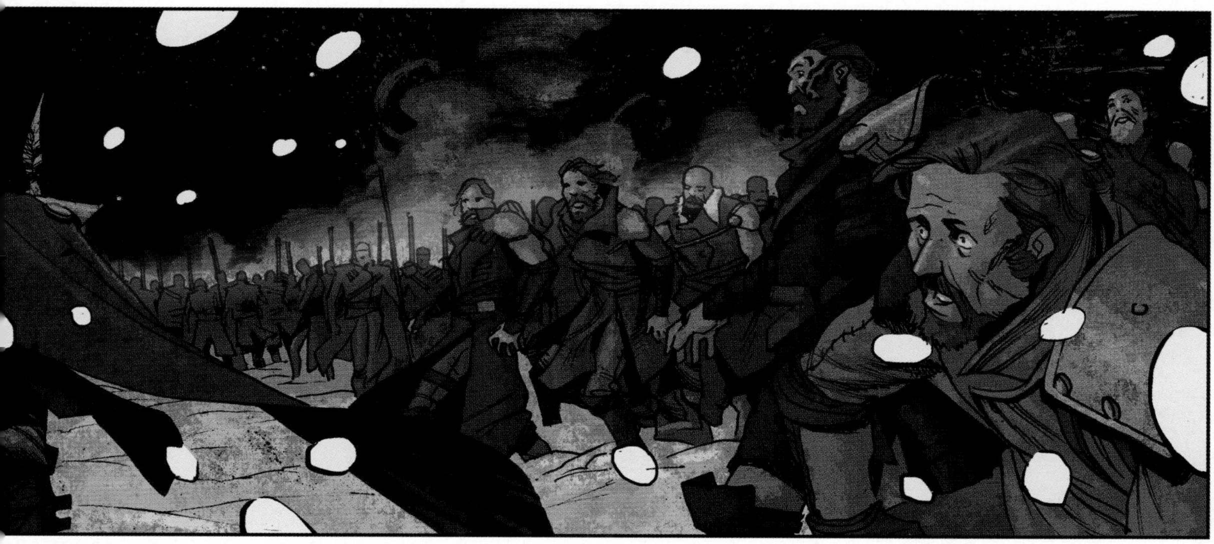

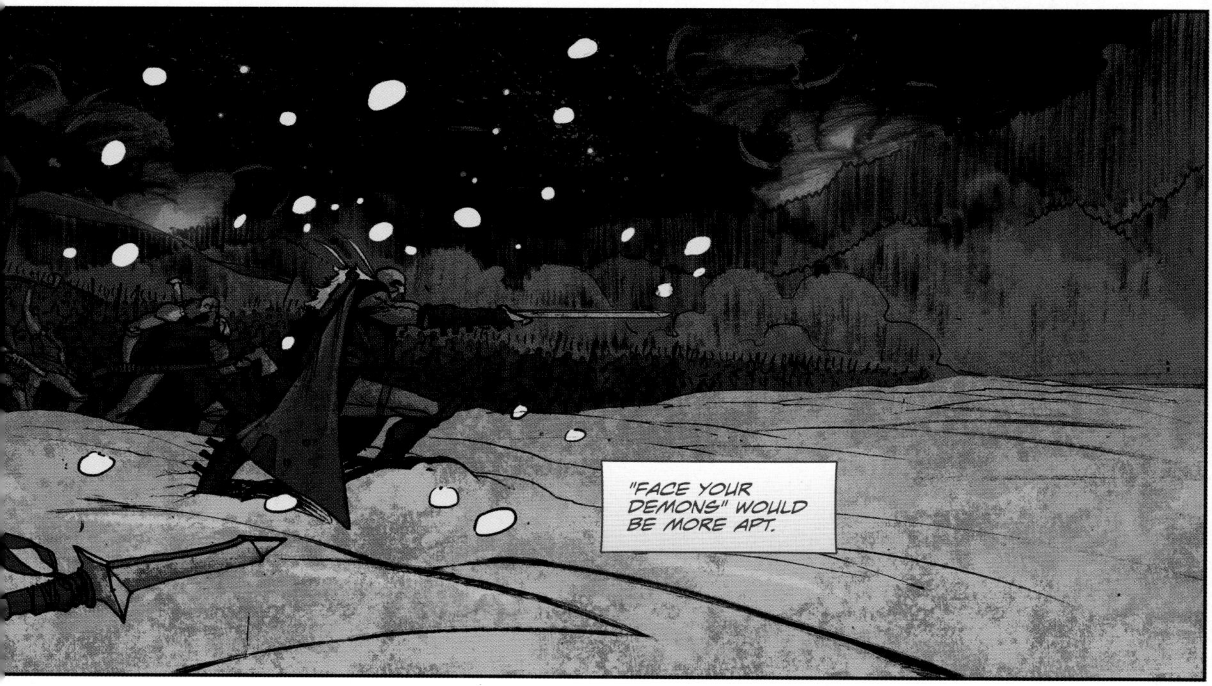
"FACE YOUR DEMONS" WOULD BE MORE APT.

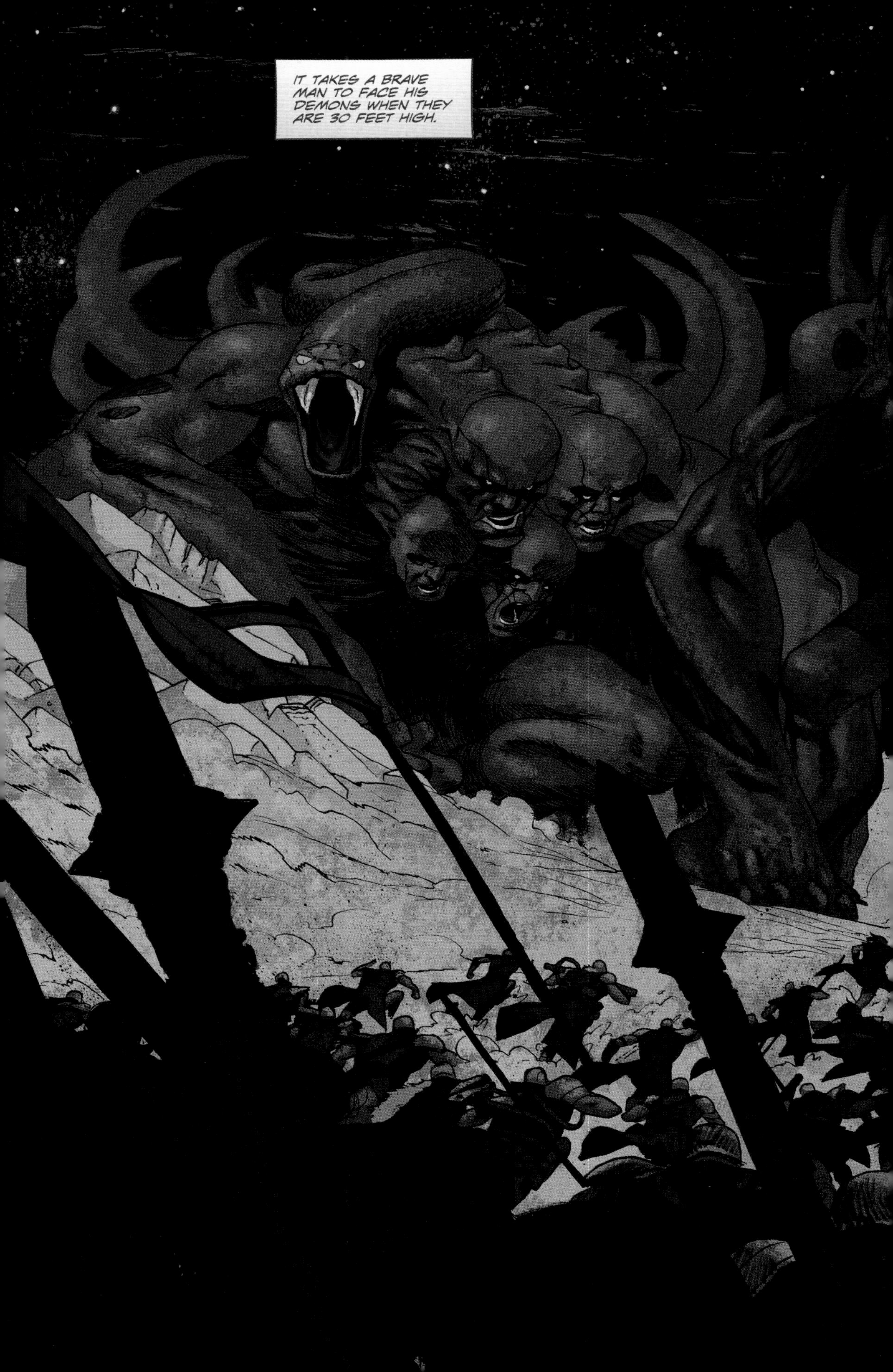
IT TAKES A BRAVE MAN TO FACE HIS DEMONS WHEN THEY ARE 30 FEET HIGH.

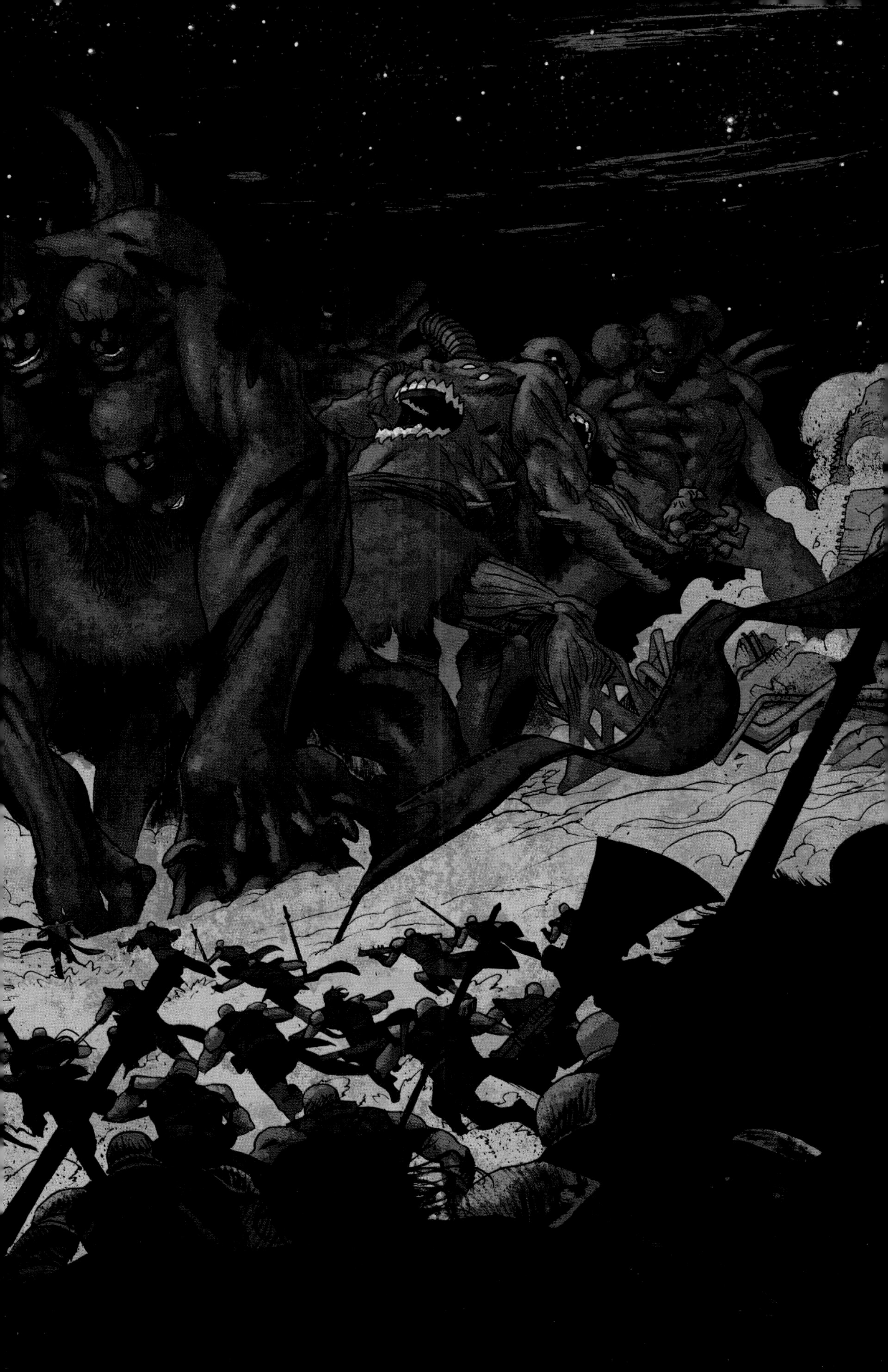

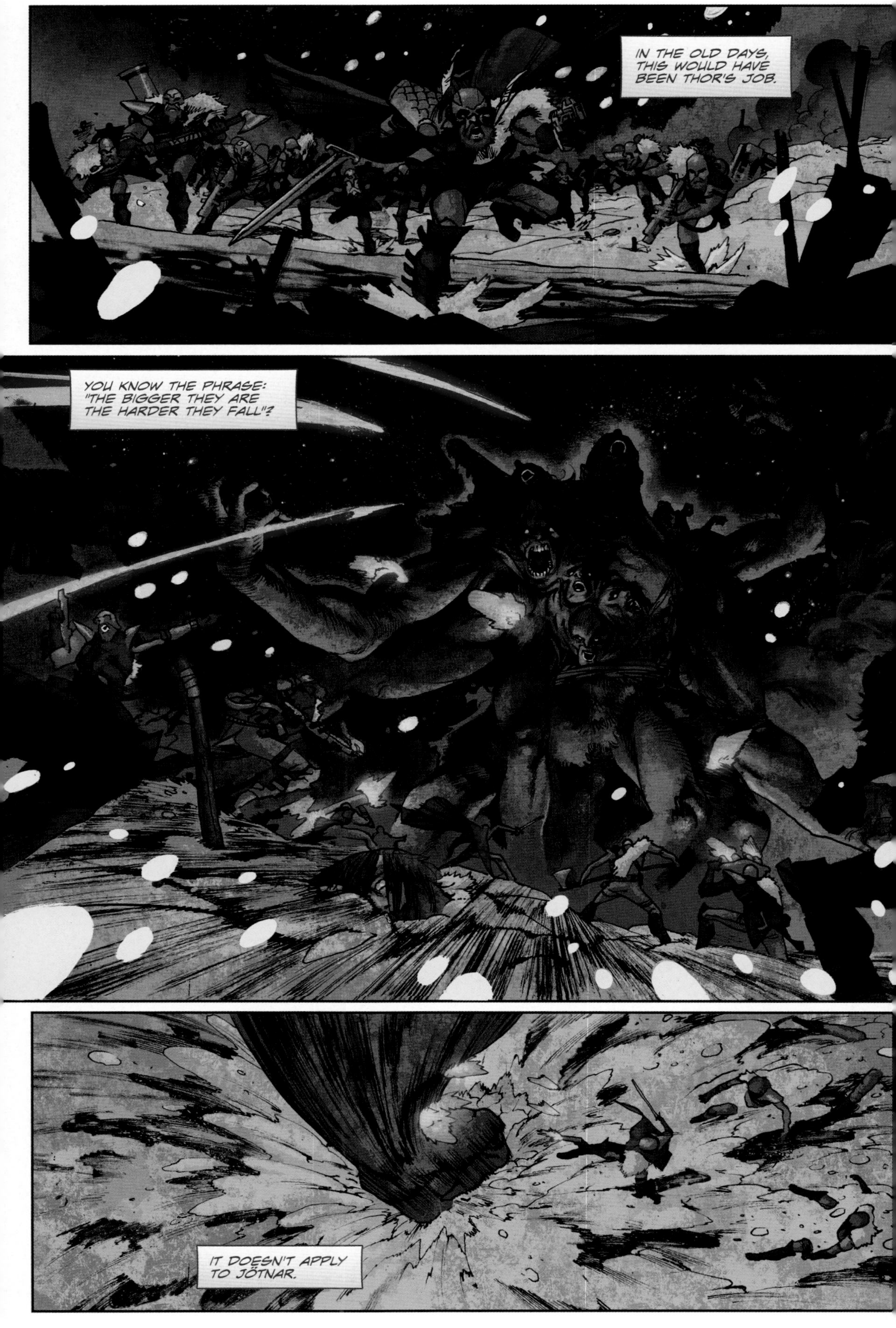
IN THE OLD DAYS, THIS WOULD HAVE BEEN THOR'S JOB.
YOU KNOW THE PHRASE: "THE BIGGER THEY ARE THE HARDER THEY FALL"?
IT DOESN'T APPLY TO JÖTNAR.

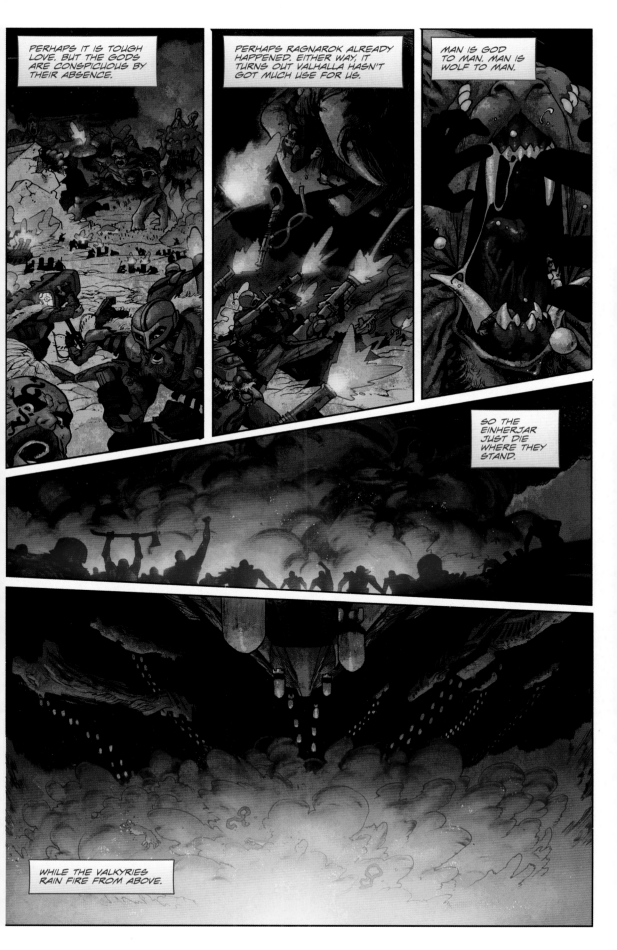

PERHAPS IT IS TOUGH LOVE. BUT THE GODS ARE CONSPICUOUS BY THEIR ABSENCE.

PERHAPS RAGNAROK ALREADY HAPPENED. EITHER WAY, IT TURNS OUT VALHALLA HASN'T GOT MUCH USE FOR US.

MAN IS GOD TO MAN. MAN IS WOLF TO MAN.

SO THE EINHERJAR JUST DIE WHERE THEY STAND.

WHILE THE VALKYRIES RAIN FIRE FROM ABOVE.

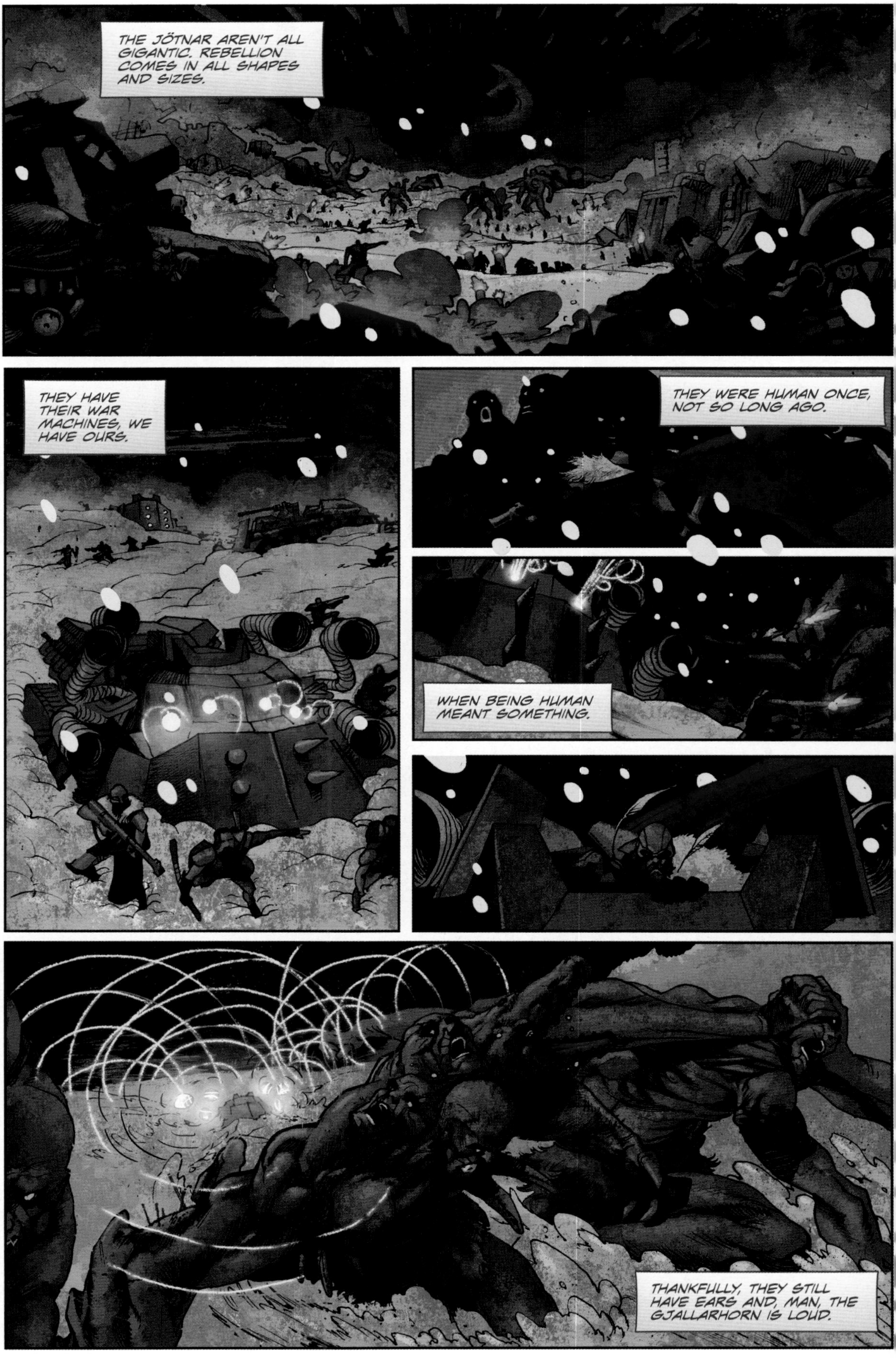
THE JÖTNAR AREN'T ALL GIGANTIC. REBELLION COMES IN ALL SHAPES AND SIZES.
THEY HAVE THEIR WAR MACHINES, WE HAVE OURS.
THEY WERE HUMAN ONCE, NOT SO LONG AGO.
WHEN BEING HUMAN MEANT SOMETHING.
THANKFULLY, THEY STILL HAVE EARS AND, MAN, THE GJALLARHORN IS LOUD.

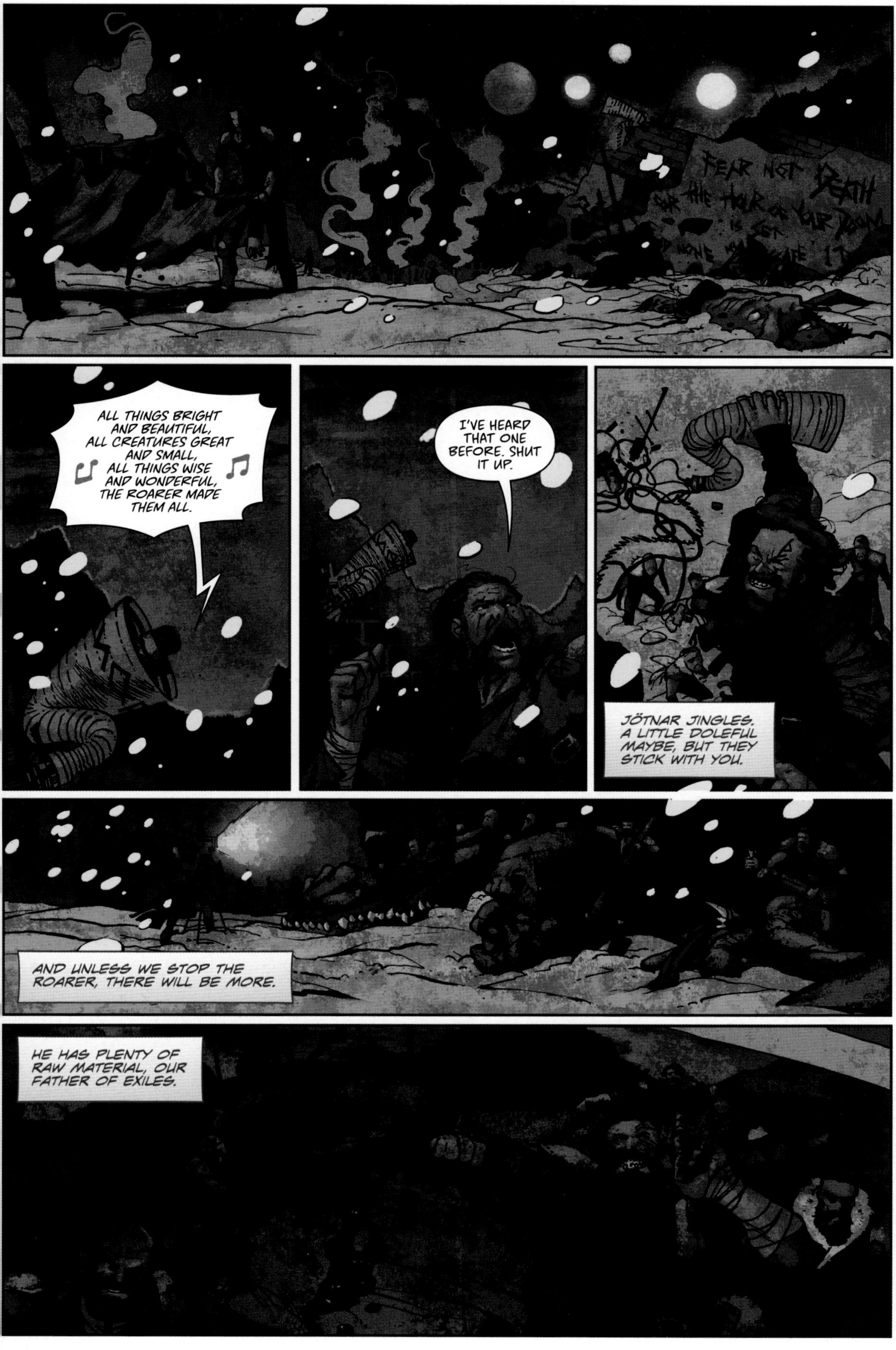
FEAR NOT DEATH
THE HOUR OF YOUR DOOM
IS SET
ALL THINGS BRIGHT AND BEAUTIFUL, ALL CREATURES GREAT AND SMALL, ALL THINGS WISE AND WONDERFUL, THE ROARER MADE THEM ALL.
I'VE HEARD THAT ONE BEFORE. SHUT IT UP.
JÖTNAR JINGLES. A LITTLE DOLEFUL MAYBE, BUT THEY STICK WITH YOU.
AND UNLESS WE STOP THE ROARER, THERE WILL BE MORE.
HE HAS PLENTY OF RAW MATERIAL, OUR FATHER OF EXILES.

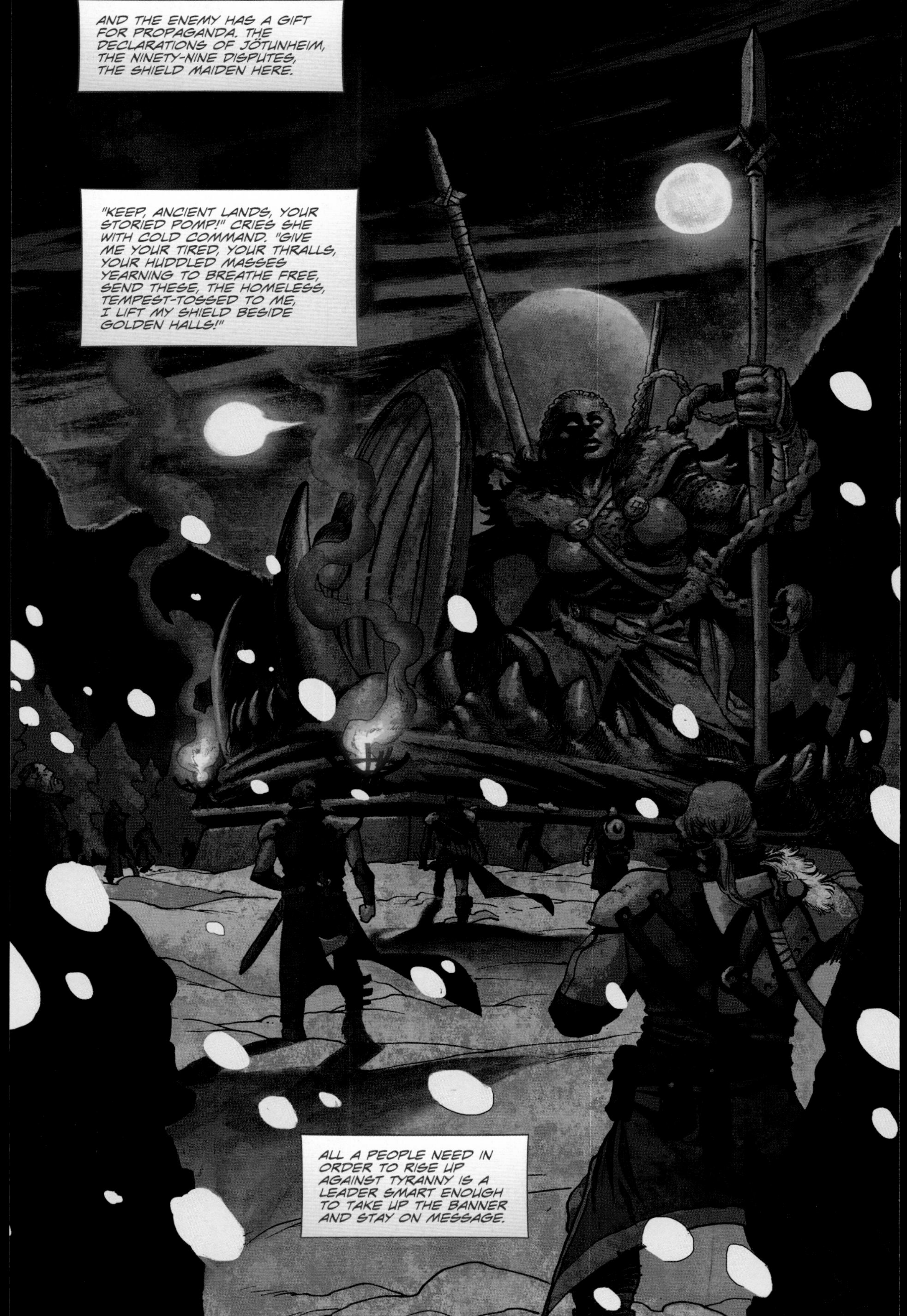
AND THE ENEMY HAS A GIFT FOR PROPAGANDA. THE DECLARATIONS OF JÖTUNHEIM, THE NINETY-NINE DISPUTES, THE SHIELD MAIDEN HERE.
"KEEP, ANCIENT LANDS, YOUR STORIED POMP!" CRIES SHE WITH COLD COMMAND. "GIVE ME YOUR TIRED, YOUR THRALLS, YOUR HUDDLED MASSES YEARNING TO BREATHE FREE, SEND THESE, THE HOMELESS, TEMPEST-TOSSED TO ME, I LIFT MY SHIELD BESIDE GOLDEN HALLS!"
ALL A PEOPLE NEED IN ORDER TO RISE UP AGAINST TYRANNY IS A LEADER SMART ENOUGH TO TAKE UP THE BANNER AND STAY ON MESSAGE.

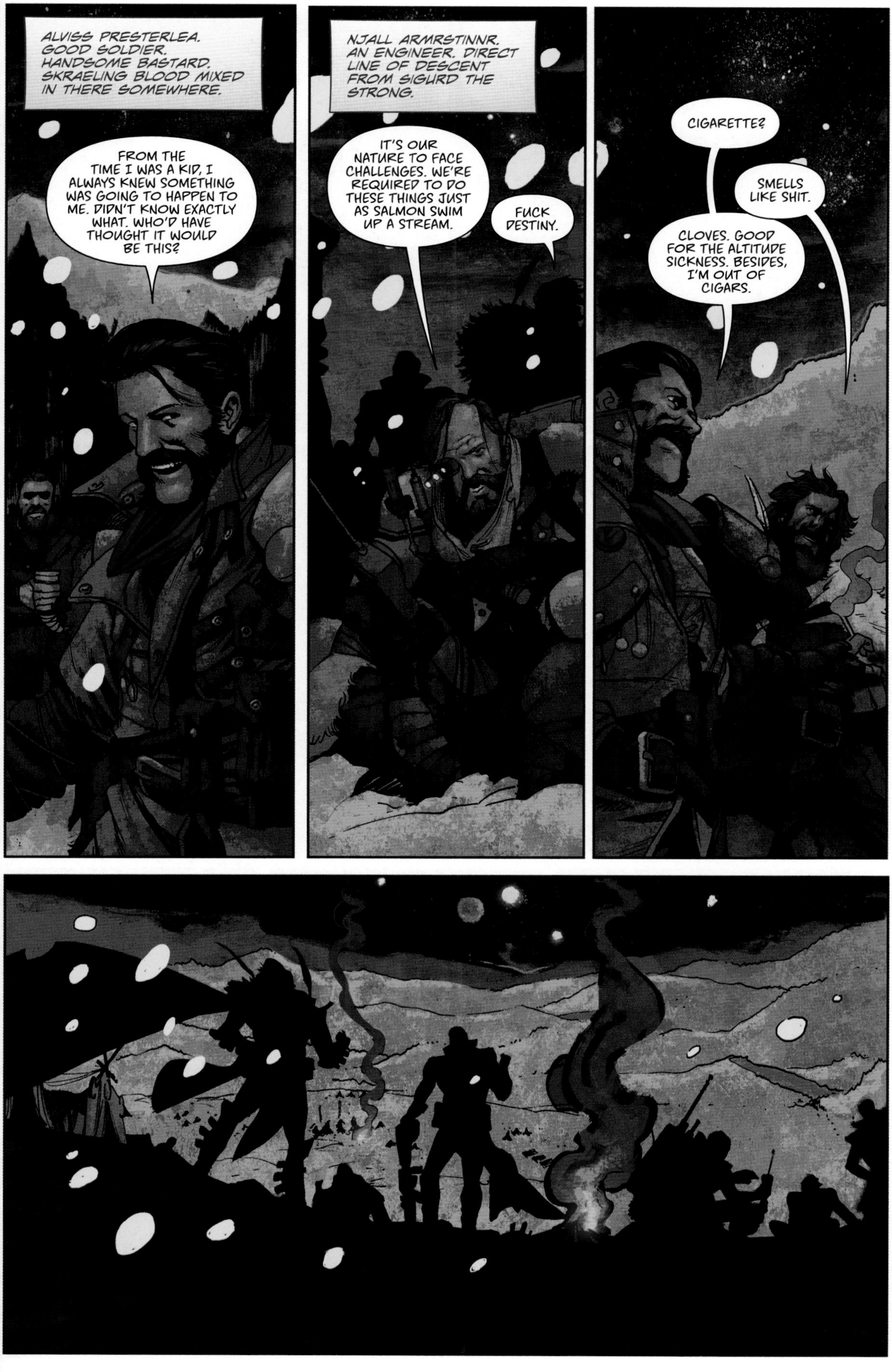
ALVISS PRESTERLEA. GOOD SOLDIER. HANDSOME BASTARD. SKRAELING BLOOD MIXED IN THERE SOMEWHERE.
FROM THE TIME I WAS A KID, I ALWAYS KNEW SOMETHING WAS GOING TO HAPPEN TO ME. DIDN'T KNOW EXACTLY WHAT. WHO'D HAVE THOUGHT IT WOULD BE THIS?
NJALL ARMRSTINNR. AN ENGINEER. DIRECT LINE OF DESCENT FROM SIGURD THE STRONG.
IT'S OUR NATURE TO FACE CHALLENGES. WE'RE REQUIRED TO DO THESE THINGS JUST AS SALMON SWIM UP A STREAM.
FUCK DESTINY.
CIGARETTE?
SMELLS LIKE SHIT.
CLOVES. GOOD FOR THE ALTITUDE SICKNESS. BESIDES, I'M OUT OF CIGARS.

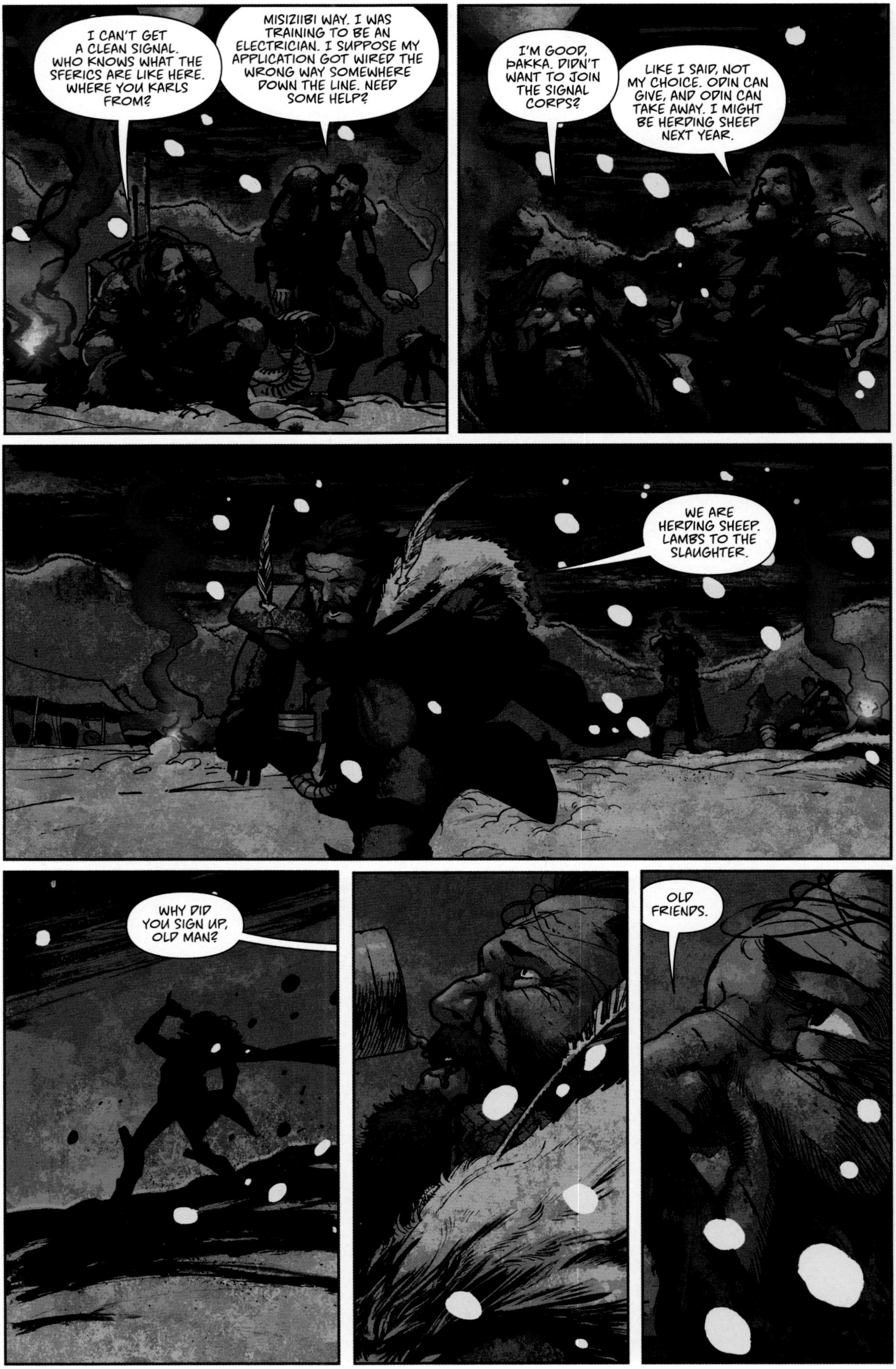
I CAN'T GET A CLEAN SIGNAL. WHO KNOWS WHAT THE SFERICS ARE LIKE HERE. WHERE YOU KARLS FROM?
MISIZIIBI WAY. I WAS TRAINING TO BE AN ELECTRICIAN. I SUPPOSE MY APPLICATION GOT WIRED THE WRONG WAY SOMEWHERE DOWN THE LINE. NEED SOME HELP?
I'M GOOD, ÞAKKA. DIDN'T WANT TO JOIN THE SIGNAL CORPS?
LIKE I SAID, NOT MY CHOICE. ODIN CAN GIVE, AND ODIN CAN TAKE AWAY. I MIGHT BE HERDING SHEEP NEXT YEAR.
WE ARE HERDING SHEEP. LAMBS TO THE SLAUGHTER.
WHY DID YOU SIGN UP, OLD MAN?
OLD FRIENDS.

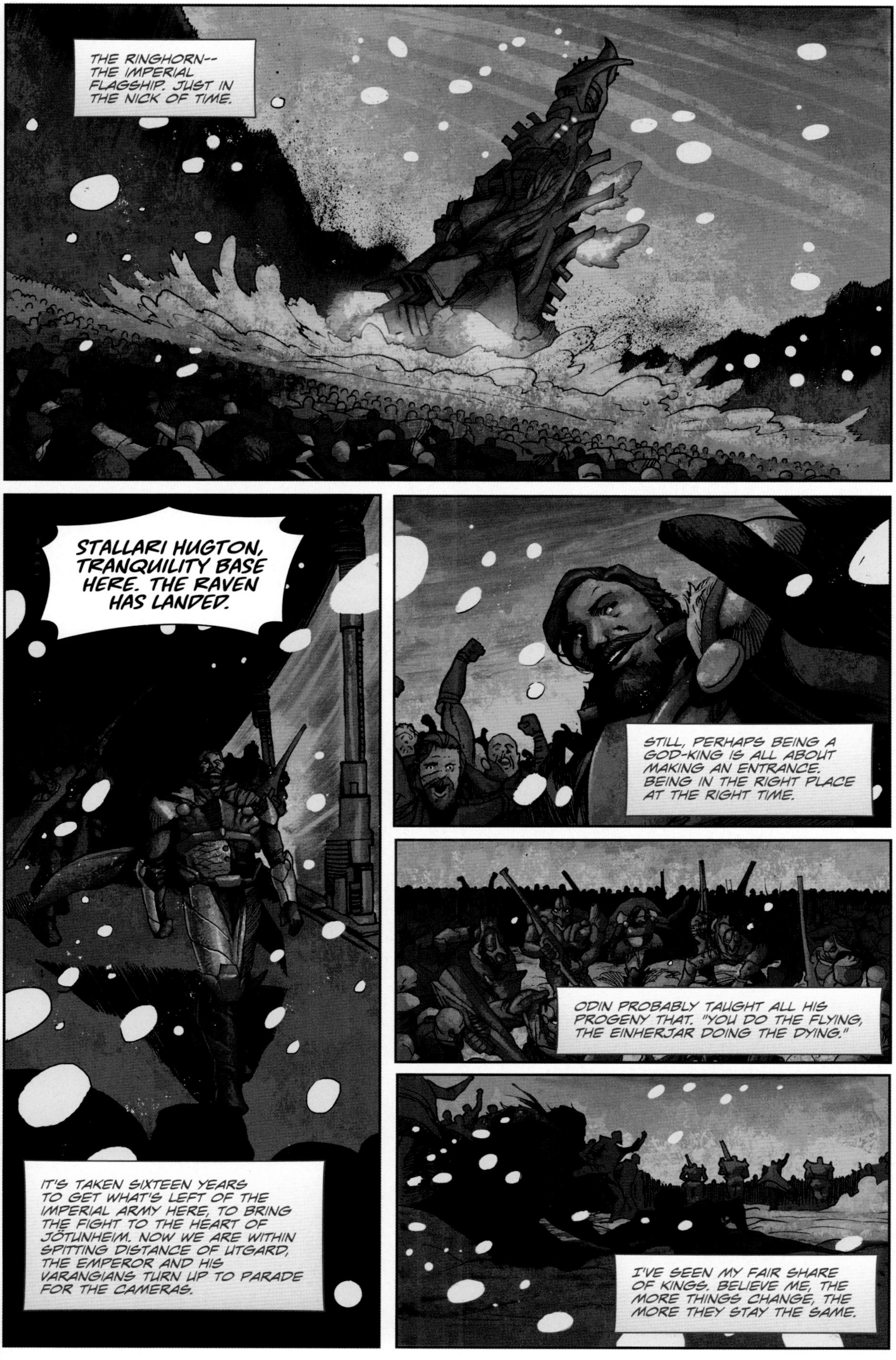
THE RINGHORN-- THE IMPERIAL FLAGSHIP. JUST IN THE NICK OF TIME.
STALLARI HUGTON, TRANQUILITY BASE HERE. THE RAVEN HAS LANDED.
STILL, PERHAPS BEING A GOD-KING IS ALL ABOUT MAKING AN ENTRANCE. BEING IN THE RIGHT PLACE AT THE RIGHT TIME.
ODIN PROBABLY TAUGHT ALL HIS PROGENY THAT. "YOU DO THE FLYING, THE EINHERJAR DOING THE DYING."
IT'S TAKEN SIXTEEN YEARS TO GET WHAT'S LEFT OF THE IMPERIAL ARMY HERE, TO BRING THE FIGHT TO THE HEART OF JÖTUNHEIM. NOW WE ARE WITHIN SPITTING DISTANCE OF UTGARD, THE EMPEROR AND HIS VARANGIANS TURN UP TO PARADE FOR THE CAMERAS.
I'VE SEEN MY FAIR SHARE OF KINGS. BELIEVE ME, THE MORE THINGS CHANGE, THE MORE THEY STAY THE SAME.

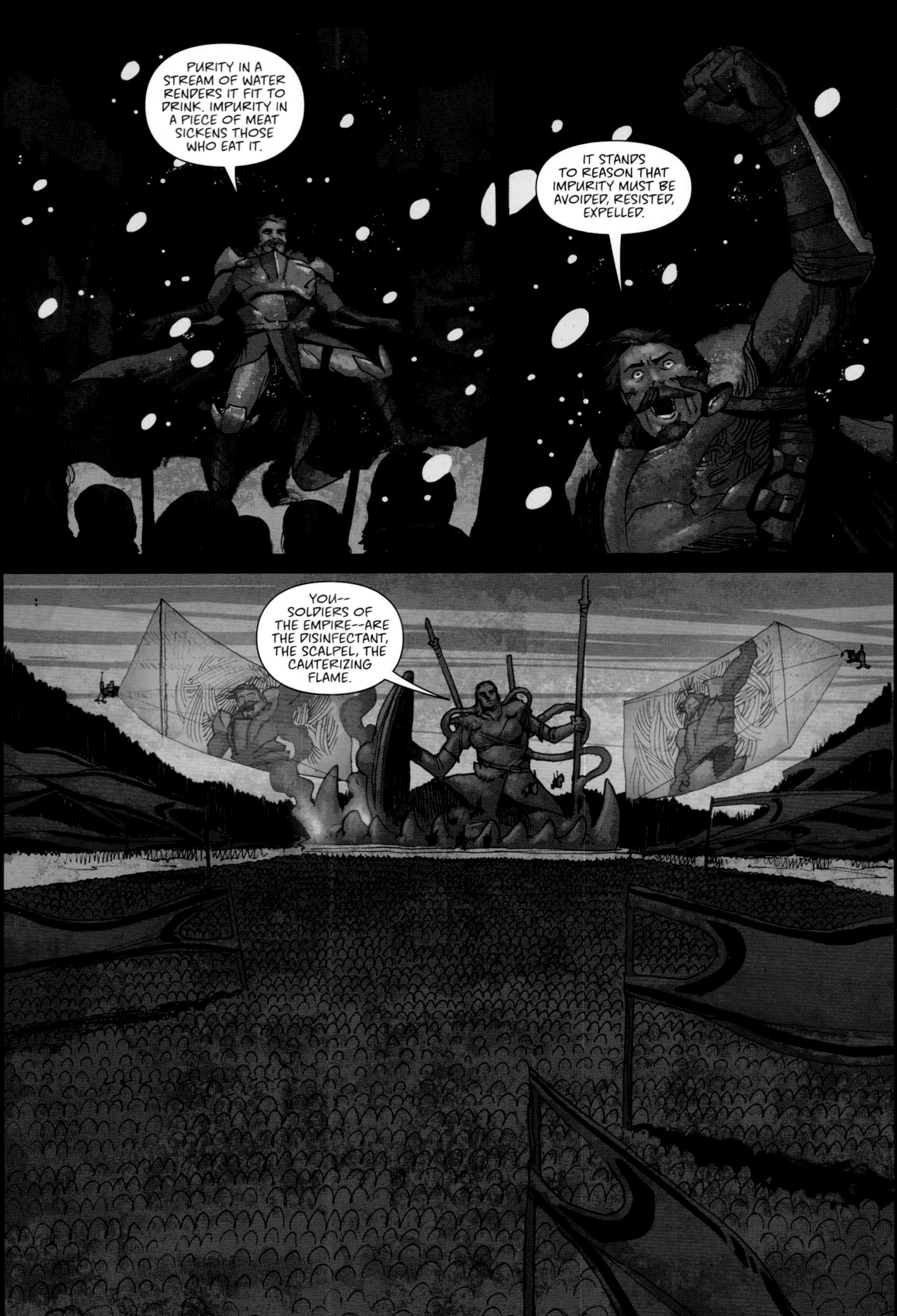
PURITY IN A STREAM OF WATER RENDERS IT FIT TO DRINK. IMPURITY IN A PIECE OF MEAT SICKENS THOSE WHO EAT IT.
IT STANDS TO REASON THAT IMPURITY MUST BE AVOIDED, RESISTED, EXPELLED.
YOU--SOLDIERS OF THE EMPIRE--ARE THE DISINFECTANT, THE SCALPEL, THE CAUTERIZING FLAME.

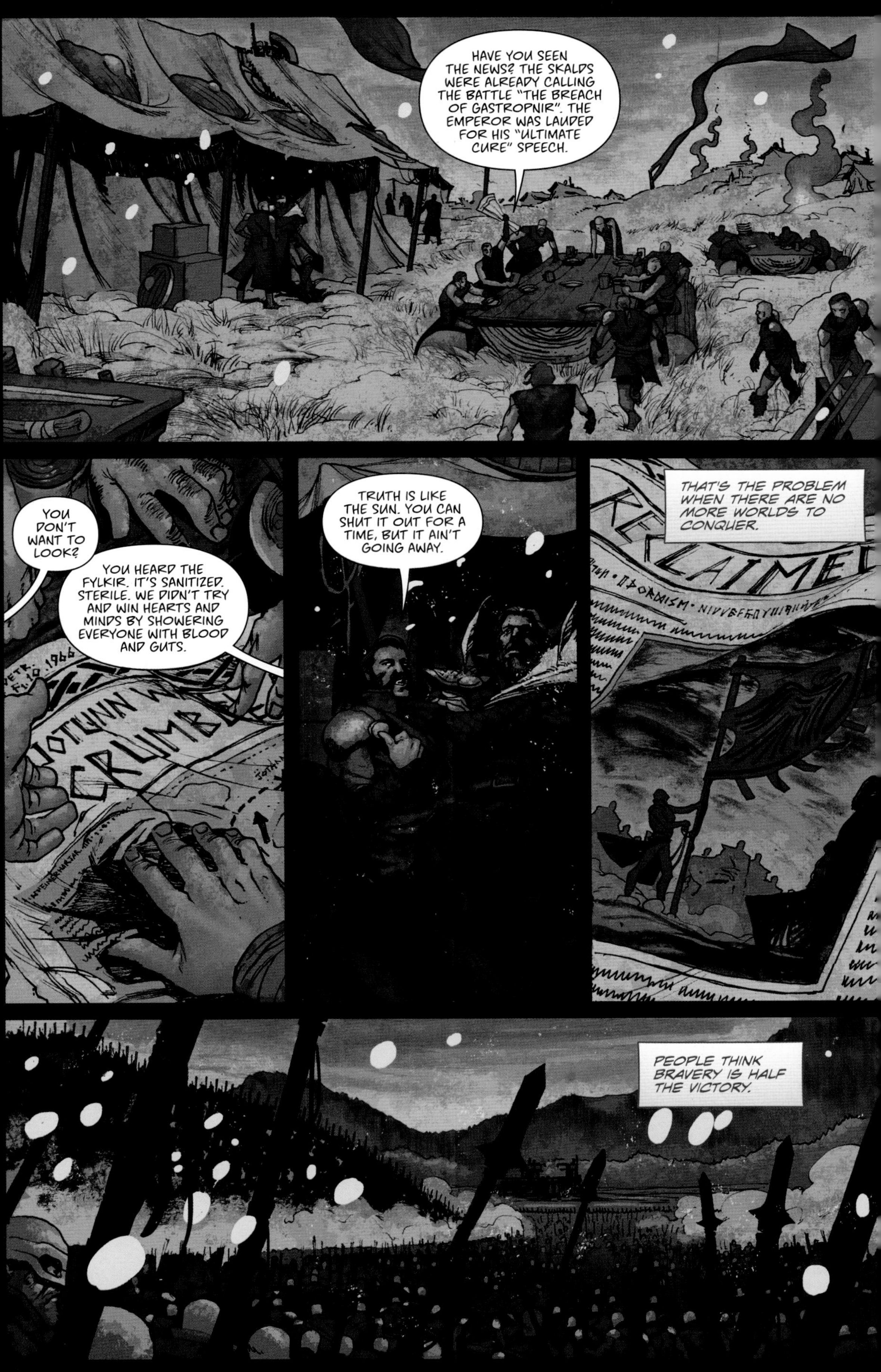
HAVE YOU SEEN THE NEWS? THE SKALDS WERE ALREADY CALLING THE BATTLE "THE BREACH OF GASTROPNIR". THE EMPEROR WAS LAUDED FOR HIS "ULTIMATE CURE" SPEECH.
YOU DON'T WANT TO LOOK?
YOU HEARD THE FYLKIR. IT'S SANITIZED. STERILE. WE DIDN'T TRY AND WIN HEARTS AND MINDS BY SHOWERING EVERYONE WITH BLOOD AND GUTS.
JOTUNN
CRUMB
TRUTH IS LIKE THE SUN. YOU CAN SHUT IT OUT FOR A TIME, BUT IT AIN'T GOING AWAY.
THAT'S THE PROBLEM WHEN THERE ARE NO MORE WORLDS TO CONQUER.
LAIME
PEOPLE THINK BRAVERY IS HALF THE VICTORY.

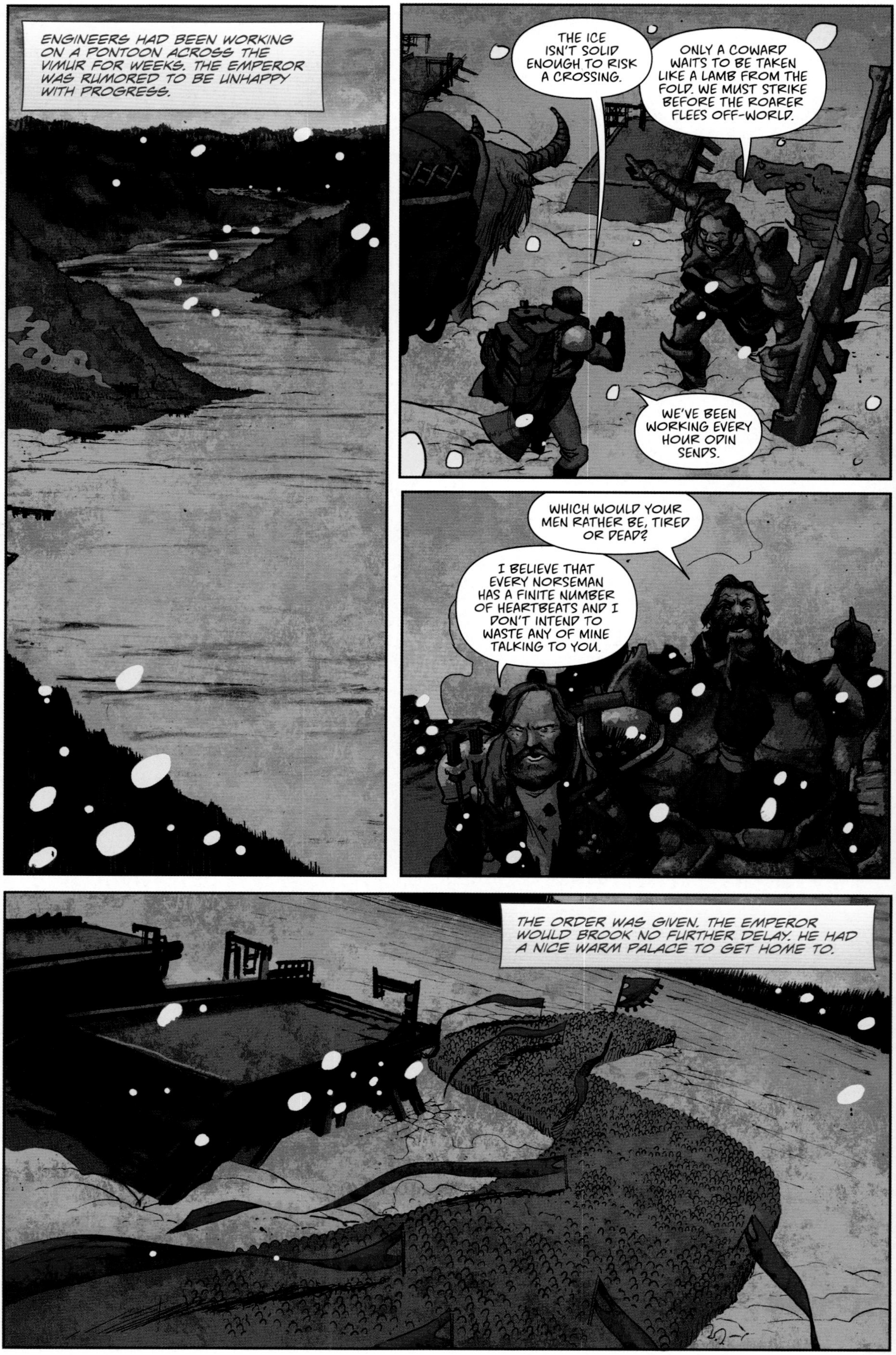
ENGINEERS HAD BEEN WORKING ON A PONTOON ACROSS THE VIMUR FOR WEEKS. THE EMPEROR WAS RUMORED TO BE UNHAPPY WITH PROGRESS.
THE ICE ISN'T SOLID ENOUGH TO RISK A CROSSING.
ONLY A COWARD WAITS TO BE TAKEN LIKE A LAMB FROM THE FOLD. WE MUST STRIKE BEFORE THE ROARER FLEES OFF-WORLD.
WE'VE BEEN WORKING EVERY HOUR ODIN SENDS.
WHICH WOULD YOUR MEN RATHER BE, TIRED OR DEAD?
I BELIEVE THAT EVERY NORSEMAN HAS A FINITE NUMBER OF HEARTBEATS AND I DON'T INTEND TO WASTE ANY OF MINE TALKING TO YOU.
THE ORDER WAS GIVEN. THE EMPEROR WOULD BROOK NO FURTHER DELAY. HE HAD A NICE WARM PALACE TO GET HOME TO.

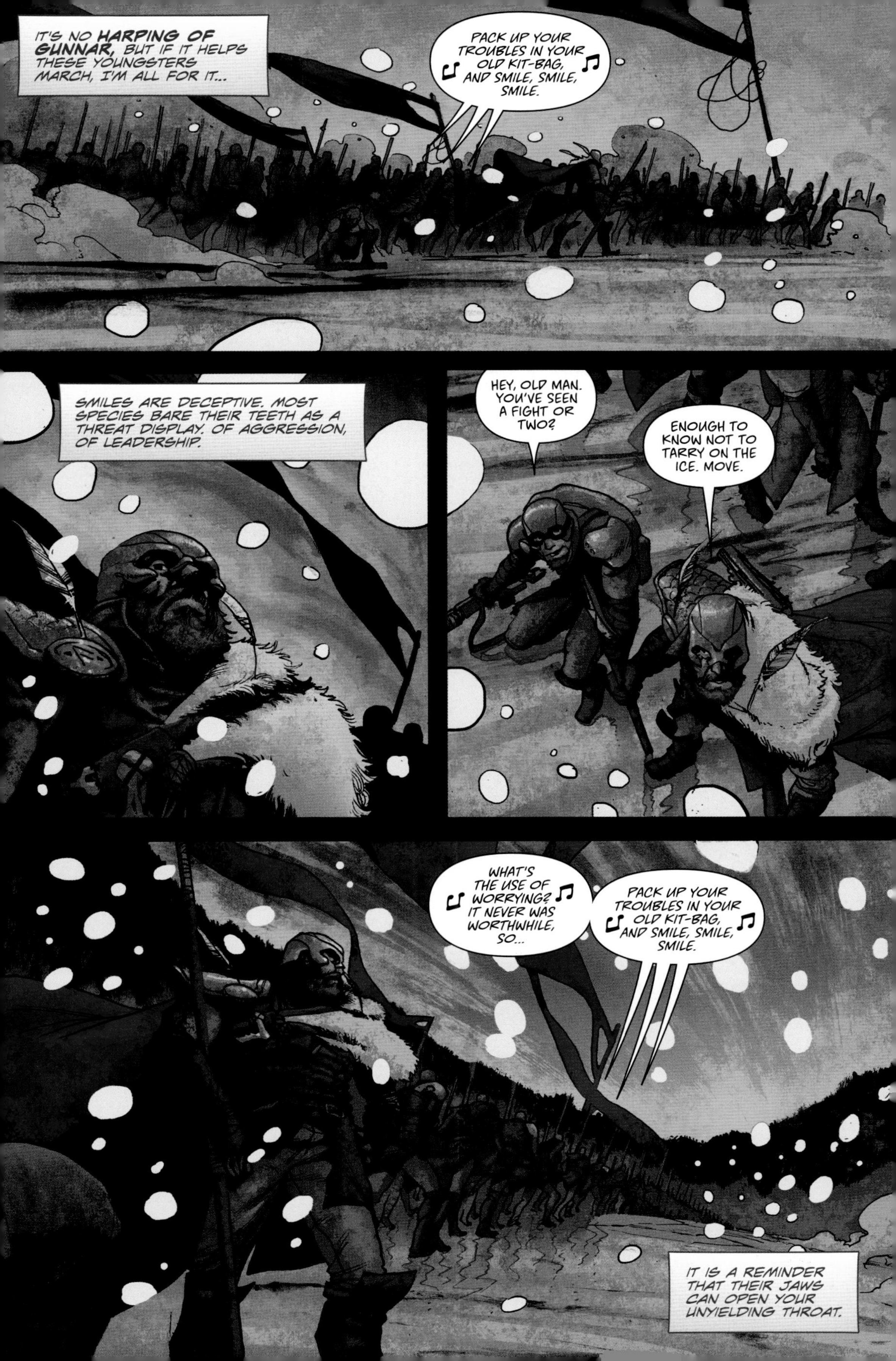
IT'S NO HARPING OF GUNNAR, BUT IF IT HELPS THESE YOUNGSTERS MARCH, I'M ALL FOR IT...
♫ PACK UP YOUR TROUBLES IN YOUR OLD KIT-BAG, AND SMILE, SMILE, SMILE. ♫
SMILES ARE DECEPTIVE. MOST SPECIES BARE THEIR TEETH AS A THREAT DISPLAY. OF AGGRESSION, OF LEADERSHIP.
HEY, OLD MAN. YOU'VE SEEN A FIGHT OR TWO?
ENOUGH TO KNOW NOT TO TARRY ON THE ICE. MOVE.
♫ WHAT'S THE USE OF WORRYING? IT NEVER WAS WORTHWHILE, SO... ♫
♫ PACK UP YOUR TROUBLES IN YOUR OLD KIT-BAG, AND SMILE, SMILE, SMILE. ♫
IT IS A REMINDER THAT THEIR JAWS CAN OPEN YOUR UNYIELDING THROAT.

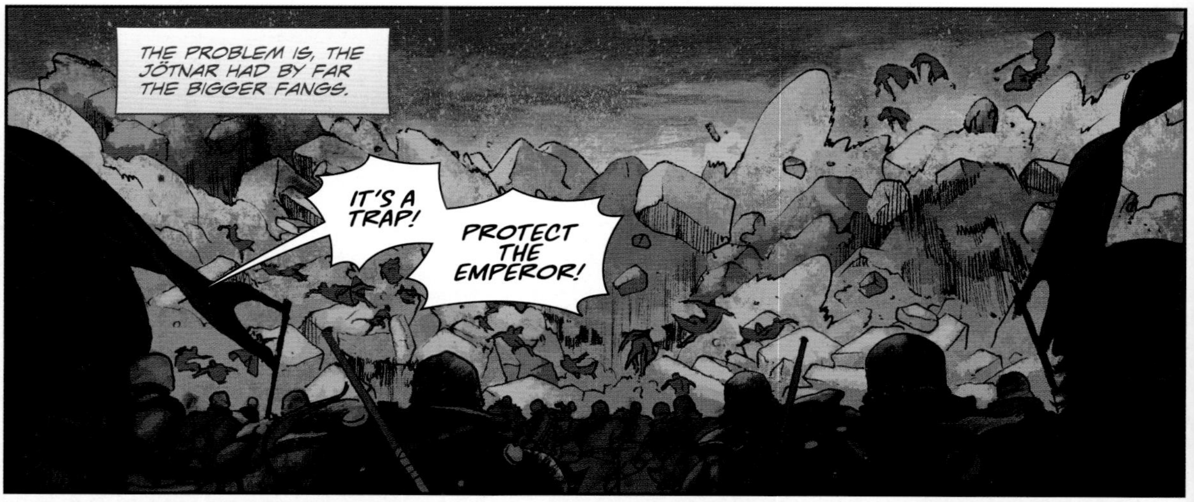
THE PROBLEM IS, THE JÖTNAR HAD BY FAR THE BIGGER FANGS.
IT'S A TRAP!
PROTECT THE EMPEROR!

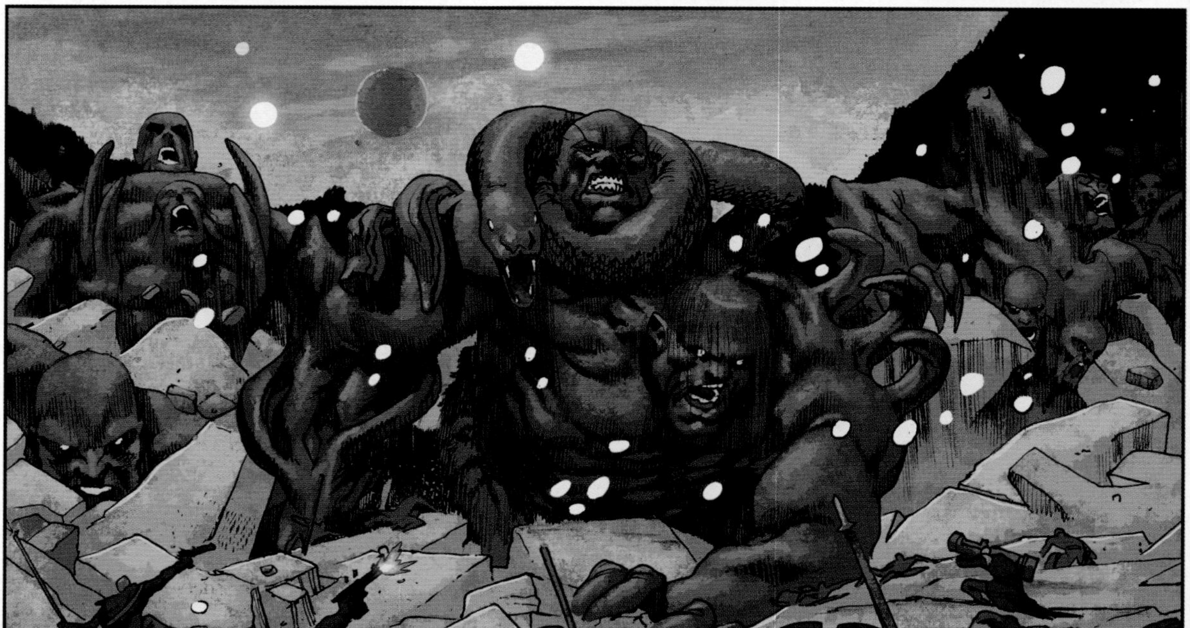

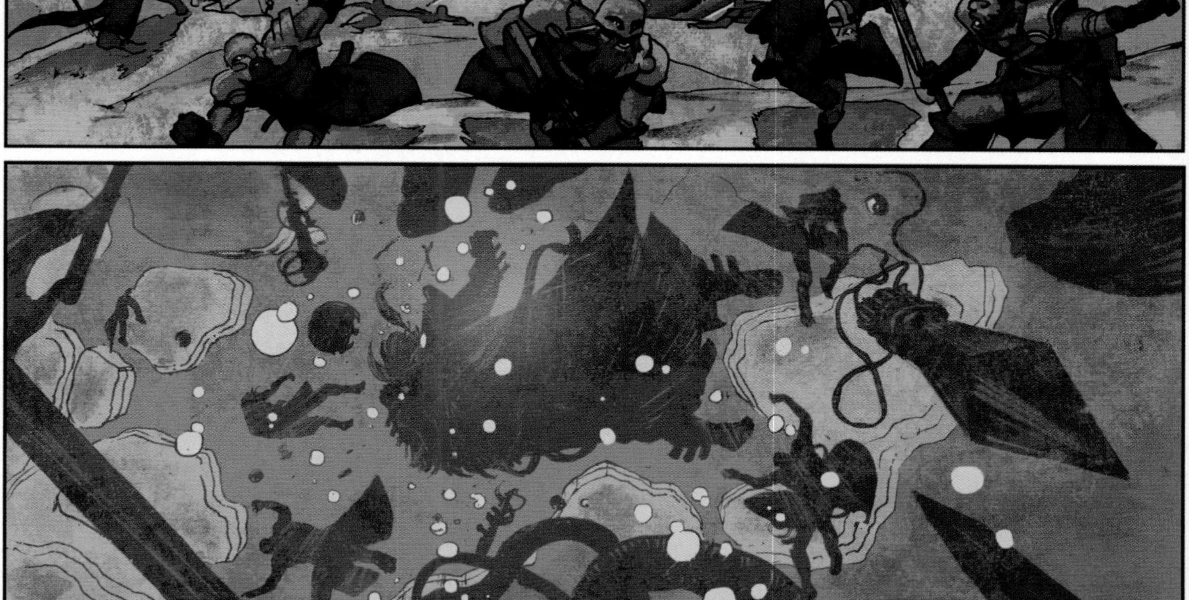

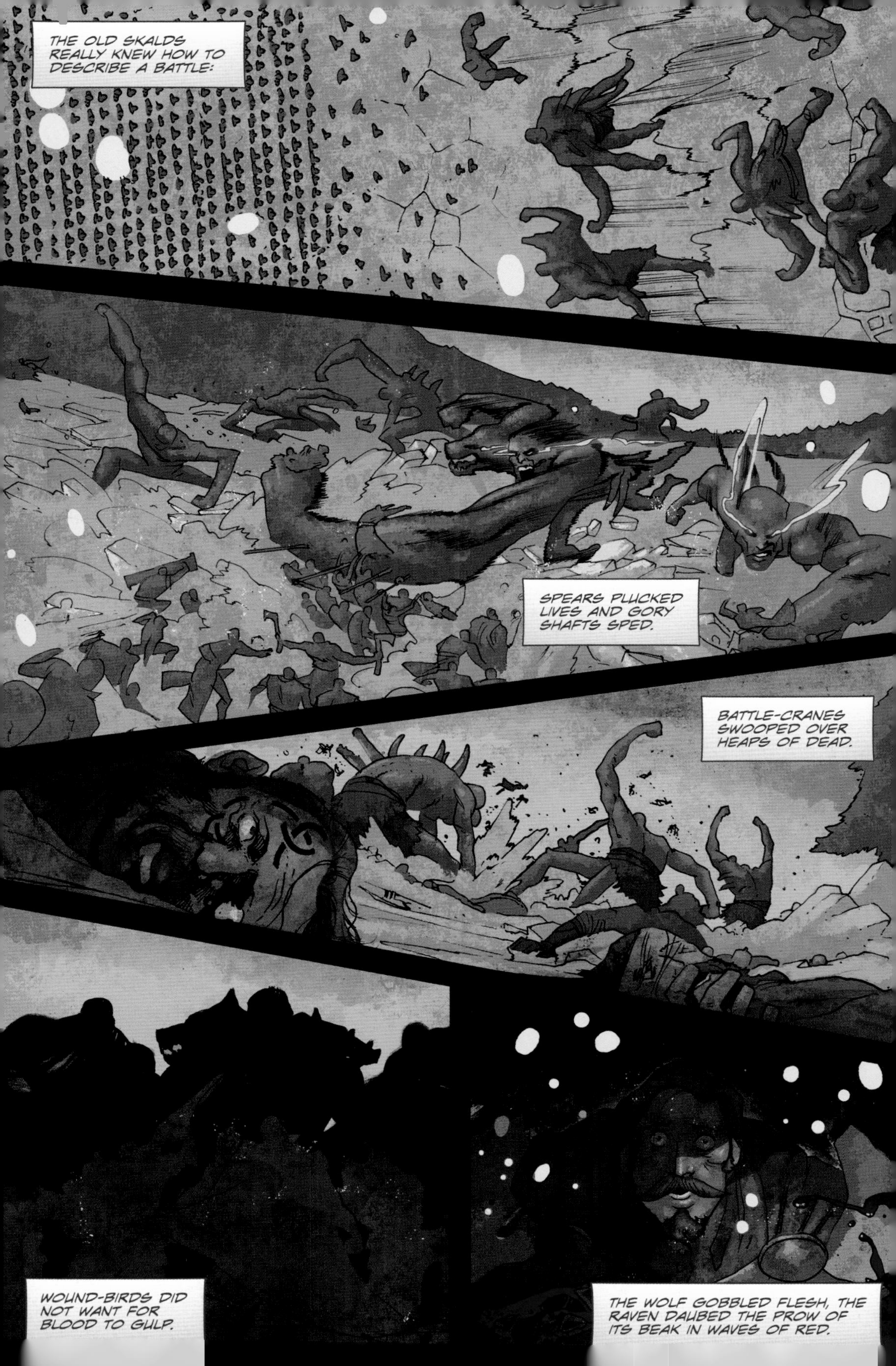
THE OLD SKALDS REALLY KNEW HOW TO DESCRIBE A BATTLE:
SPEARS PLUCKED LIVES AND GORY SHAFTS SPED.
BATTLE-CRANES SWOOPED OVER HEAPS OF DEAD.
WOUND-BIRDS DID NOT WANT FOR BLOOD TO GULP.
THE WOLF GOBBLED FLESH, THE RAVEN DAUBED THE PROW OF ITS BEAK IN WAVES OF RED.

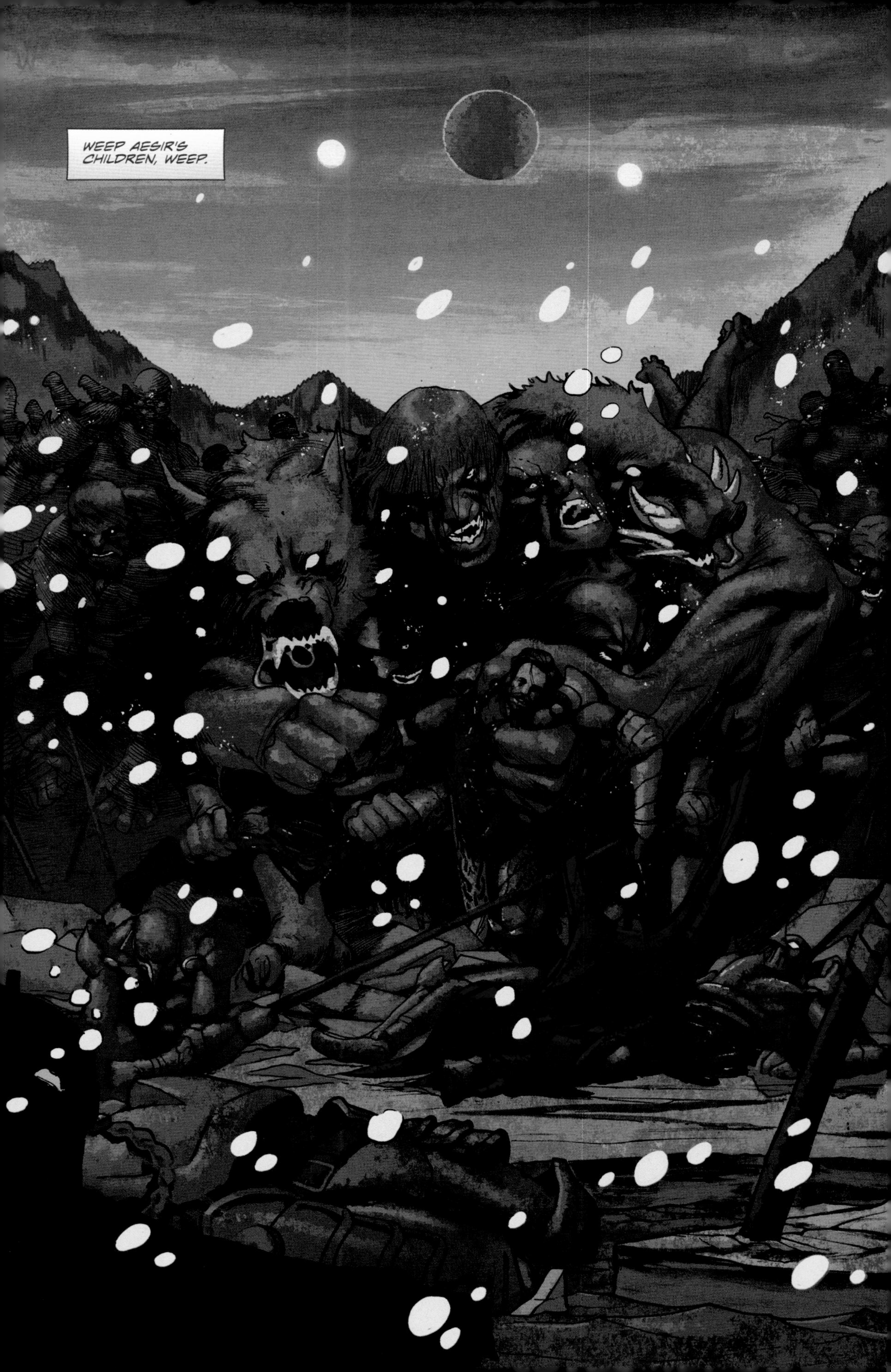
WEEP AESIR'S CHILDREN, WEEP.

MEN
OF THE
EMPIRE

SPEAKING OUT OF A FULL HEART, MAY I SAY HOW **GLORIOUSLY** OUR
TROOPS HAVE UPHELD THE FINEST TRADITIONS OF THE NORSE
DURING THIS STRUGGLE STILL IN PROGRESS?

CLOUD SCRAPERS.
SHADOWS ON THE SKY.
DEVOURERS.

IT DOESN'T MATTER **WHAT** YOU CALL OUR ENEMY.
THEY BRING ONLY **DEATH**.

THE DAY MAY DAWN WHEN OUR **SLEEPLESS VALOUR**, **UNTIRING RESOURCE**,
AND **IMPERISHABLE VIRTUE** WILL ENABLE TORMENTED GENERATIONS TO MARCH
FORTH, SERENE AND TRIUMPHANT, FROM THE HIDEOUS EPOCH IN WHICH WE HAVE
TO DWELL. UNTIL THEN, **NEVER** FLINCH, **NEVER** WEARY, **NEVER** DESPAIR.

RALLY TO THE RAVEN BANNER

IF THE *FATHER OF MONSTERS* WINS, NO HOME IN THE **NINE WORLDS**
WILL BE SAFE! WIVES, DAUGHTERS, MOTHERS WILL
BE AT THE MERCY OF OUR FOE.

YOUR EMPIRE NEEDS YOU

ENLIST
NOW

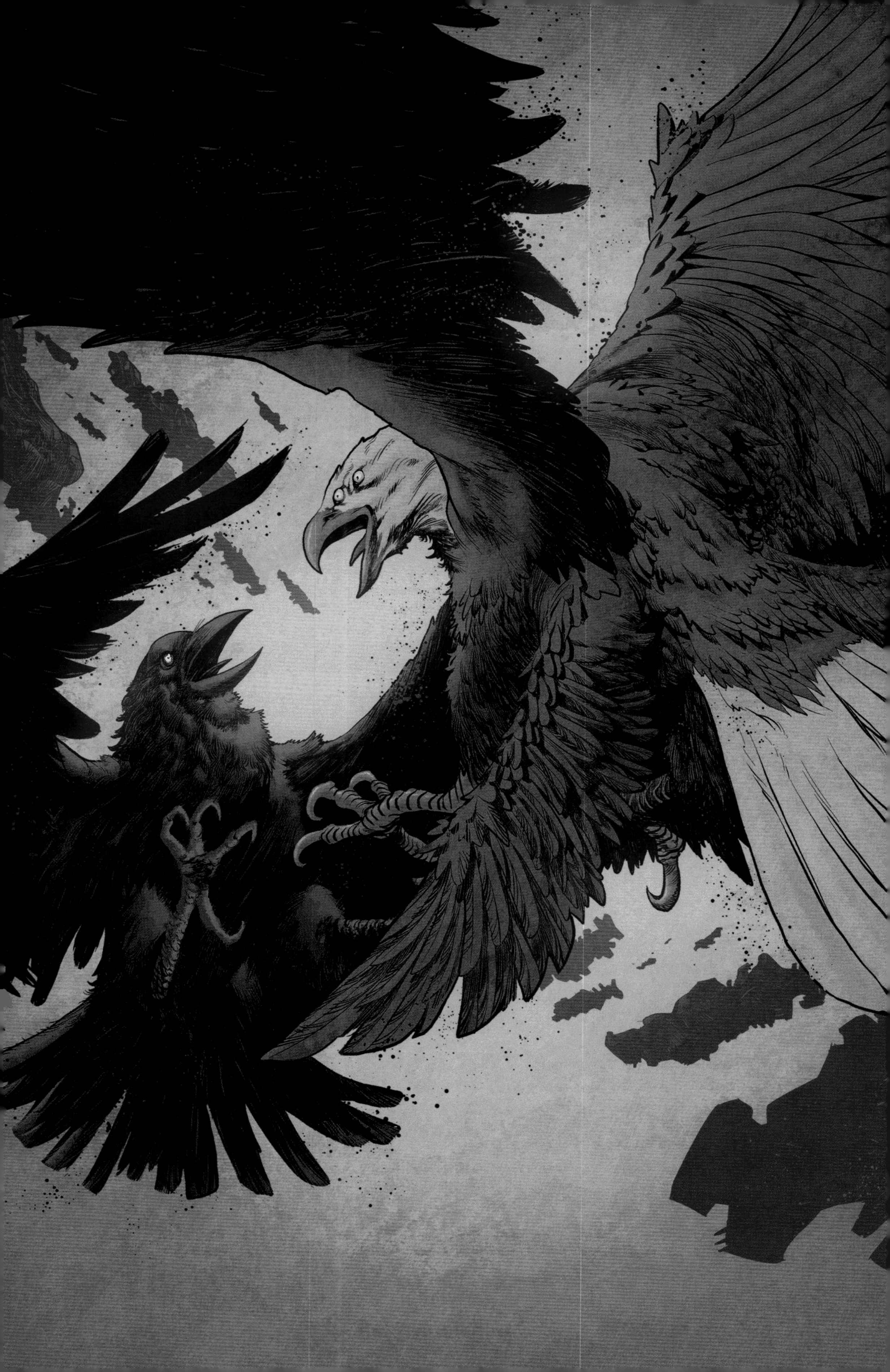

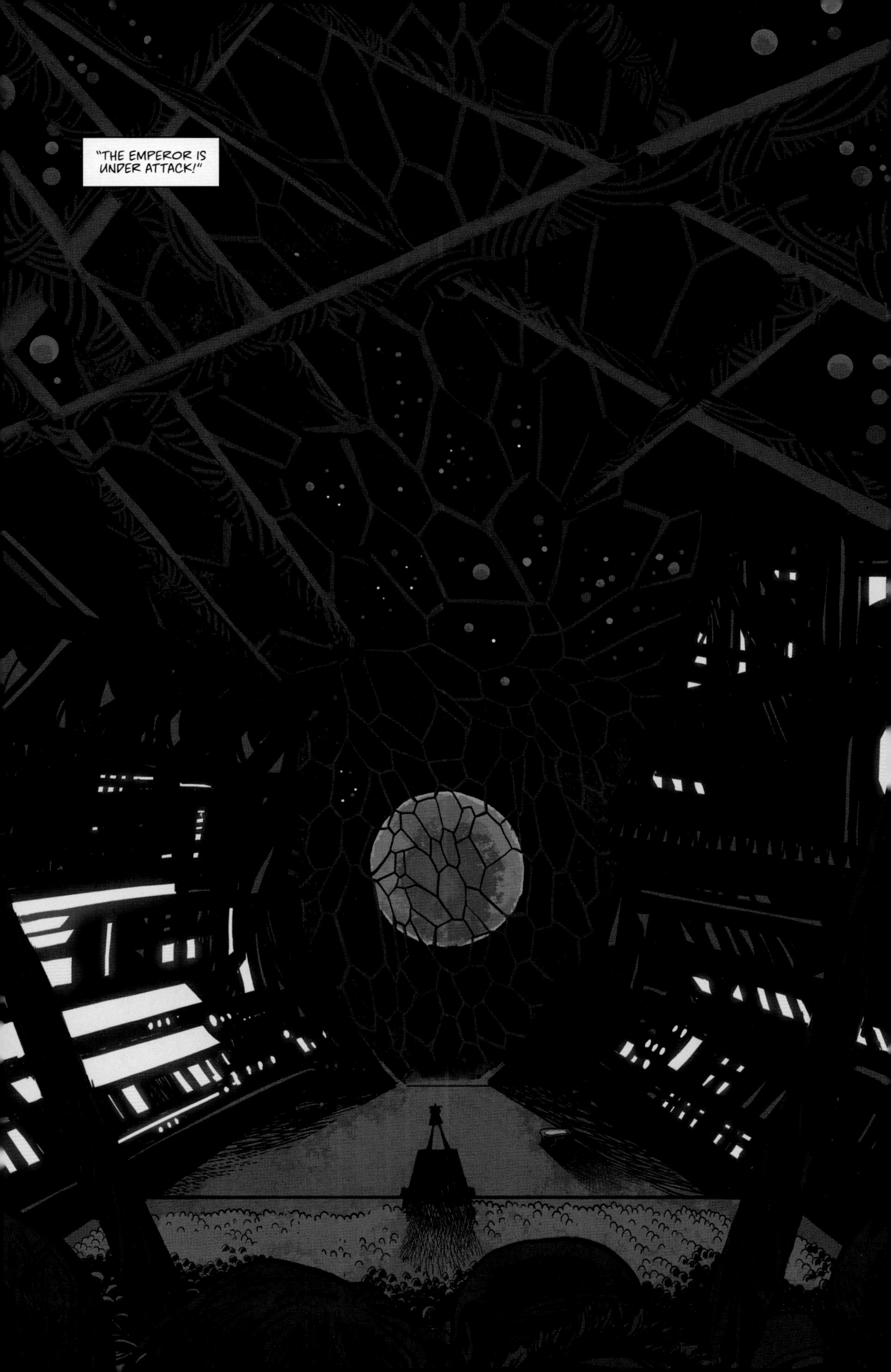
"THE EMPEROR IS UNDER ATTACK!"

"MANNERHEIM! WE MUST SEND REINFORCEMENTS!"
ARE YOU LISTENING? BY MY HALL AND ROOF! I'LL NOT STAND IDLE WHILE YOU SHILLY-SHALLY. IT'S A SLAUGHTER DOWN THERE.
PREPARE MY KARVE. I'LL LEAD THE RELIEF PERSONALLY.

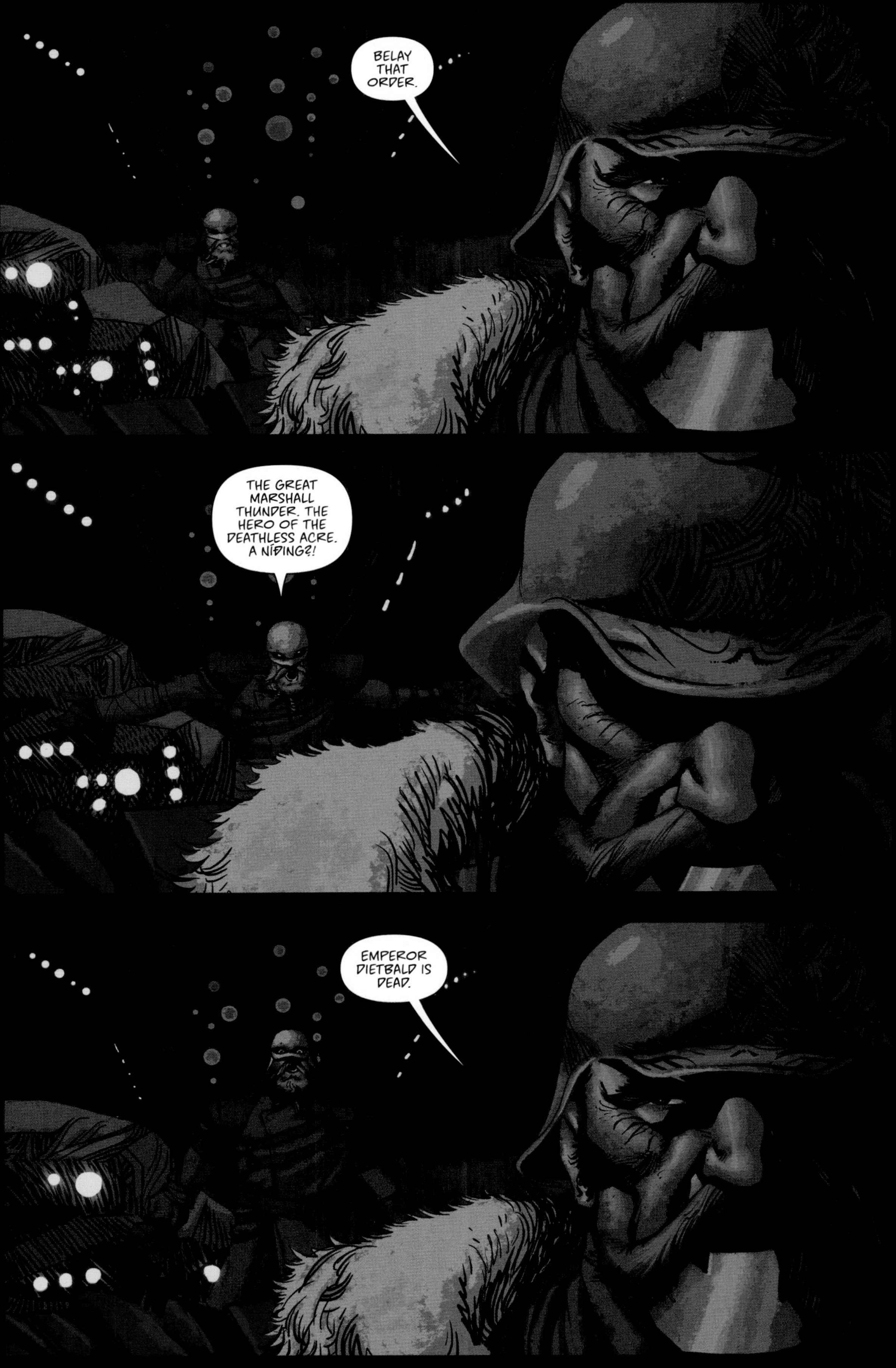
BELAY THAT ORDER.
THE GREAT MARSHALL THUNDER. THE HERO OF THE DEATHLESS ACRE. A NÍÐING?!
EMPEROR DIETBALD IS DEAD.

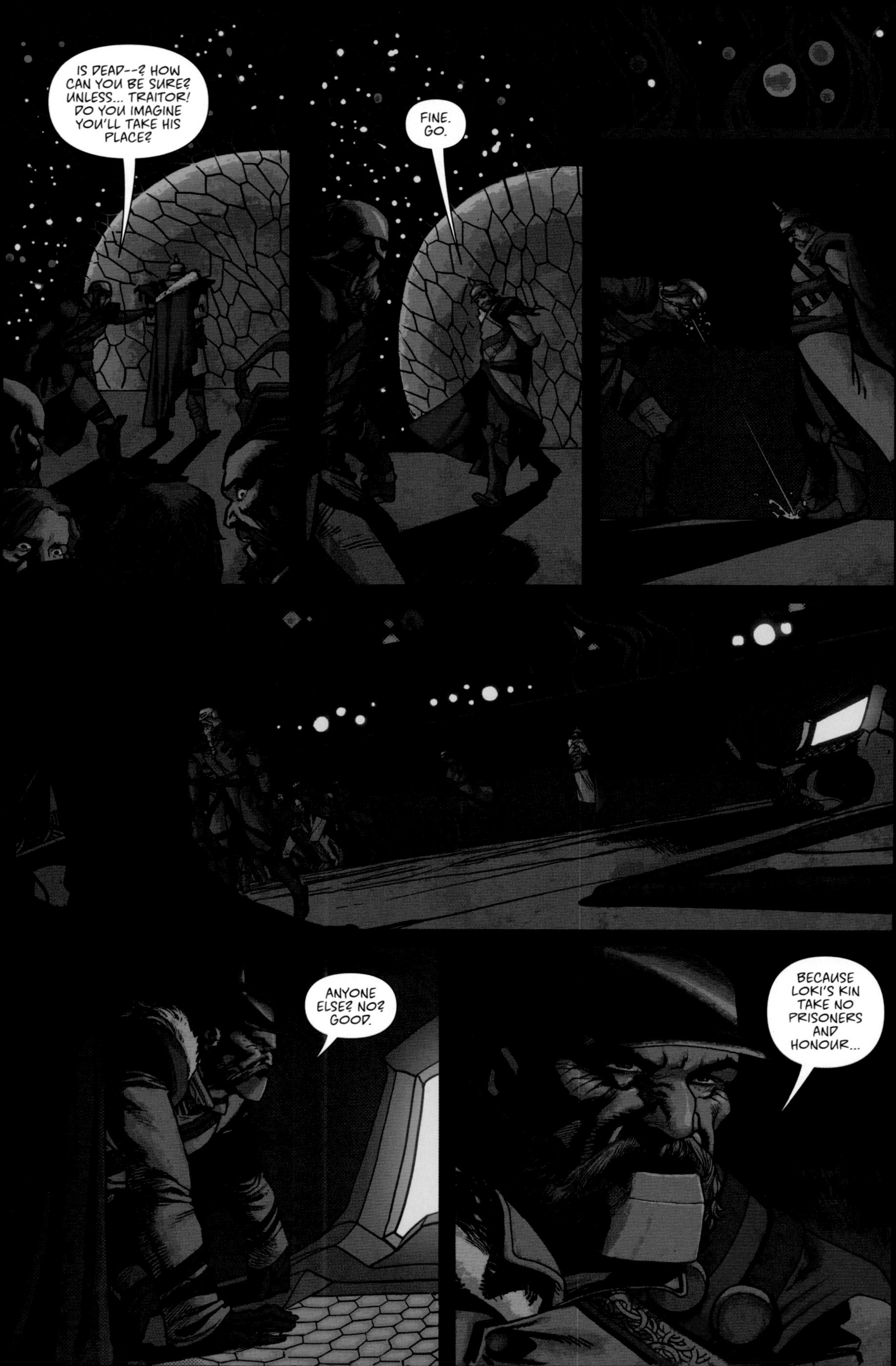
IS DEAD--? HOW CAN YOU BE SURE? UNLESS... TRAITOR! DO YOU IMAGINE YOU'LL TAKE HIS PLACE?
FINE. GO.
ANYONE ELSE? NO? GOOD.
BECAUSE LOKI'S KIN TAKE NO PRISONERS AND HONOUR...

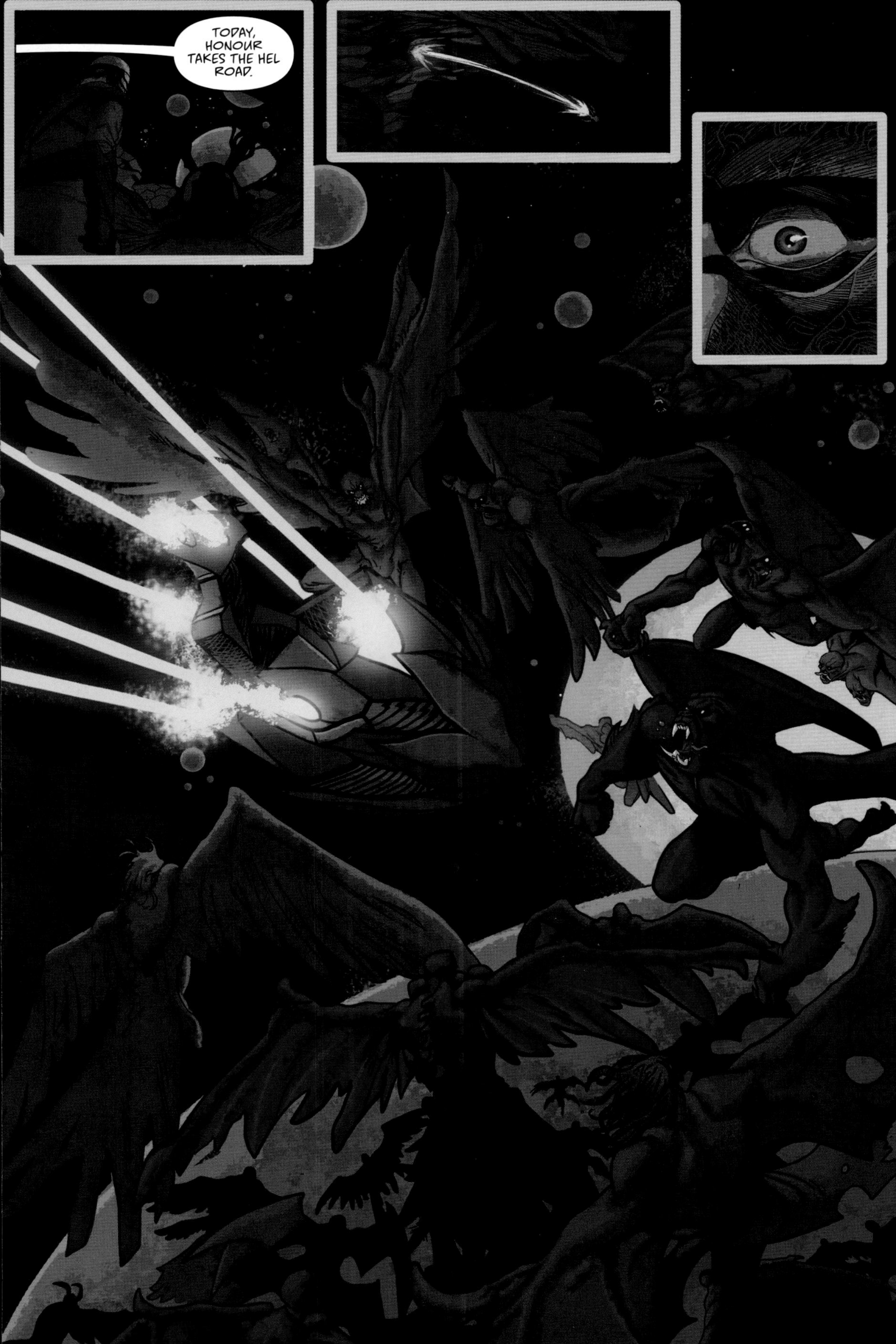
TODAY, HONOUR TAKES THE HEL ROAD.

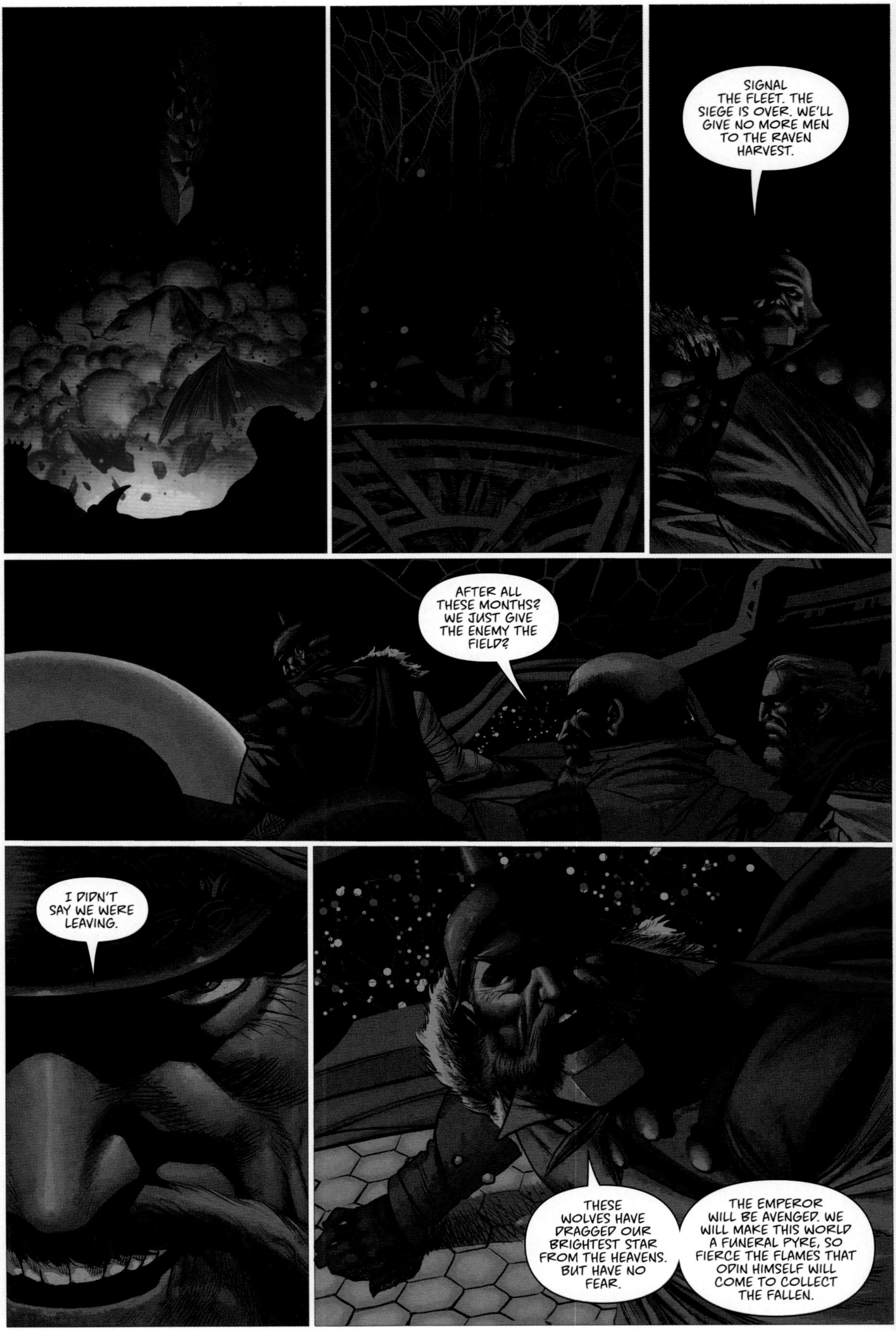
SIGNAL THE FLEET. THE SIEGE IS OVER. WE'LL GIVE NO MORE MEN TO THE RAVEN HARVEST.
AFTER ALL THESE MONTHS? WE JUST GIVE THE ENEMY THE FIELD?
I DIDN'T SAY WE WERE LEAVING.
THESE WOLVES HAVE DRAGGED OUR BRIGHTEST STAR FROM THE HEAVENS. BUT HAVE NO FEAR.
THE EMPEROR WILL BE AVENGED. WE WILL MAKE THIS WORLD A FUNERAL PYRE, SO FIERCE THE FLAMES THAT ODIN HIMSELF WILL COME TO COLLECT THE FALLEN.

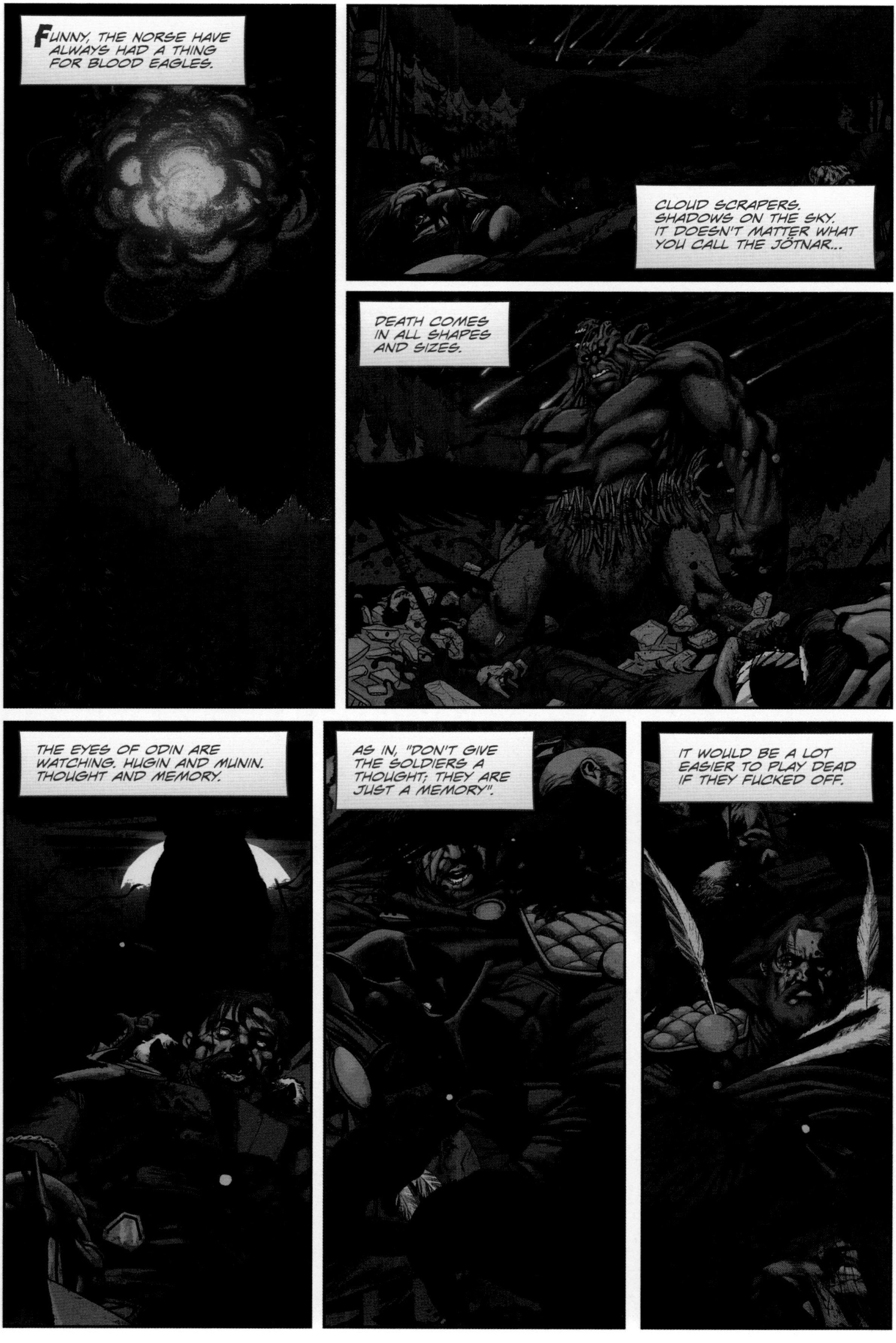
FUNNY, THE NORSE HAVE ALWAYS HAD A THING FOR BLOOD EAGLES.
CLOUD SCRAPERS. SHADOWS ON THE SKY. IT DOESN'T MATTER WHAT YOU CALL THE JÖTNAR...
DEATH COMES IN ALL SHAPES AND SIZES.
THE EYES OF ODIN ARE WATCHING. HUGIN AND MUNIN. THOUGHT AND MEMORY.
AS IN, "DON'T GIVE THE SOLDIERS A THOUGHT; THEY ARE JUST A MEMORY".
IT WOULD BE A LOT EASIER TO PLAY DEAD IF THEY FUCKED OFF.

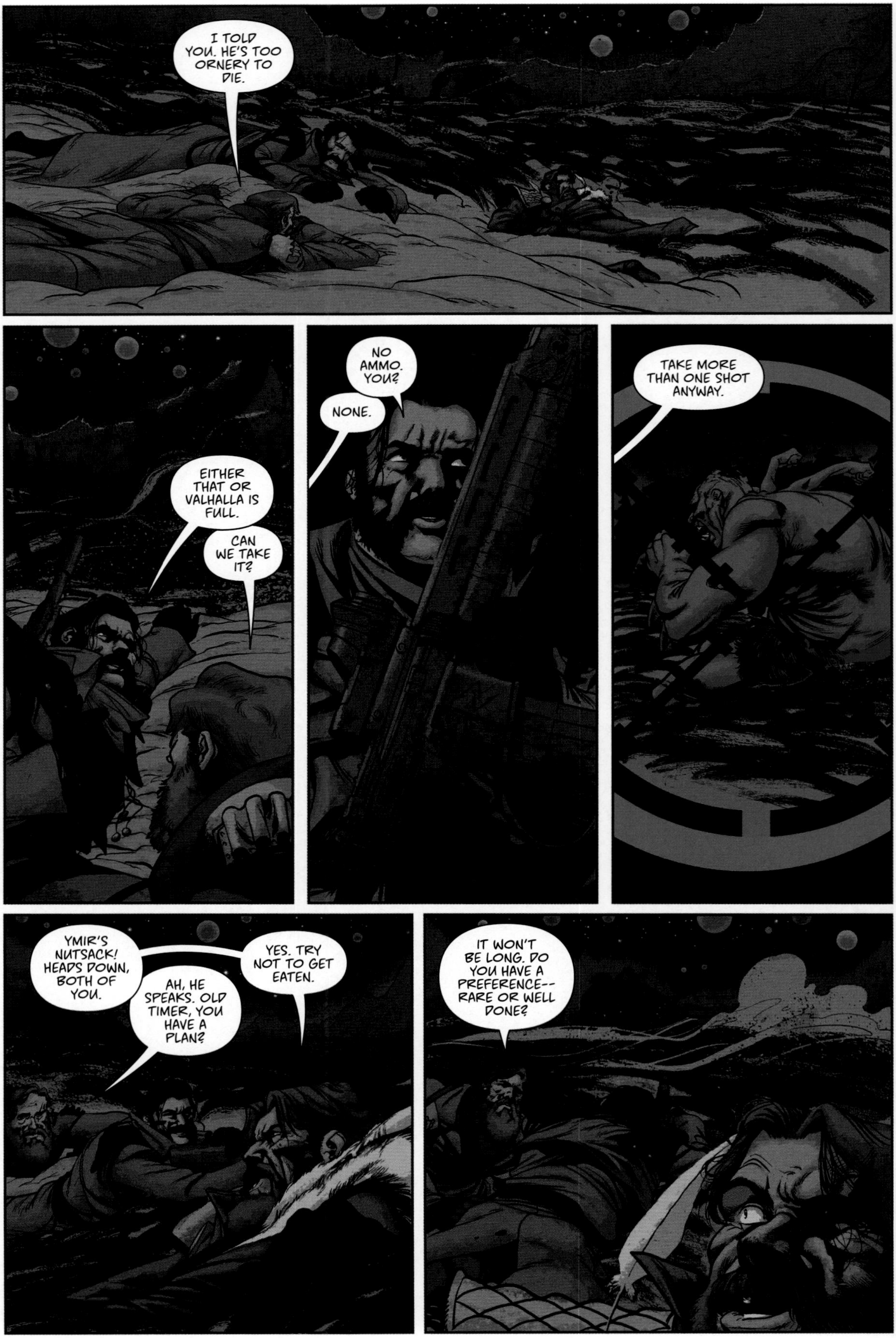
I TOLD YOU. HE'S TOO ORNERY TO DIE.
EITHER THAT OR VALHALLA IS FULL.
CAN WE TAKE IT?
NO AMMO. YOU?
NONE.
TAKE MORE THAN ONE SHOT ANYWAY.
YMIR'S NUTSACK! HEADS DOWN, BOTH OF YOU.
YES. TRY NOT TO GET EATEN.
AH, HE SPEAKS. OLD TIMER, YOU HAVE A PLAN?
IT WON'T BE LONG. DO YOU HAVE A PREFERENCE-- RARE OR WELL DONE?

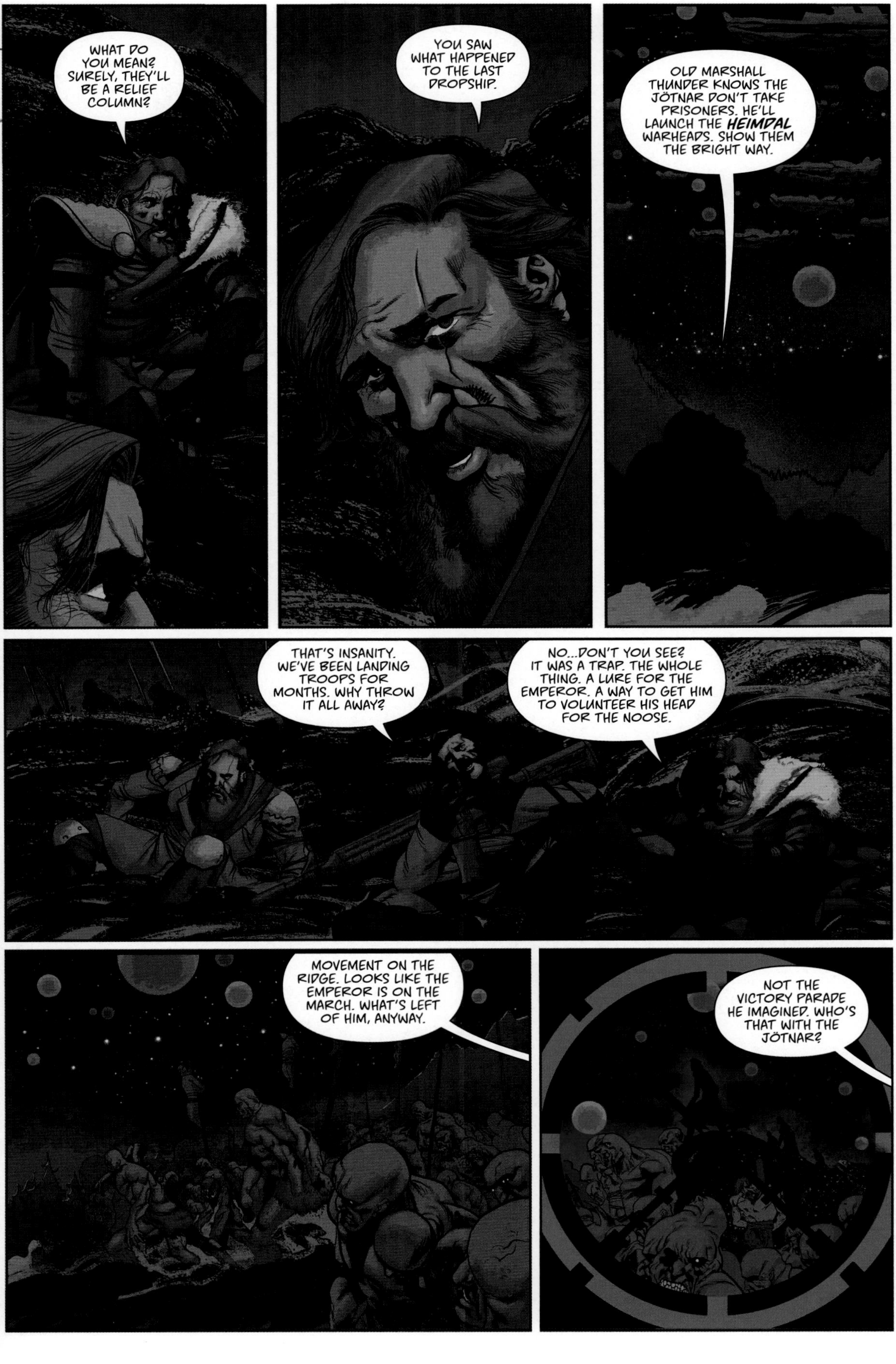
WHAT DO YOU MEAN? SURELY, THEY'LL BE A RELIEF COLUMN?
YOU SAW WHAT HAPPENED TO THE LAST DROPSHIP.
OLD MARSHALL THUNDER KNOWS THE JÖTNAR DON'T TAKE PRISONERS. HE'LL LAUNCH THE ***HEIMDAL*** WARHEADS. SHOW THEM THE BRIGHT WAY.
THAT'S INSANITY. WE'VE BEEN LANDING TROOPS FOR MONTHS. WHY THROW IT ALL AWAY?
NO...DON'T YOU SEE? IT WAS A TRAP. THE WHOLE THING. A LURE FOR THE EMPEROR. A WAY TO GET HIM TO VOLUNTEER HIS HEAD FOR THE NOOSE.
MOVEMENT ON THE RIDGE. LOOKS LIKE THE EMPEROR IS ON THE MARCH. WHAT'S LEFT OF HIM, ANYWAY.
NOT THE VICTORY PARADE HE IMAGINED. WHO'S THAT WITH THE JÖTNAR?

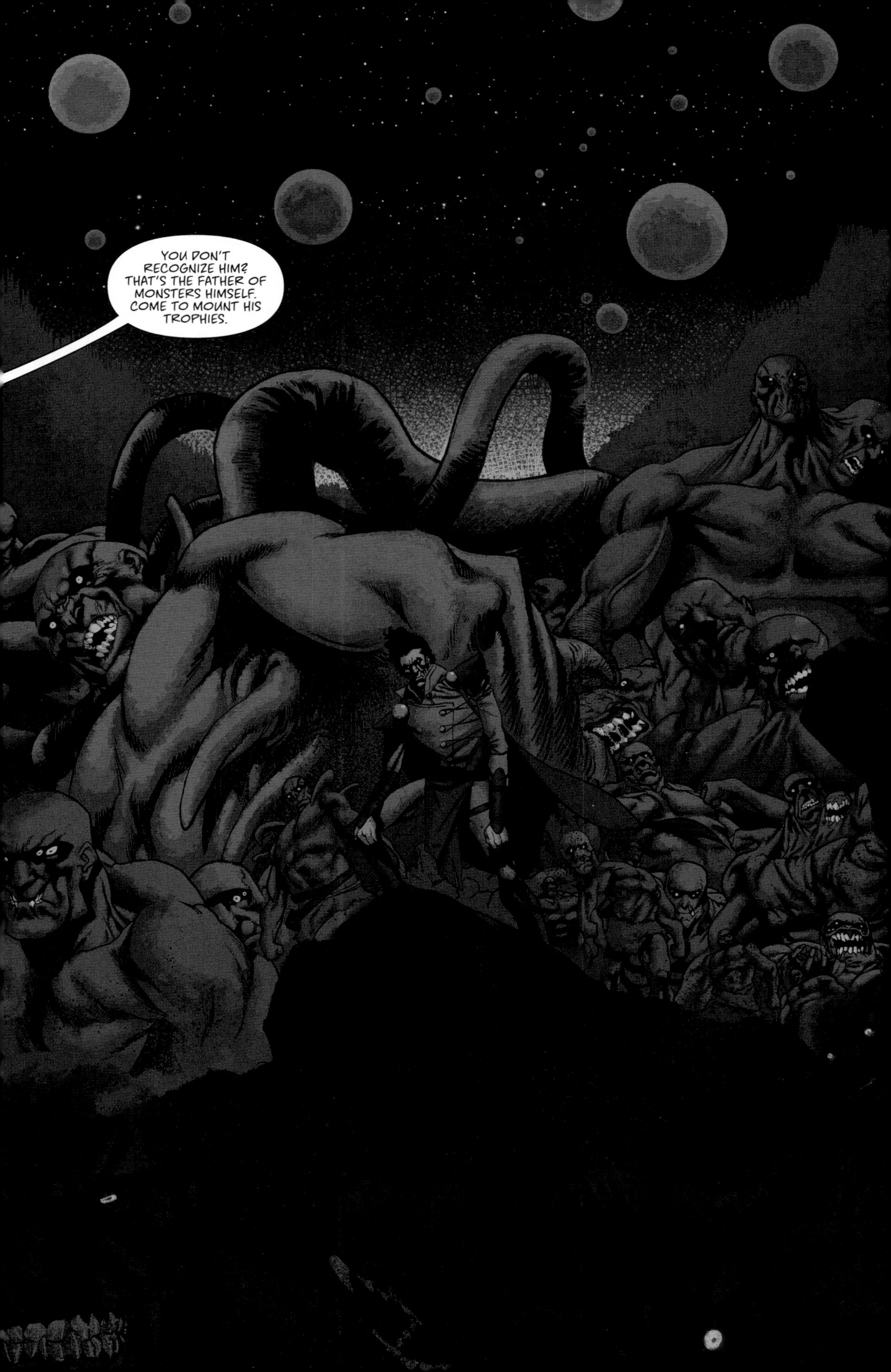
YOU DON'T RECOGNIZE HIM? THAT'S THE FATHER OF MONSTERS HIMSELF. COME TO MOUNT HIS TROPHIES.

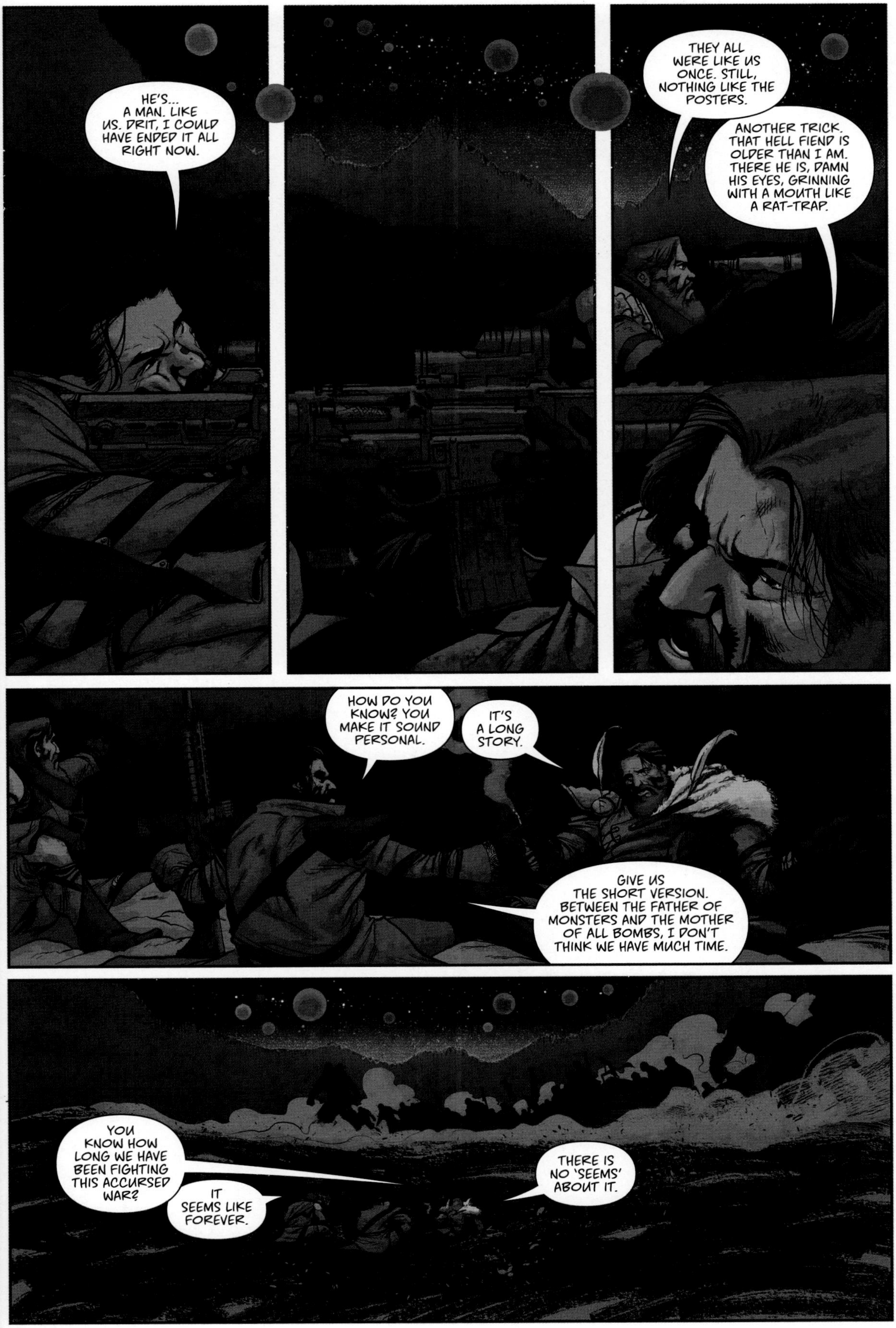
HE'S... A MAN. LIKE US. DRIT, I COULD HAVE ENDED IT ALL RIGHT NOW.
THEY ALL WERE LIKE US ONCE. STILL, NOTHING LIKE THE POSTERS.
ANOTHER TRICK. THAT HELL FIEND IS OLDER THAN I AM. THERE HE IS, DAMN HIS EYES, GRINNING WITH A MOUTH LIKE A RAT-TRAP.
HOW DO YOU KNOW? YOU MAKE IT SOUND PERSONAL.
IT'S A LONG STORY.
GIVE US THE SHORT VERSION. BETWEEN THE FATHER OF MONSTERS AND THE MOTHER OF ALL BOMBS, I DON'T THINK WE HAVE MUCH TIME.
YOU KNOW HOW LONG WE HAVE BEEN FIGHTING THIS ACCURSED WAR?
IT SEEMS LIKE FOREVER.
THERE IS NO 'SEEMS' ABOUT IT.

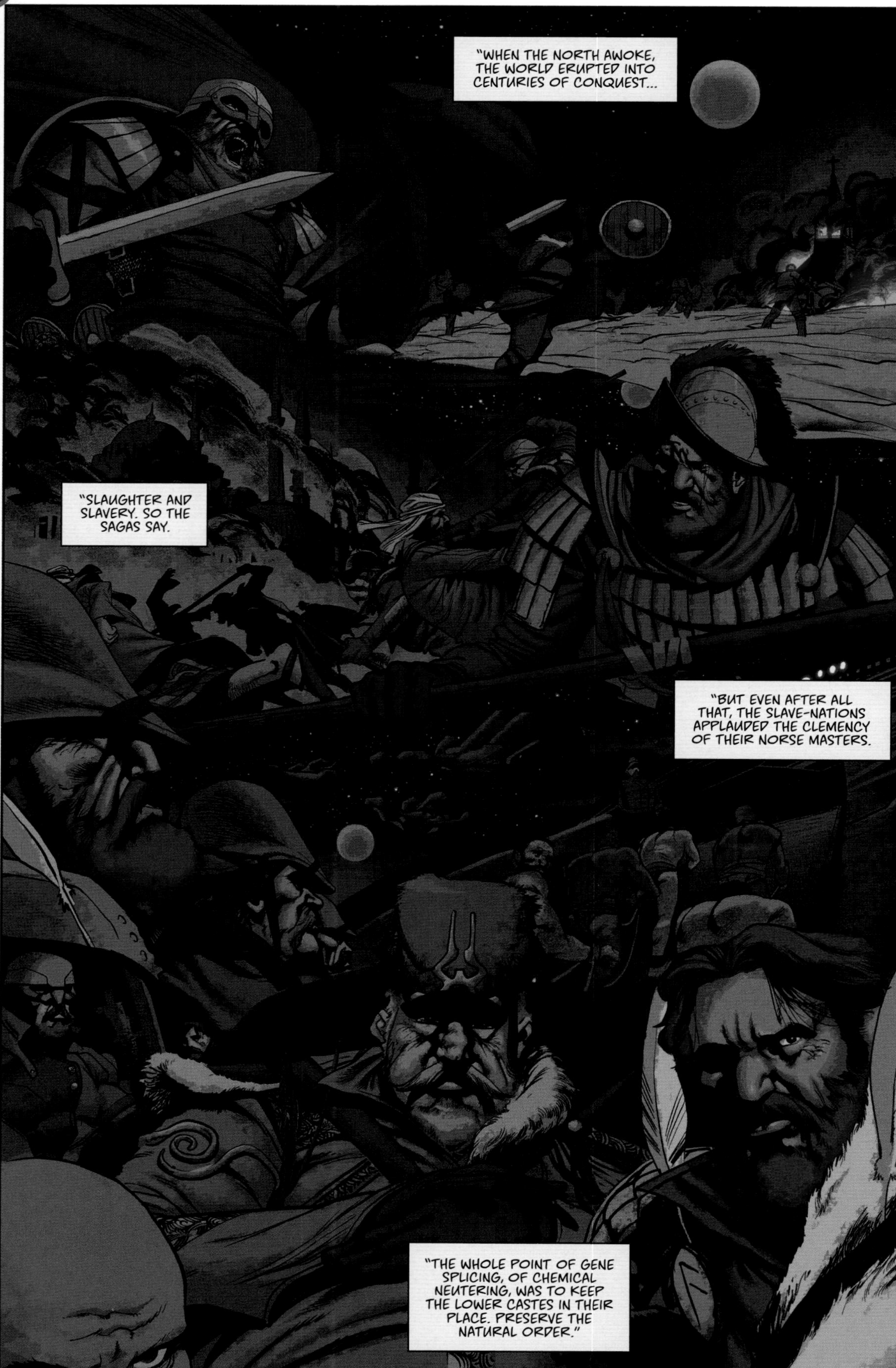
"WHEN THE NORTH AWOKE, THE WORLD ERUPTED INTO CENTURIES OF CONQUEST...
"SLAUGHTER AND SLAVERY. SO THE SAGAS SAY.
"BUT EVEN AFTER ALL THAT, THE SLAVE-NATIONS APPLAUDED THE CLEMENCY OF THEIR NORSE MASTERS.
"THE WHOLE POINT OF GENE SPLICING, OF CHEMICAL NEUTERING, WAS TO KEEP THE LOWER CASTES IN THEIR PLACE. PRESERVE THE NATURAL ORDER."

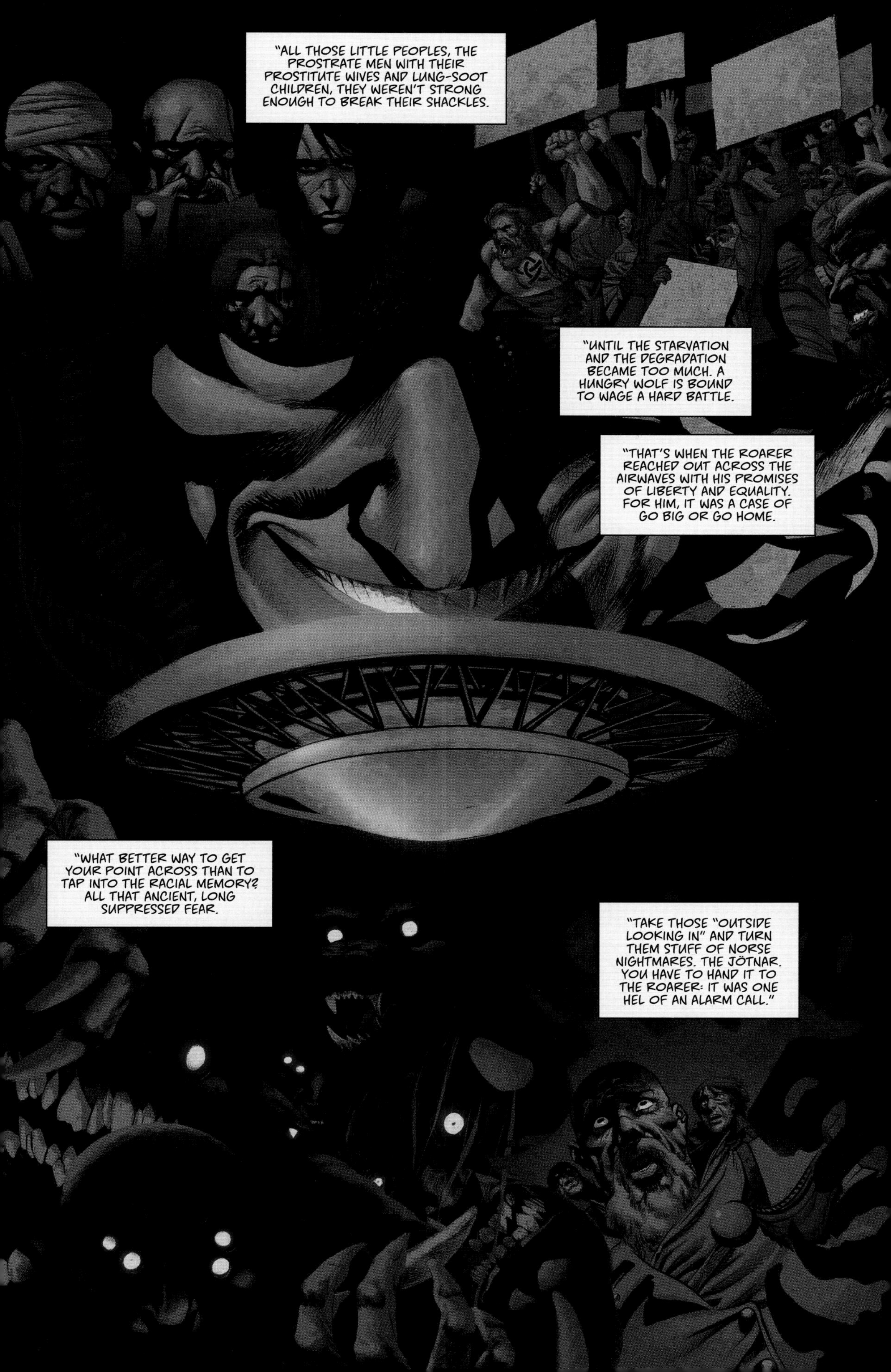
"ALL THOSE LITTLE PEOPLES, THE PROSTRATE MEN WITH THEIR PROSTITUTE WIVES AND LUNG-SOOT CHILDREN, THEY WEREN'T STRONG ENOUGH TO BREAK THEIR SHACKLES.
"UNTIL THE STARVATION AND THE DEGRADATION BECAME TOO MUCH. A HUNGRY WOLF IS BOUND TO WAGE A HARD BATTLE.
"THAT'S WHEN THE ROARER REACHED OUT ACROSS THE AIRWAVES WITH HIS PROMISES OF LIBERTY AND EQUALITY. FOR HIM, IT WAS A CASE OF GO BIG OR GO HOME.
"WHAT BETTER WAY TO GET YOUR POINT ACROSS THAN TO TAP INTO THE RACIAL MEMORY? ALL THAT ANCIENT, LONG SUPPRESSED FEAR.
"TAKE THOSE "OUTSIDE LOOKING IN" AND TURN THEM STUFF OF NORSE NIGHTMARES. THE JÖTNAR. YOU HAVE TO HAND IT TO THE ROARER: IT WAS ONE HEL OF AN ALARM CALL."

YOU SOME KIND OF WALKING, TALKING HISTORY BOOK? NEXT, YOU'RE GOING TO TELL ME YOU SAW ALL THIS WITH YOUR OWN EYES.

I WAS. NEMO MORITURUS PRAESUMITUR MENTIRI.

LATIN?

A DEAD LANGUAGE FOR A DYING DECLARATION. "NO-ONE ON THE POINT OF DEATH SHOULD BE PRESUMED TO BE LYING."

SEE THIS? A GIFT FROM THE FYLKIR, WHEN WE TOOK OLD ENGLAND. AND THAT'S HOW I KNOW THE ROARER. WE FOUGHT TOGETHER IN THOSE DAYS, SIDE BY SIDE IN THE SHIELD WALL.

WELL, IT'S A GREAT STORY. I'M GLAD I HEARD IT BEFORE I DIE.

HA. I KEPT IT QUIET ALL THESE YEARS. DIDN'T THINK ANYONE WOULD BELIEVE IT.

DON'T LOOK AT ME. WHEN I WAS A BOY, I ALWAYS SAW MYSELF AS A HERO IN SAGAS AND AT THE THINGSPIELE. I GREW UP BELIEVING THIS KINDA CRAP IMPLICITLY.

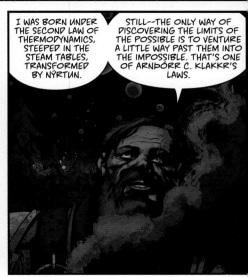

I WAS BORN UNDER THE SECOND LAW OF THERMODYNAMICS, STEEPED IN THE STEAM TABLES, TRANSFORMED BY NÝRTUN.

STILL--THE ONLY WAY OF DISCOVERING THE LIMITS OF THE POSSIBLE IS TO VENTURE A LITTLE WAY PAST THEM INTO THE IMPOSSIBLE. THAT'S ONE OF ARNÞÓRR C. KLAKKR'S LAWS.

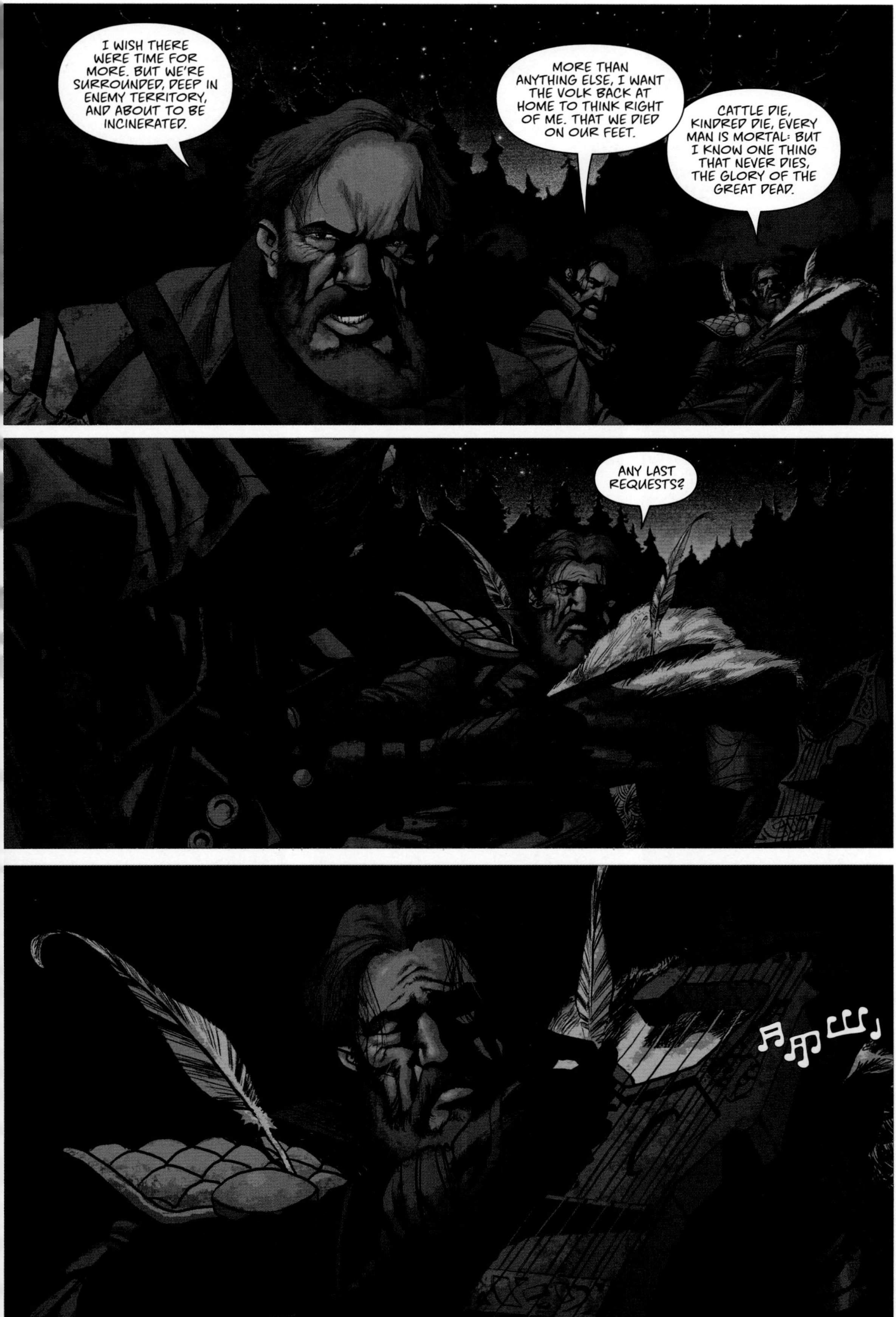
I WISH THERE WERE TIME FOR MORE. BUT WE'RE SURROUNDED, DEEP IN ENEMY TERRITORY, AND ABOUT TO BE INCINERATED.
MORE THAN ANYTHING ELSE, I WANT THE VOLK BACK AT HOME TO THINK RIGHT OF ME. THAT WE DIED ON OUR FEET.
CATTLE DIE, KINDRED DIE, EVERY MAN IS MORTAL: BUT I KNOW ONE THING THAT NEVER DIES, THE GLORY OF THE GREAT DEAD.
ANY LAST REQUESTS?

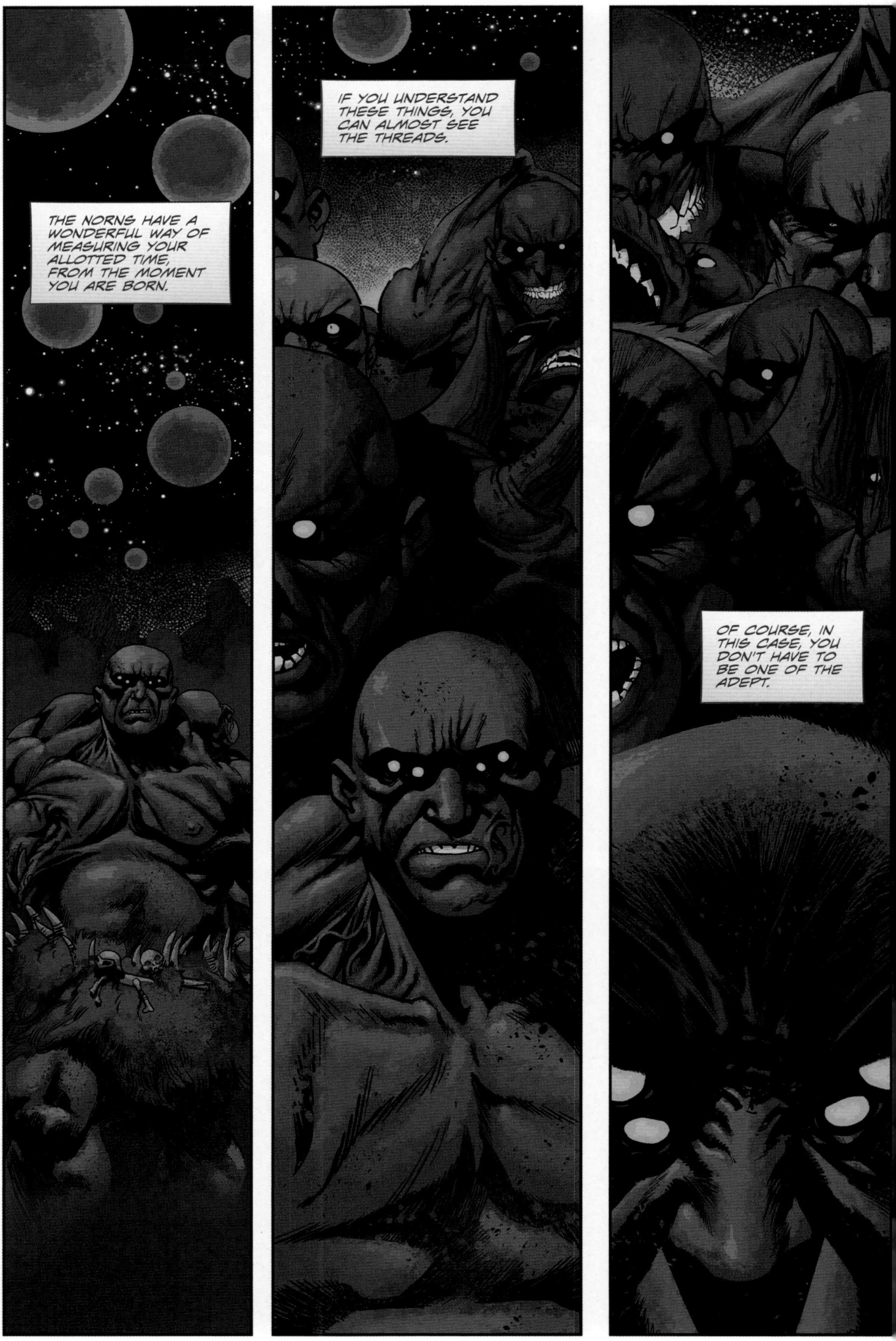
THE NORNS HAVE A WONDERFUL WAY OF MEASURING YOUR ALLOTTED TIME, FROM THE MOMENT YOU ARE BORN.
IF YOU UNDERSTAND THESE THINGS, YOU CAN ALMOST SEE THE THREADS.
OF COURSE, IN THIS CASE, YOU DON'T HAVE TO BE ONE OF THE ADEPT.

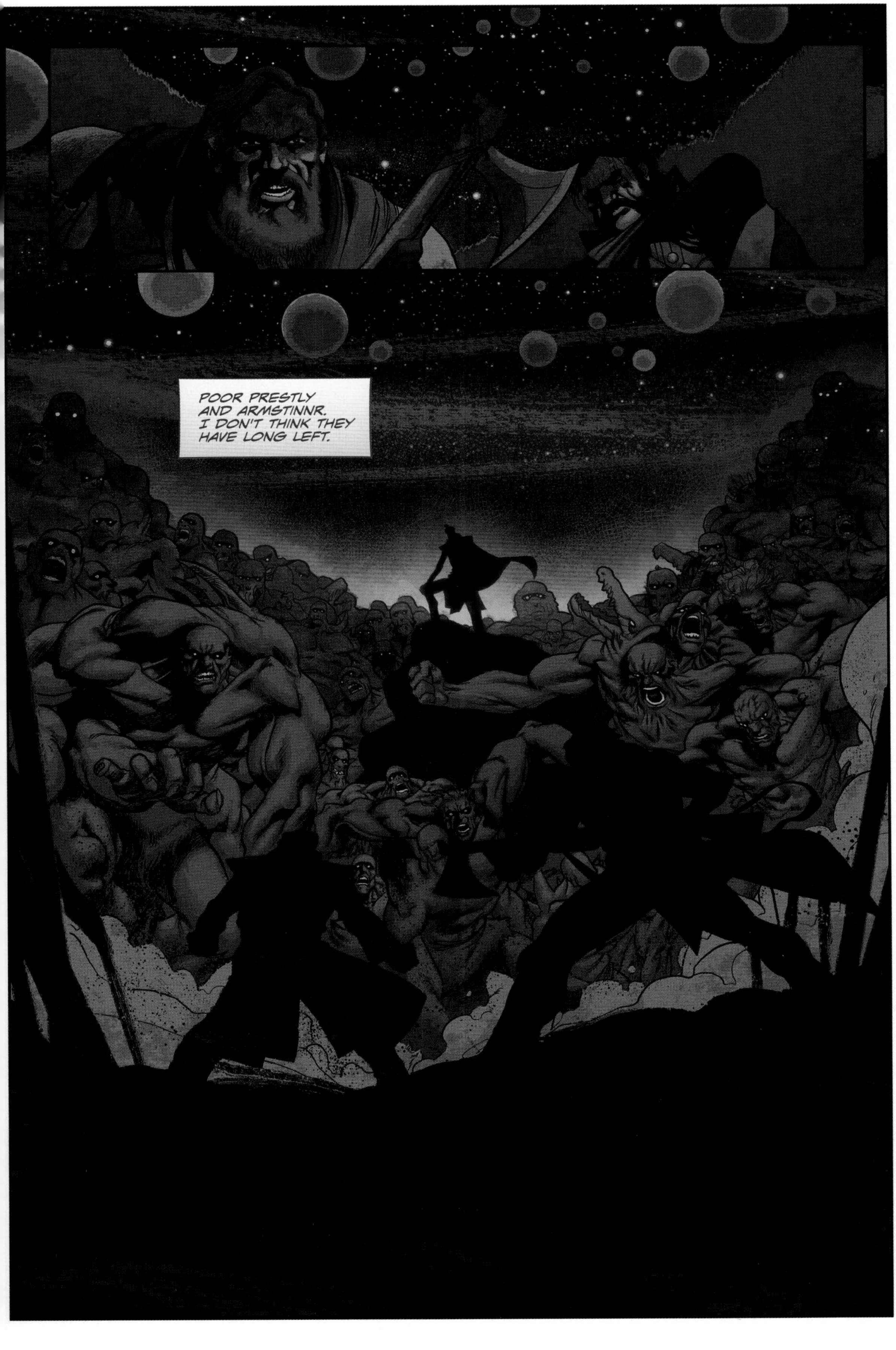
POOR PRESTLY AND ARMSTINNR. I DON'T THINK THEY HAVE LONG LEFT.

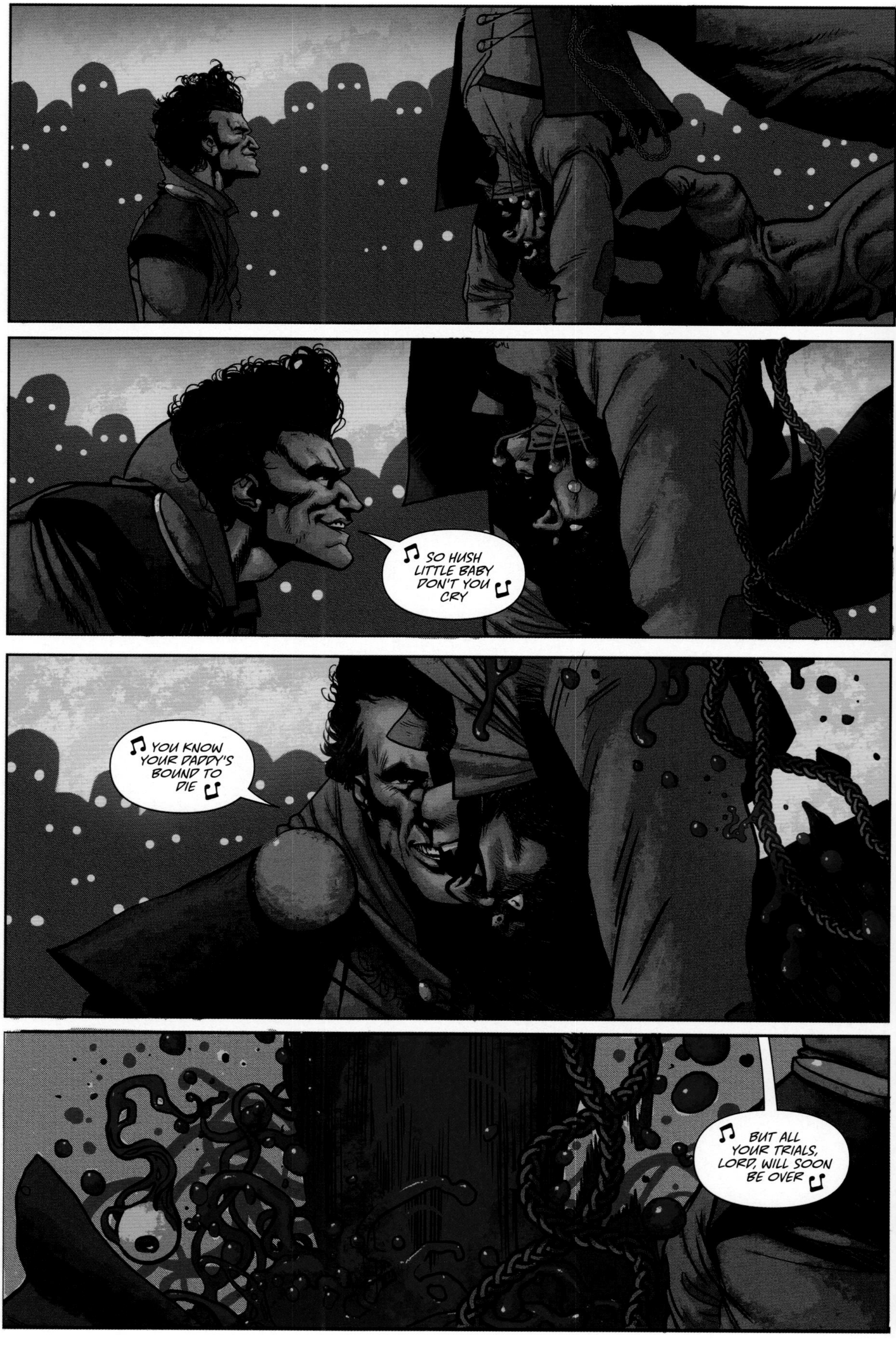
♫ SO HUSH LITTLE BABY DON'T YOU CRY ♫
♫ YOU KNOW YOUR DADDY'S BOUND TO DIE ♫
♫ BUT ALL YOUR TRIALS, LORD, WILL SOON BE OVER ♫

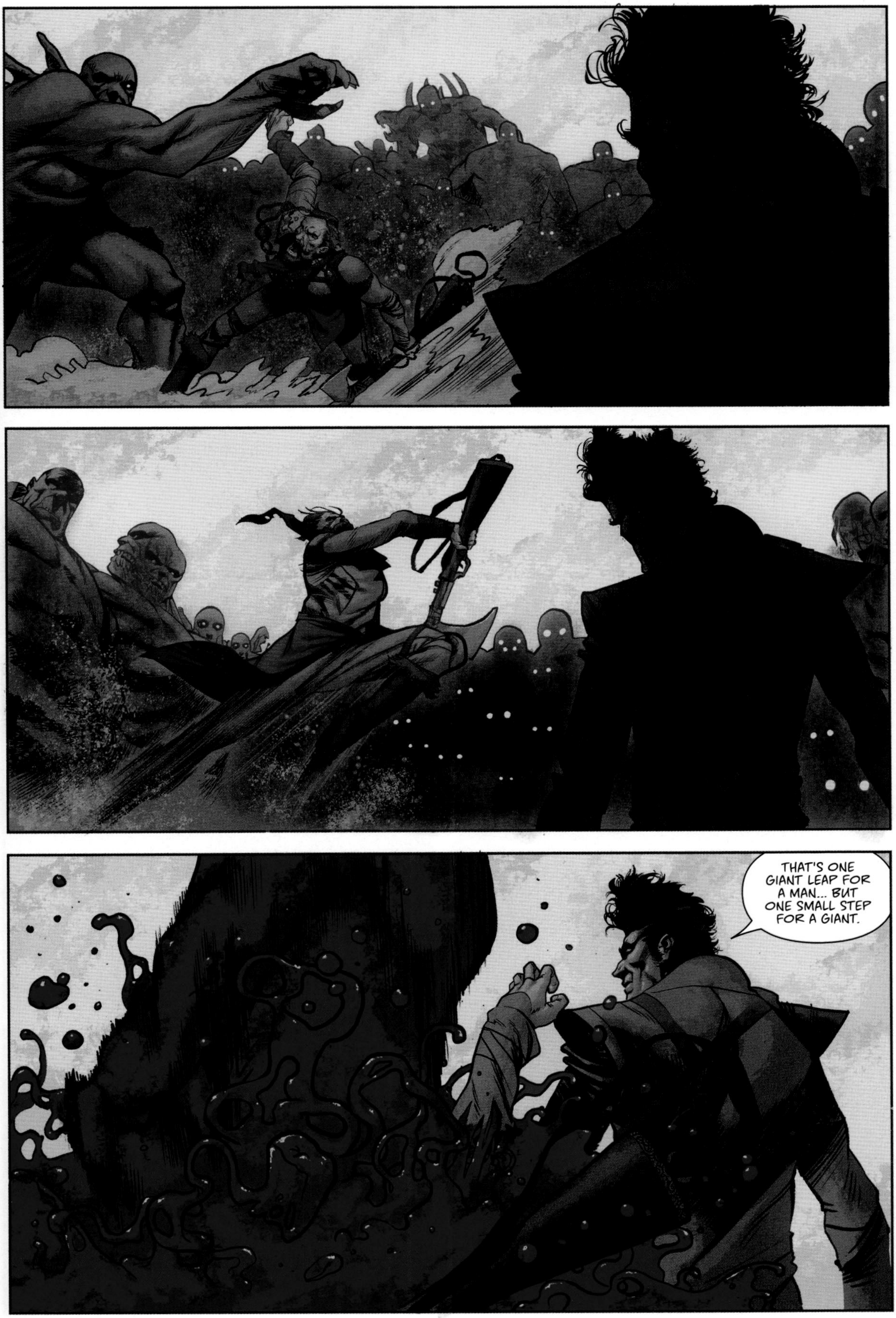
THAT'S ONE GIANT LEAP FOR A MAN... BUT ONE SMALL STEP FOR A GIANT.

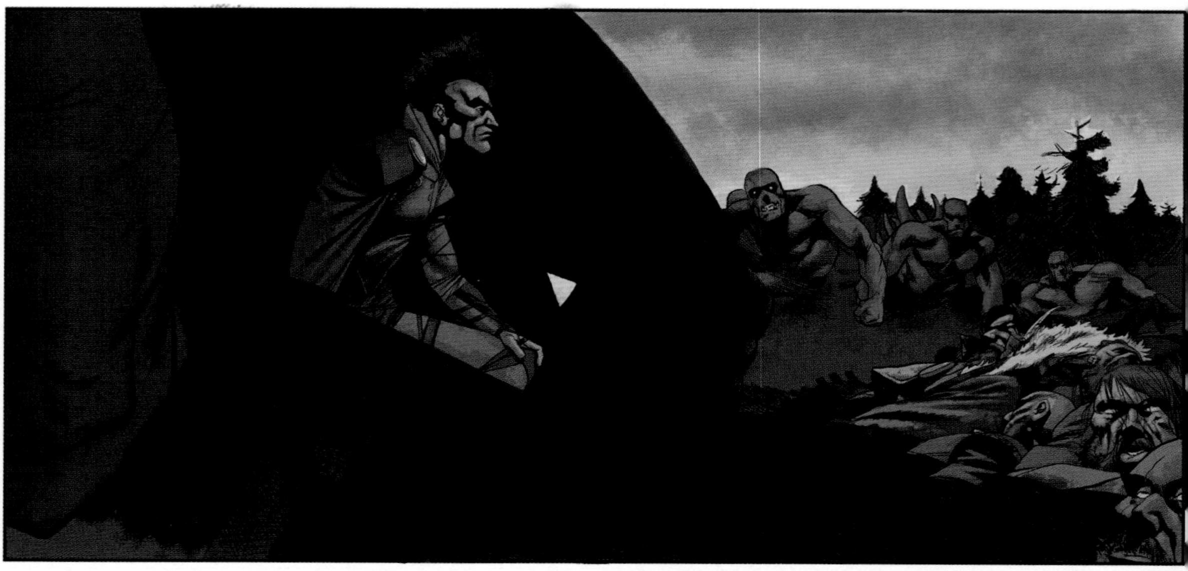
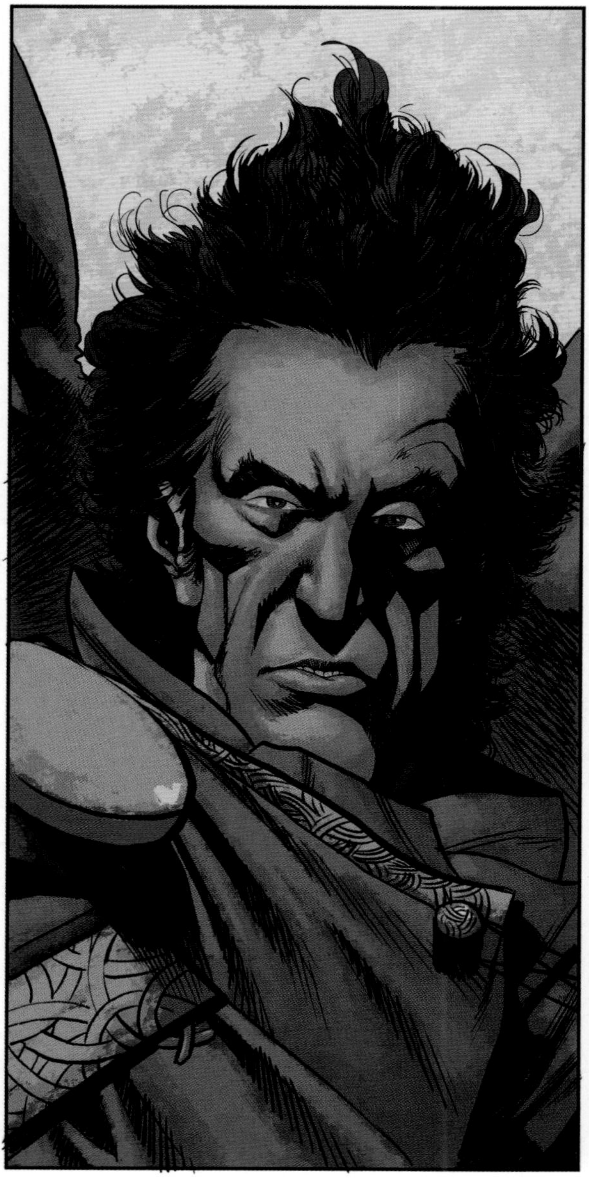
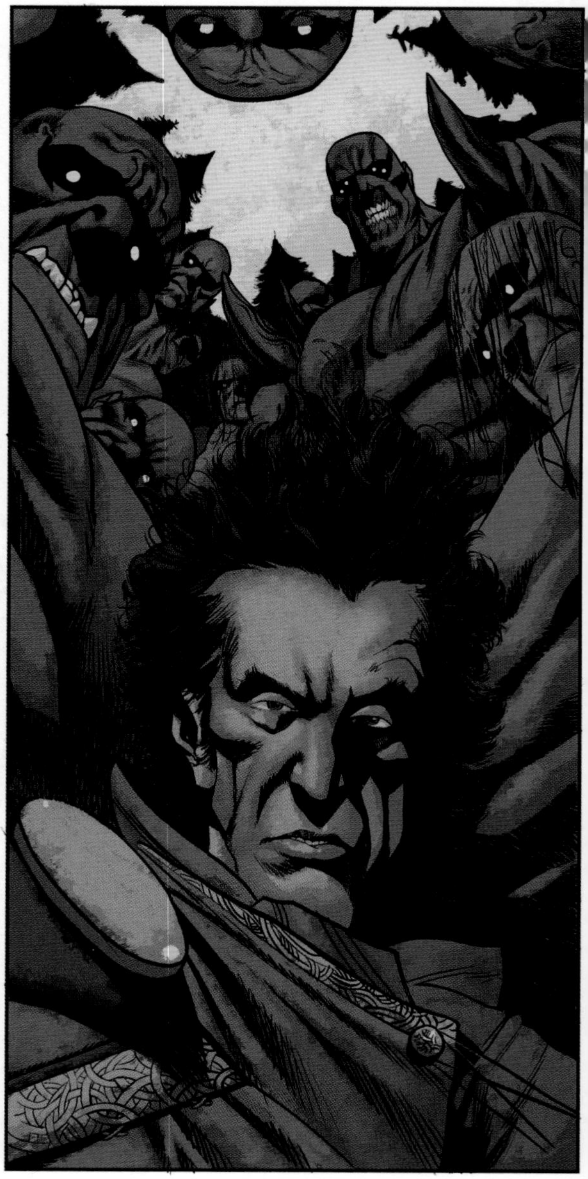

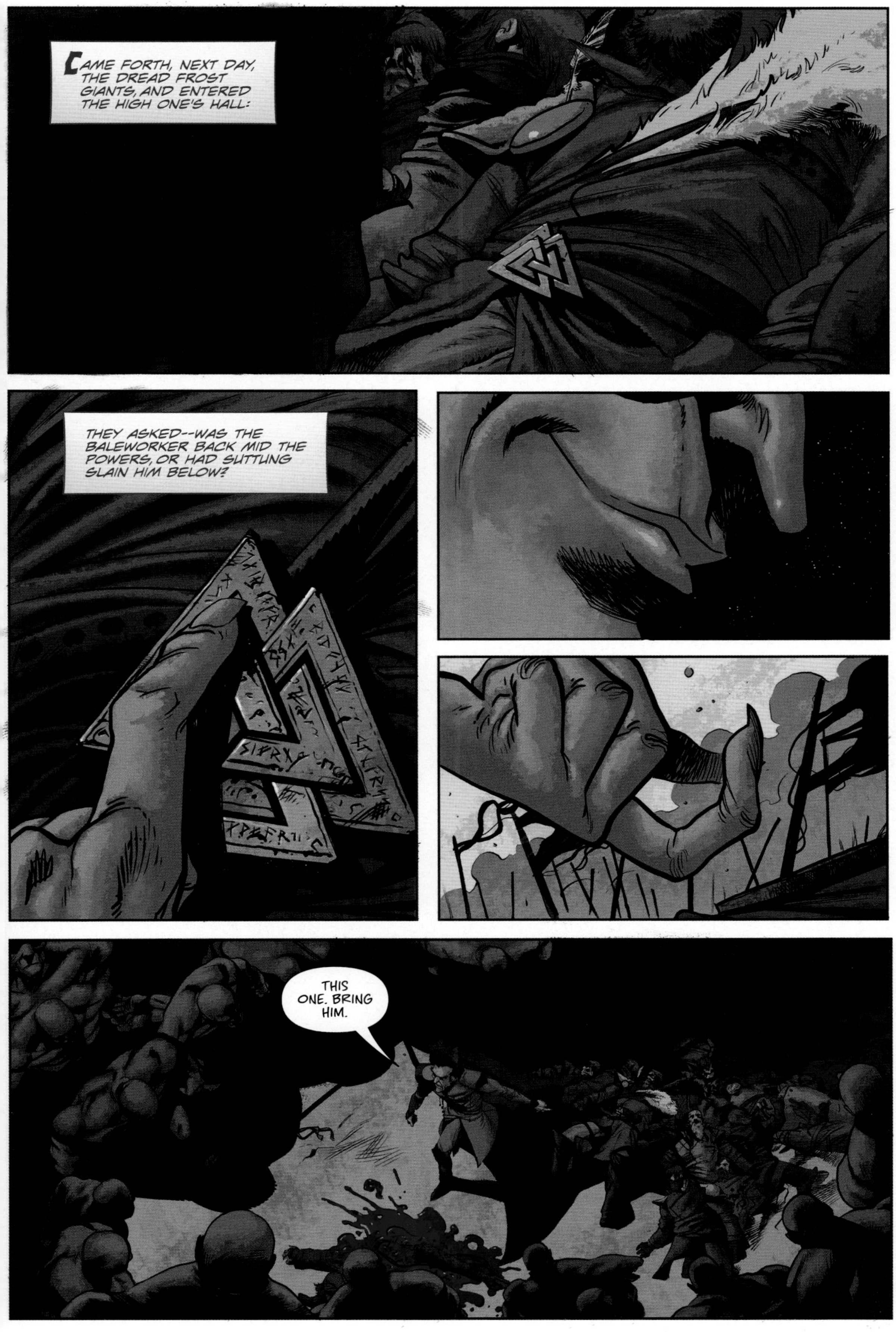
CAME FORTH, NEXT DAY, THE DREAD FROST GIANTS, AND ENTERED THE HIGH ONE'S HALL:
THEY ASKED--WAS THE BALEWORKER BACK MID THE POWERS, OR HAD SUTTUNG SLAIN HIM BELOW?
THIS ONE. BRING HIM.

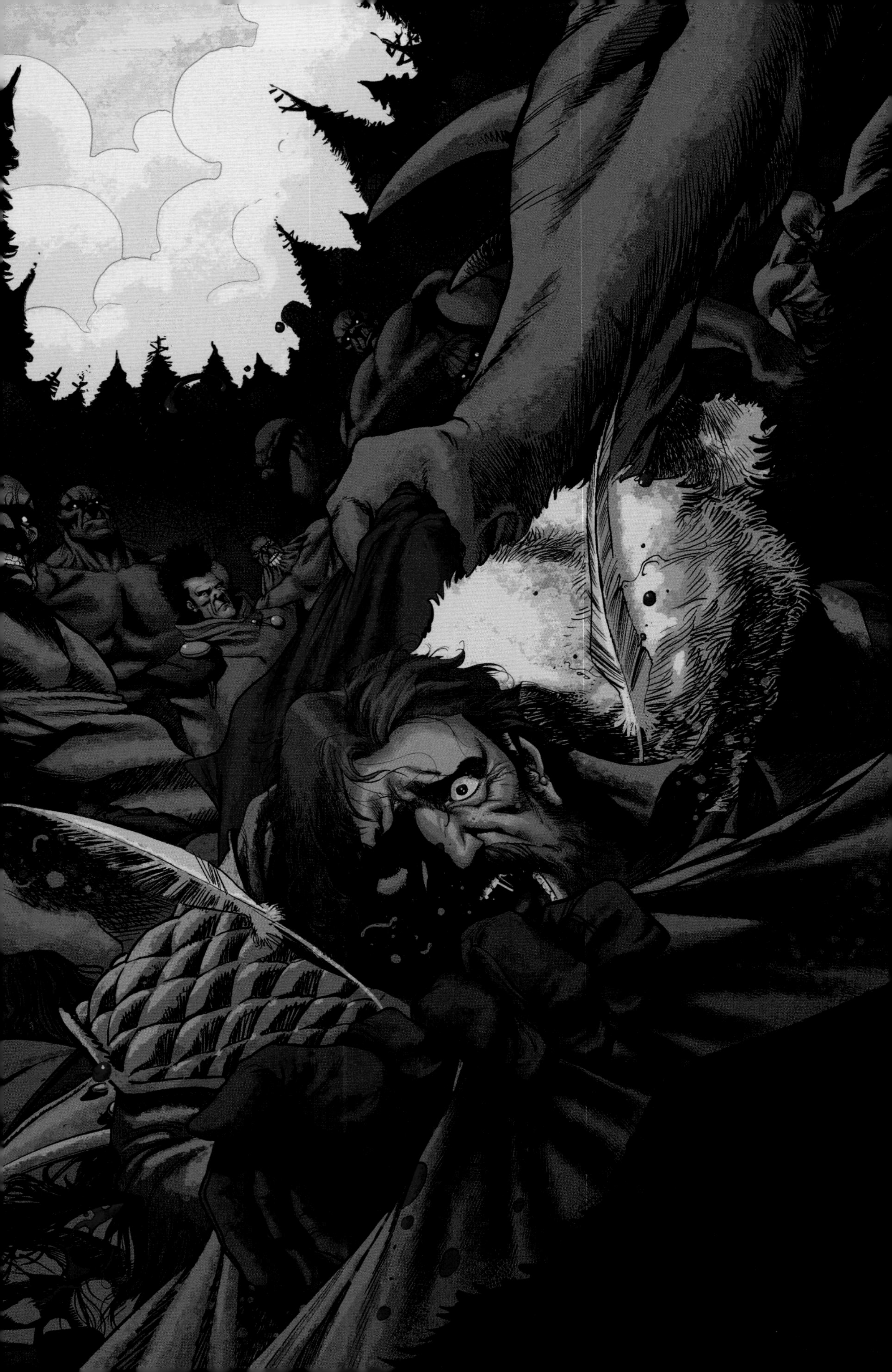

MEN
OF THE
EMPIRE

THE **GRATITUDE** OF EVERY HOME IN MIDGARD,
AND INDEED THROUGHOUT THE **NINE WORLDS**,
GOES OUT TO THE NORSE **AIRMEN** WHO,

UNDAUNTED BY ODDS

UNWEARIED IN THEIR **CONSTANT CHALLENGE** AND **MORTAL DANGER**,
ARE **TURNING THE TIDE** OF THE JÖTUNN WAR BY THEIR

PROWESS
AND BY THEIR
DEVOTION.

NEVER IN THE FIELD OF INHUMAN CONFLICT WAS
SO MUCH OWED BY **SO MANY** TO **SO FEW.**

THEY SHALL **MOUNT UP** WITH **WINGS AS RAVENS;**
THEY SHALL **SOAR** AND **NOT BE WEARY;**
AND THEY SHALL **SWOOP** AND **NOT BE FAINT.**

YOUR EMPEROR NEEDS YOU
TO MAINTAIN THE HONOUR
AND GLORY OF THE

UNITED
KINGDOMS

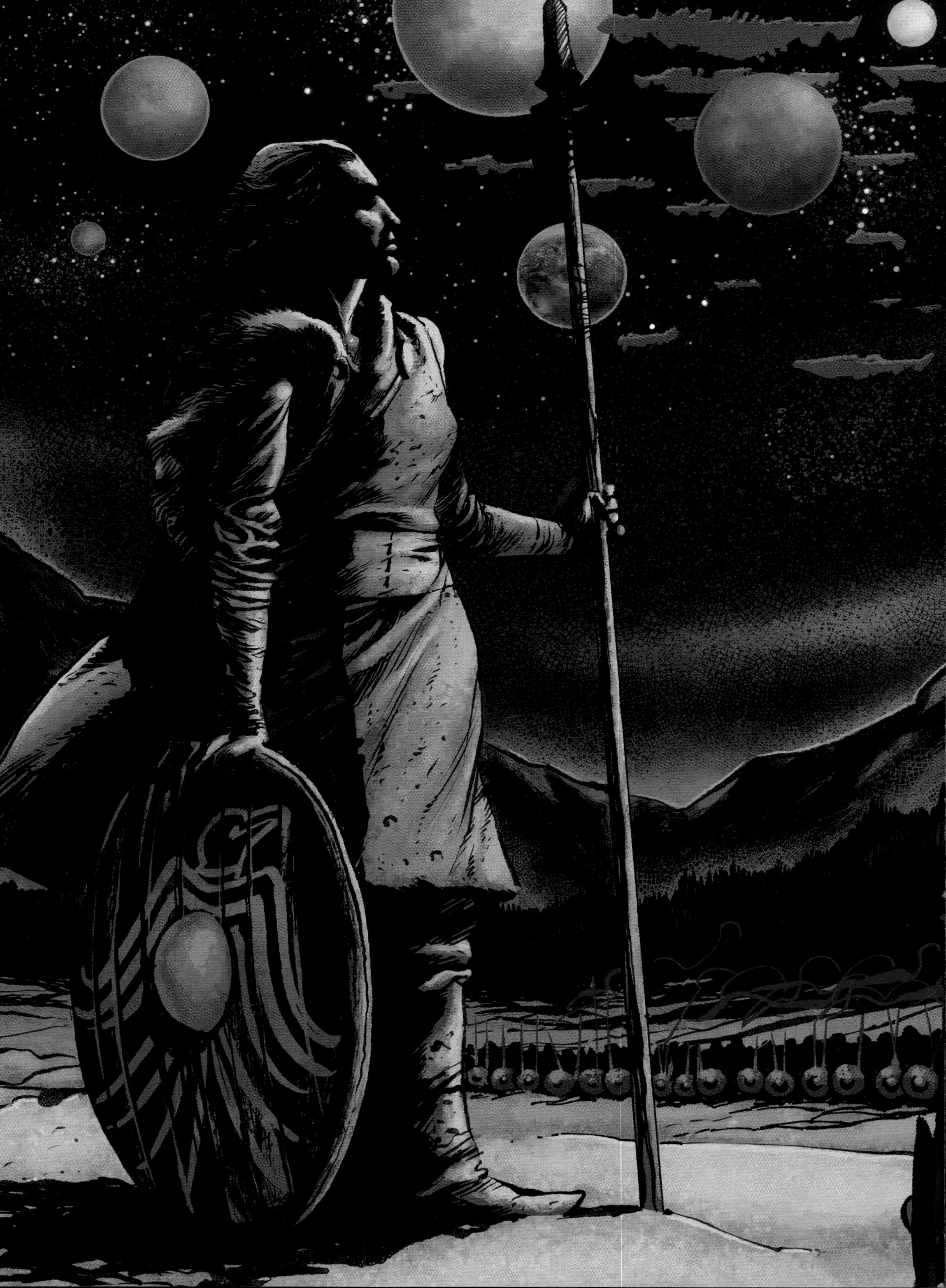

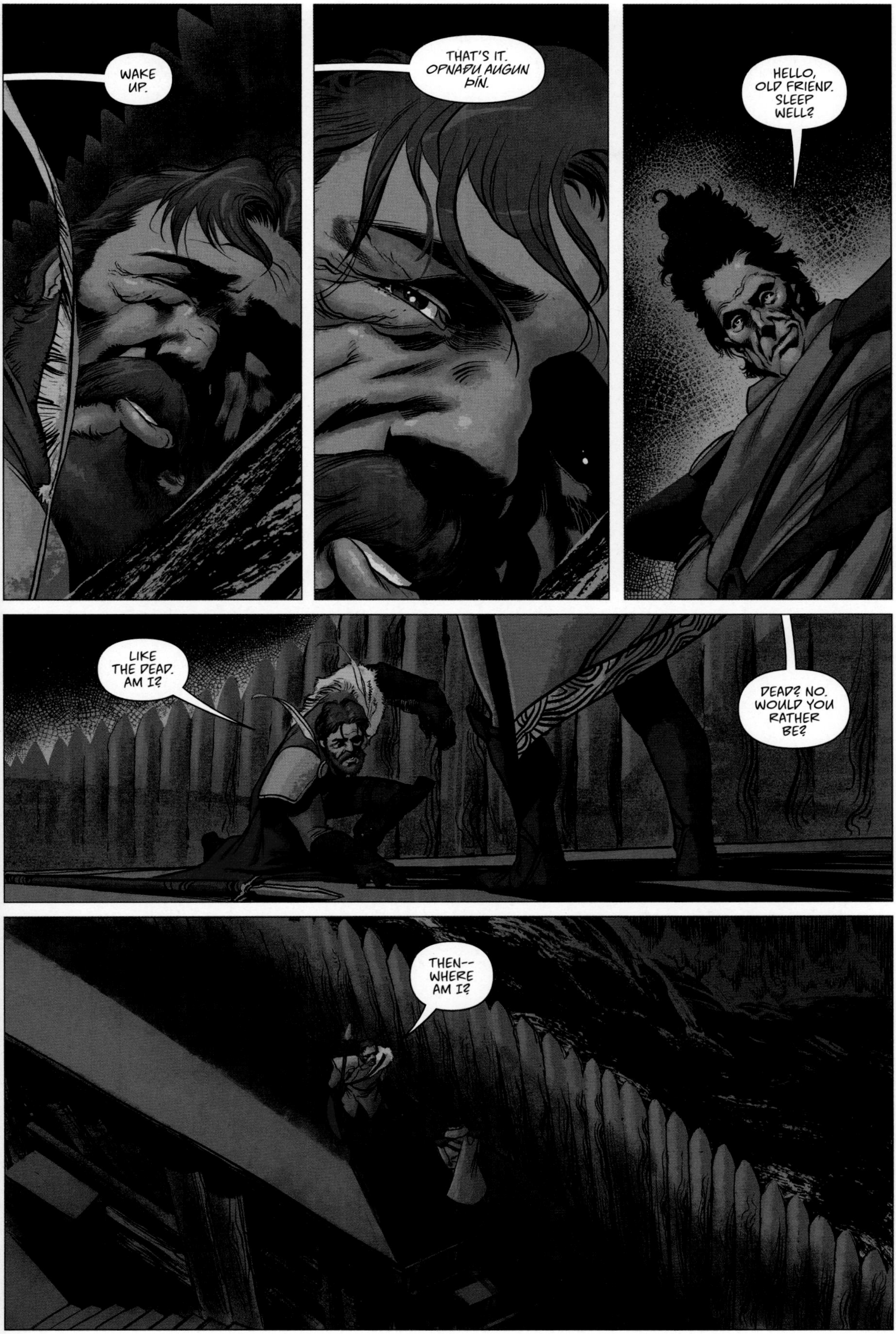
WAKE UP.
THAT'S IT. OPNAÐU AUGUN ÞÍN.
HELLO, OLD FRIEND. SLEEP WELL?
LIKE THE DEAD. AM I?
DEAD? NO. WOULD YOU RATHER BE?
THEN-- WHERE AM I?

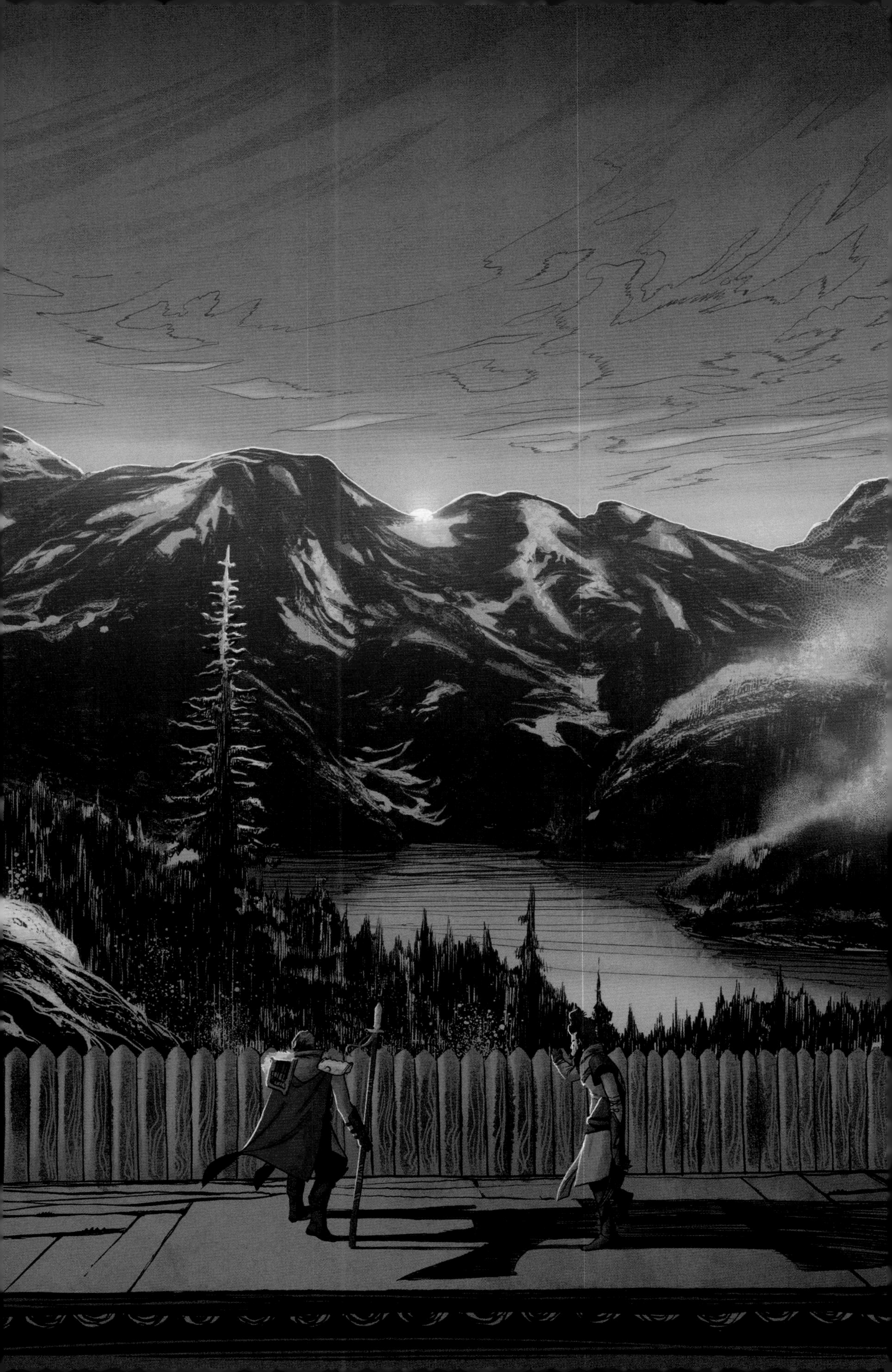

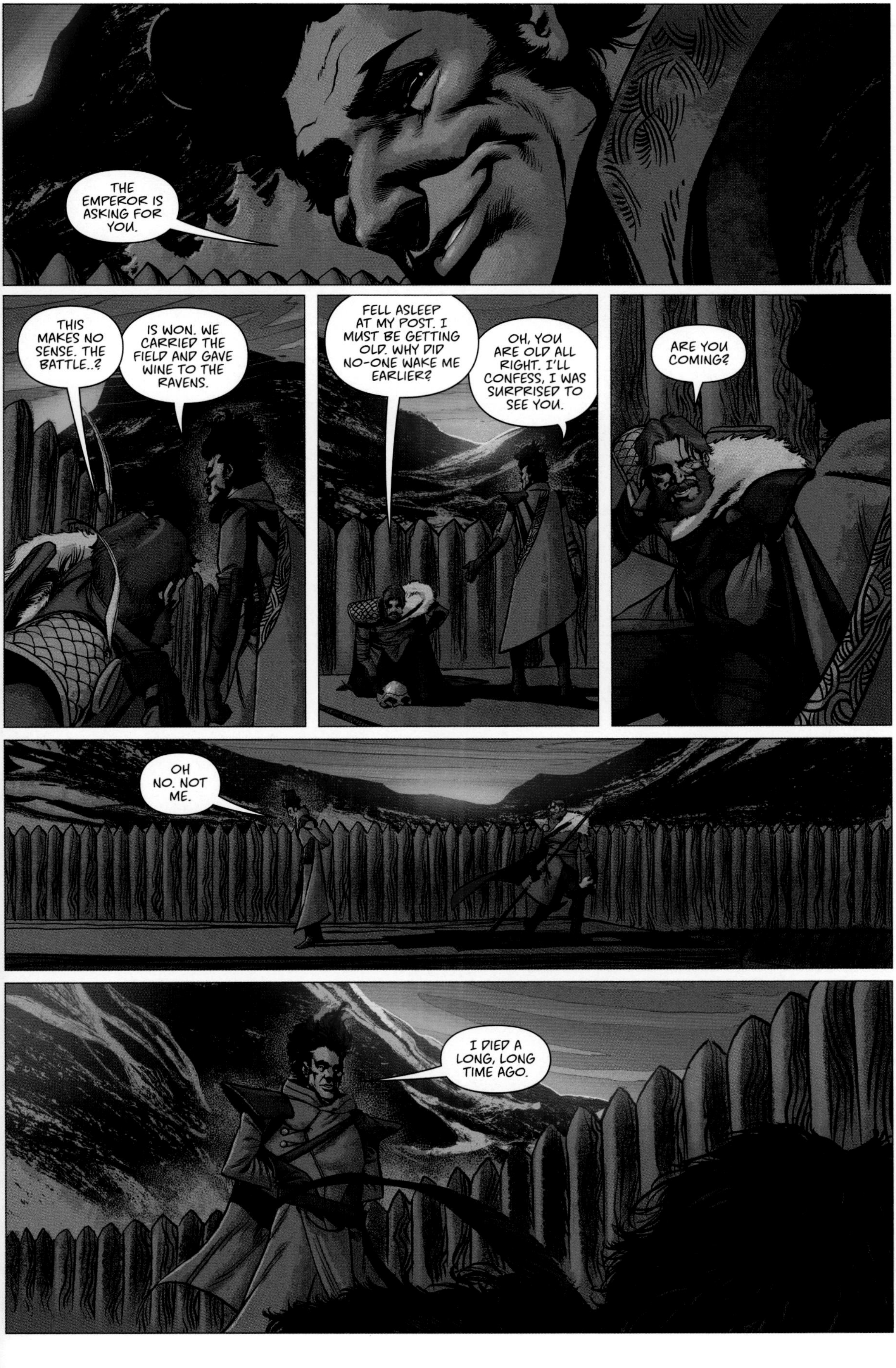
THE EMPEROR IS ASKING FOR YOU.
THIS MAKES NO SENSE. THE BATTLE..?
IS WON. WE CARRIED THE FIELD AND GAVE WINE TO THE RAVENS.
FELL ASLEEP AT MY POST. I MUST BE GETTING OLD. WHY DID NO-ONE WAKE ME EARLIER?
OH, YOU ARE OLD ALL RIGHT. I'LL CONFESS, I WAS SURPRISED TO SEE YOU.
ARE YOU COMING?
OH NO. NOT ME.
I DIED A LONG, LONG TIME AGO.

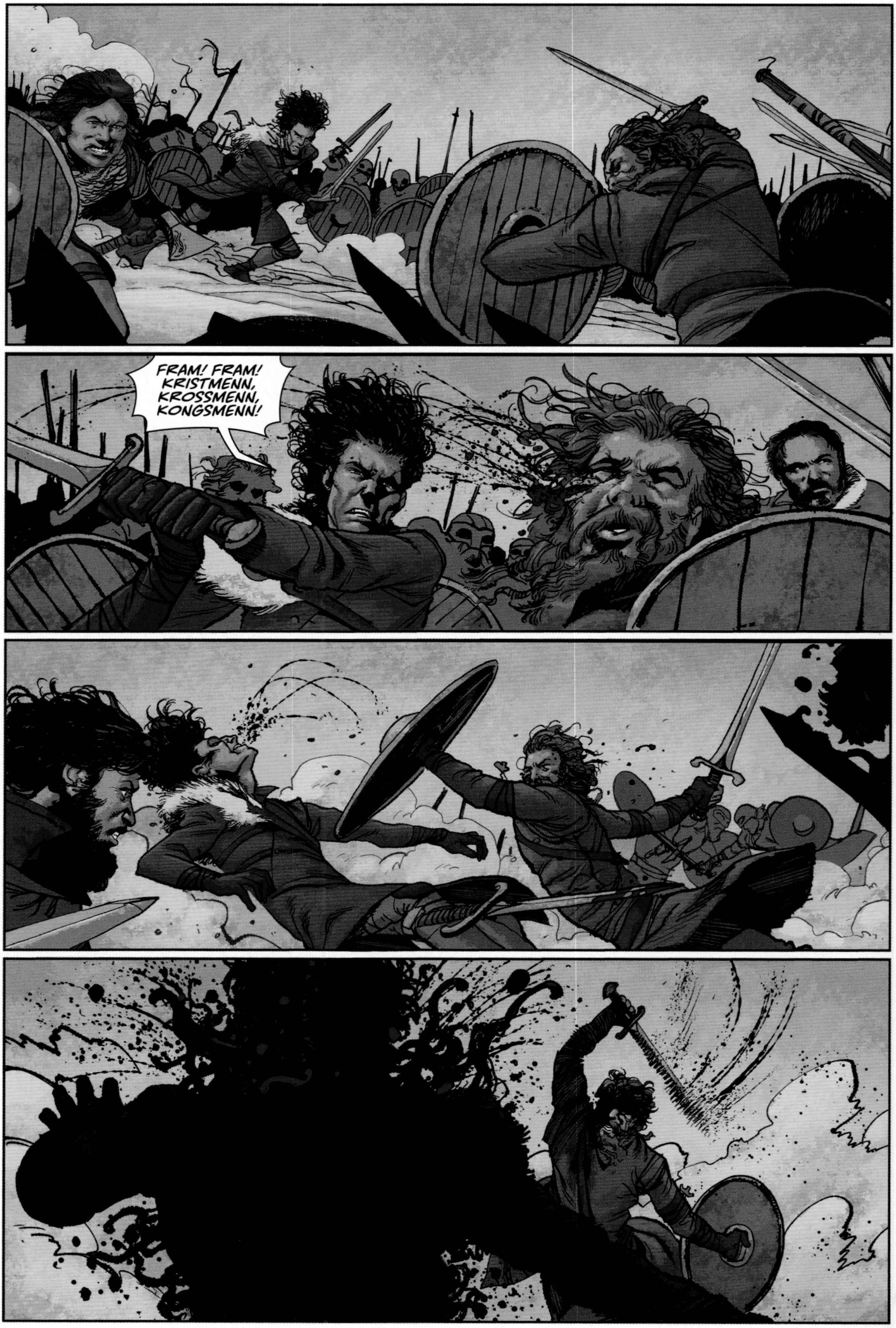
FRAM! FRAM! KRISTMENN, KROSSMENN, KONGSMENN!

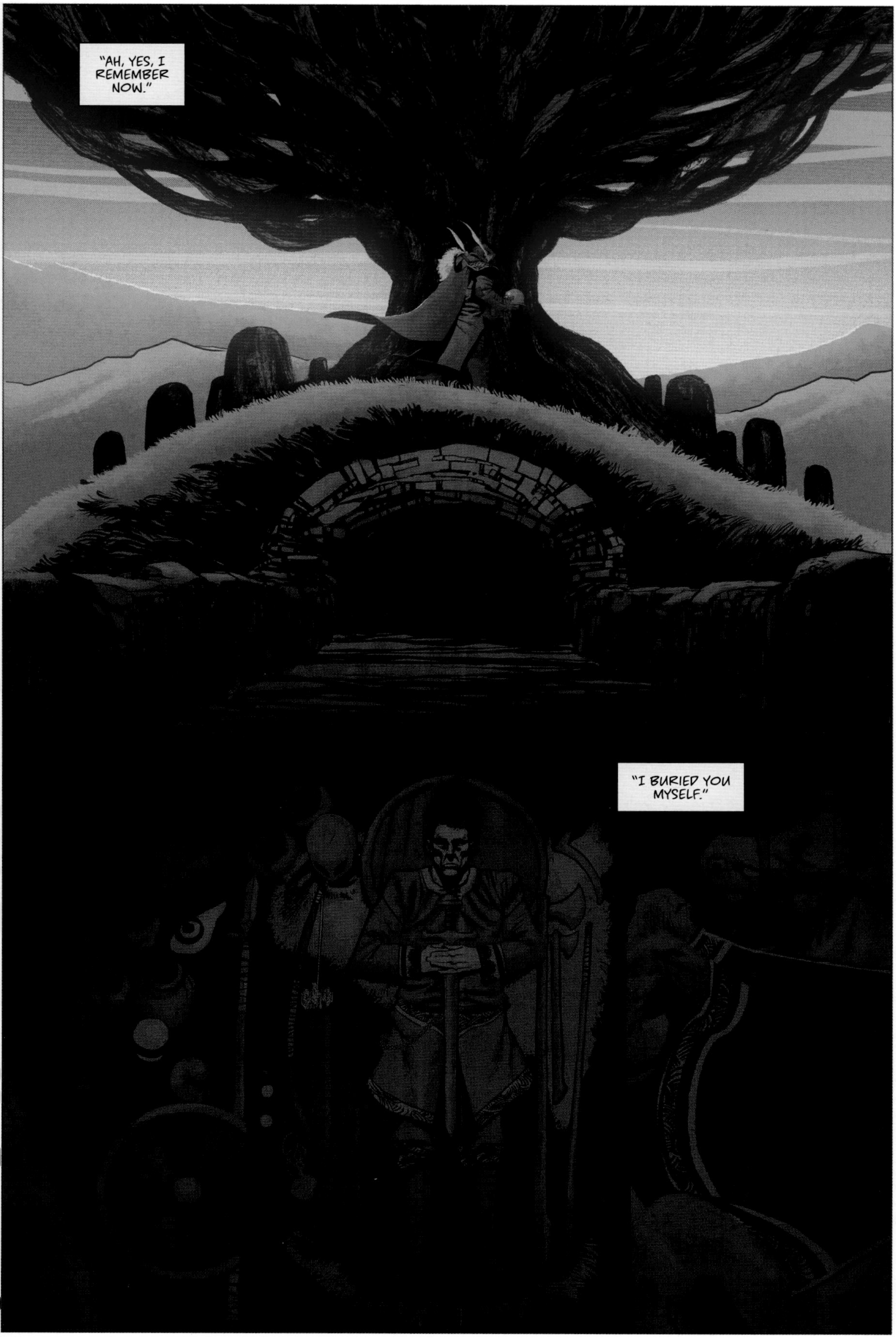
"AH, YES, I REMEMBER NOW."
"I BURIED YOU MYSELF."

TRAPPED WITH A DRAUGR.

A WIGHT, BURIED IN HIS BARROW-MOUND.

SOMEWHERE BETWEEN LIFE AND DEATH.

DOES IT LOOK LIKE HIM? THOSE STARVED LIPS, GAPING IN THE GLOOM. HARD TO TELL.

THEN AGAIN, JEALOUS OF LIFE, THE DRAUGR CAN CHANGE THEIR SHAPE. TO WATCH OVER THEIR BIRTHRIGHT. TO GUARD THEIR POSSESSIONS.

IT'S THE VOICE. AND THE GLOW OF FOX FIRE. THAT GAVE HIM AWAY. THAT HAUNTS ME STILL.

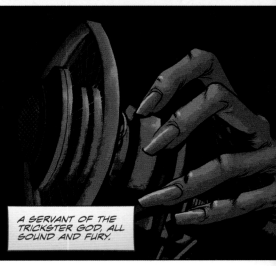

A SERVANT OF THE TRICKSTER GOD, ALL SOUND AND FURY.

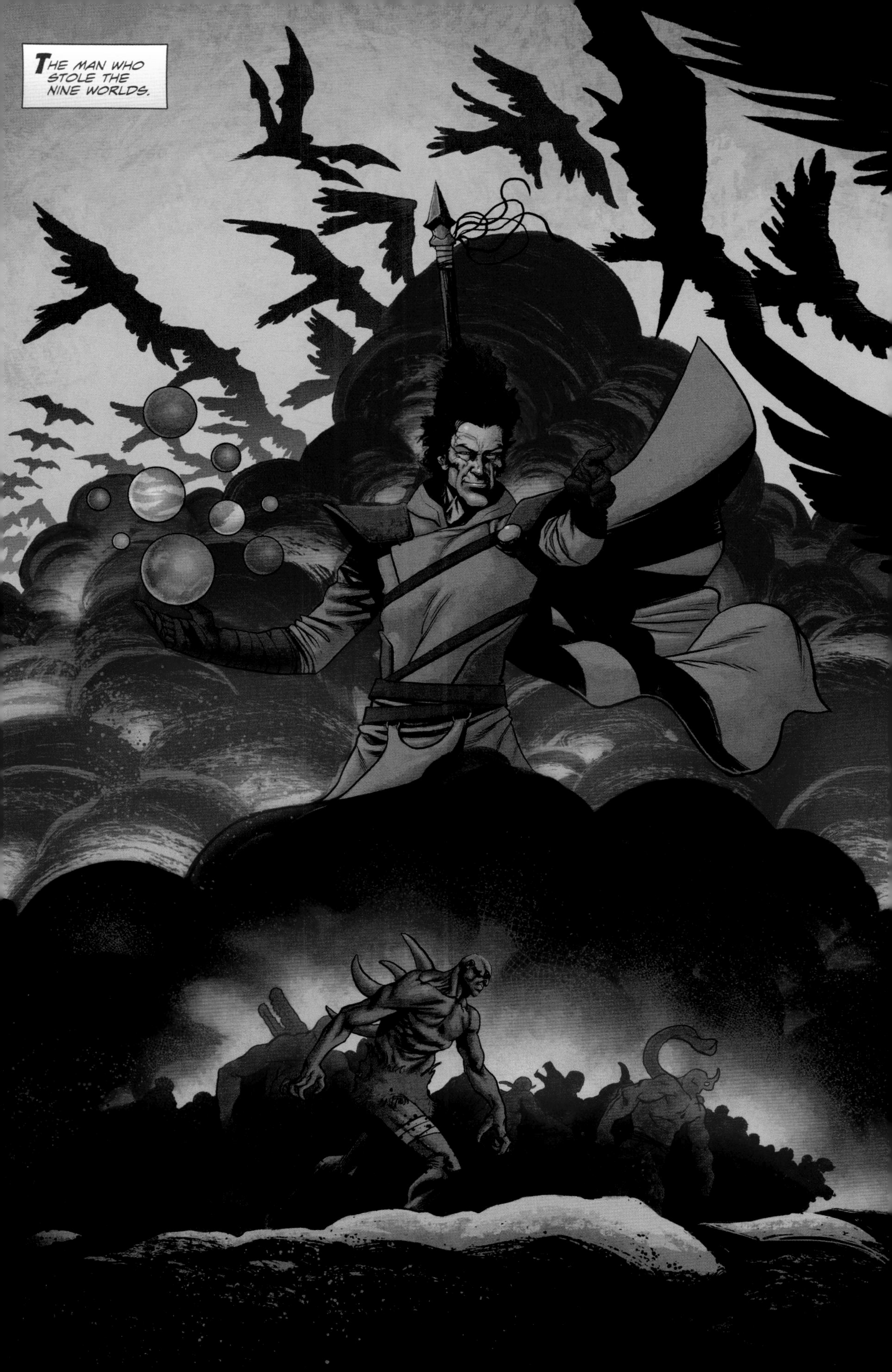
THE MAN WHO STOLE THE NINE WORLDS.

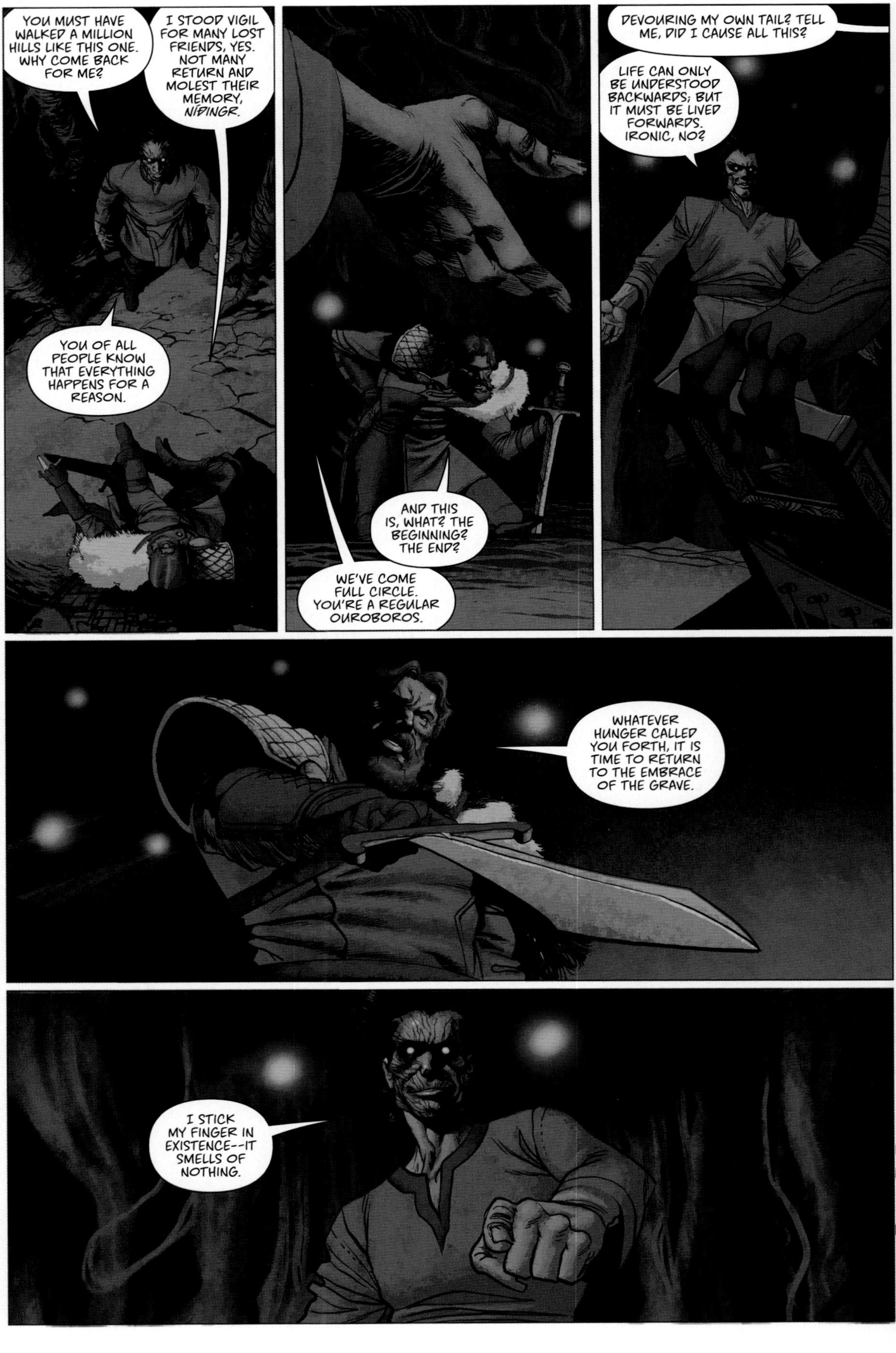
YOU MUST HAVE WALKED A MILLION HILLS LIKE THIS ONE. WHY COME BACK FOR ME?
I STOOD VIGIL FOR MANY LOST FRIENDS, YES. NOT MANY RETURN AND MOLEST THEIR MEMORY, *NÍÐINGR.*
YOU OF ALL PEOPLE KNOW THAT EVERYTHING HAPPENS FOR A REASON.
AND THIS IS, WHAT? THE BEGINNING? THE END?
WE'VE COME FULL CIRCLE. YOU'RE A REGULAR OUROBOROS.
DEVOURING MY OWN TAIL? TELL ME, DID I CAUSE ALL THIS?
LIFE CAN ONLY BE UNDERSTOOD BACKWARDS; BUT IT MUST BE LIVED FORWARDS. IRONIC, NO?
WHATEVER HUNGER CALLED YOU FORTH, IT IS TIME TO RETURN TO THE EMBRACE OF THE GRAVE.
I STICK MY FINGER IN EXISTENCE--IT SMELLS OF NOTHING.

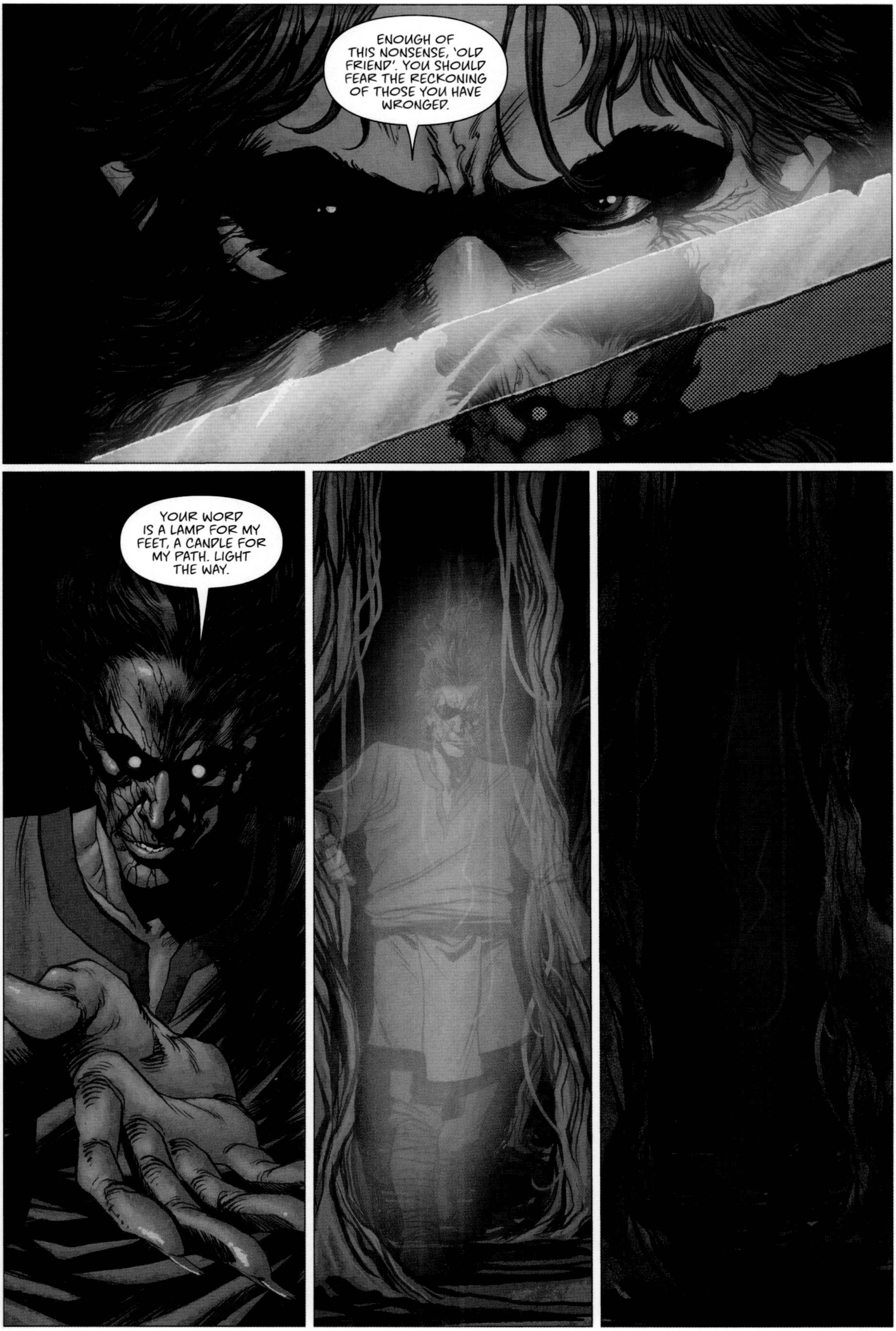
ENOUGH OF THIS NONSENSE, 'OLD FRIEND'. YOU SHOULD FEAR THE RECKONING OF THOSE YOU HAVE WRONGED.
YOUR WORD IS A LAMP FOR MY FEET, A CANDLE FOR MY PATH. LIGHT THE WAY.

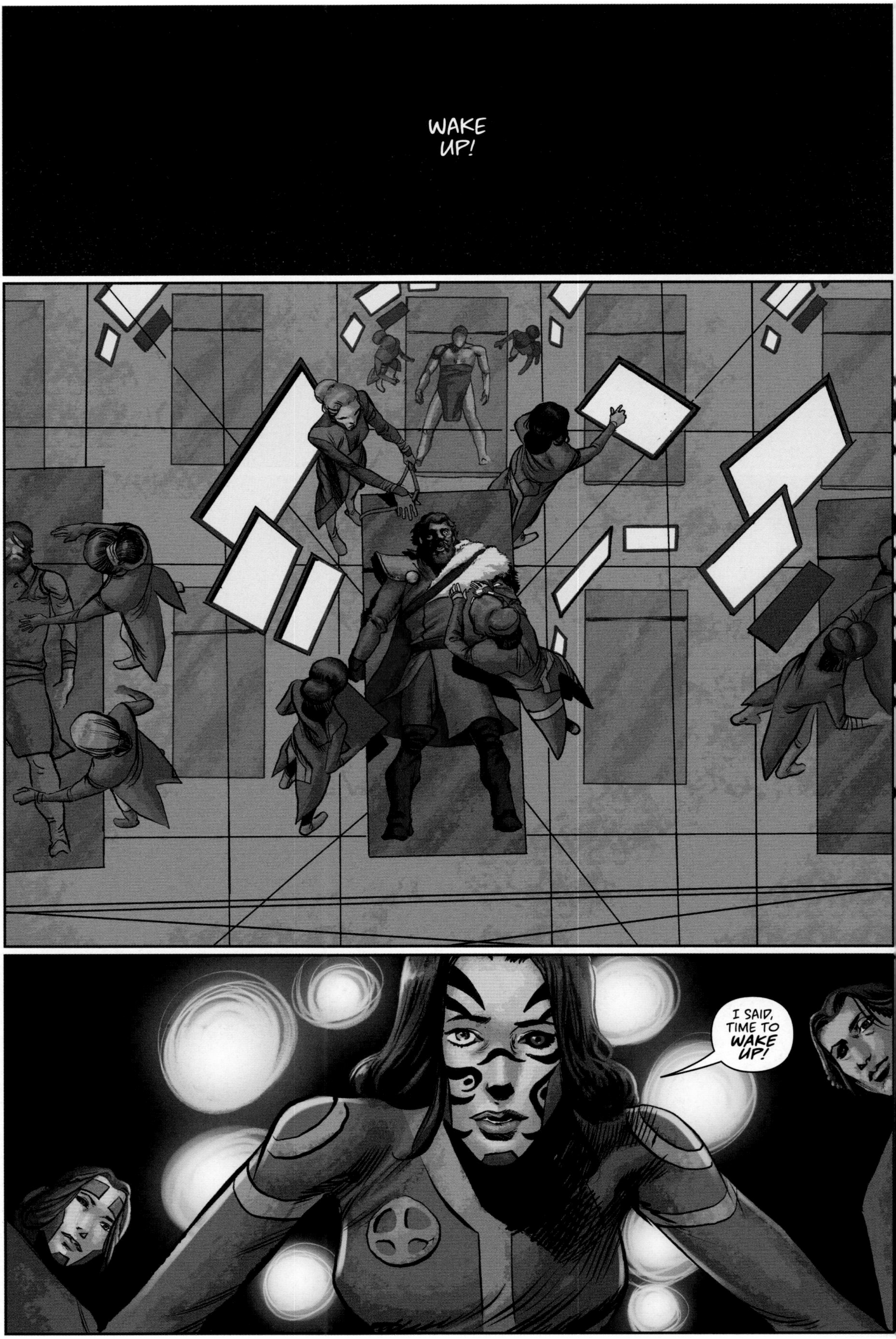
WAKE UP!
I SAID, TIME TO WAKE UP!

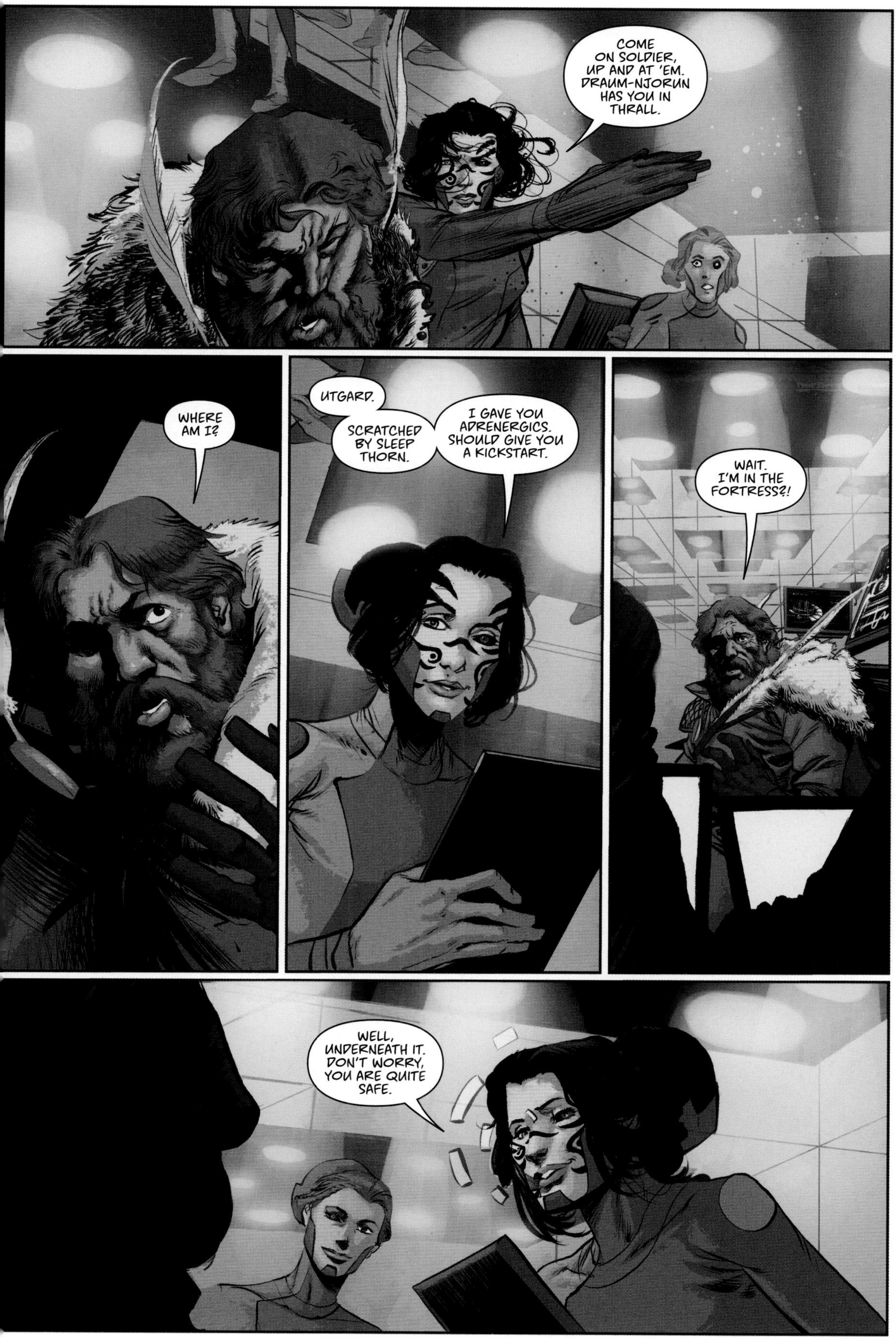
COME ON SOLDIER, UP AND AT 'EM. DRAUM-NJORUN HAS YOU IN THRALL.
WHERE AM I?
UTGARD.
SCRATCHED BY SLEEP THORN.
I GAVE YOU ADRENERGICS. SHOULD GIVE YOU A KICKSTART.
WAIT. I'M IN THE FORTRESS?!
WELL, UNDERNEATH IT. DON'T WORRY, YOU ARE QUITE SAFE.

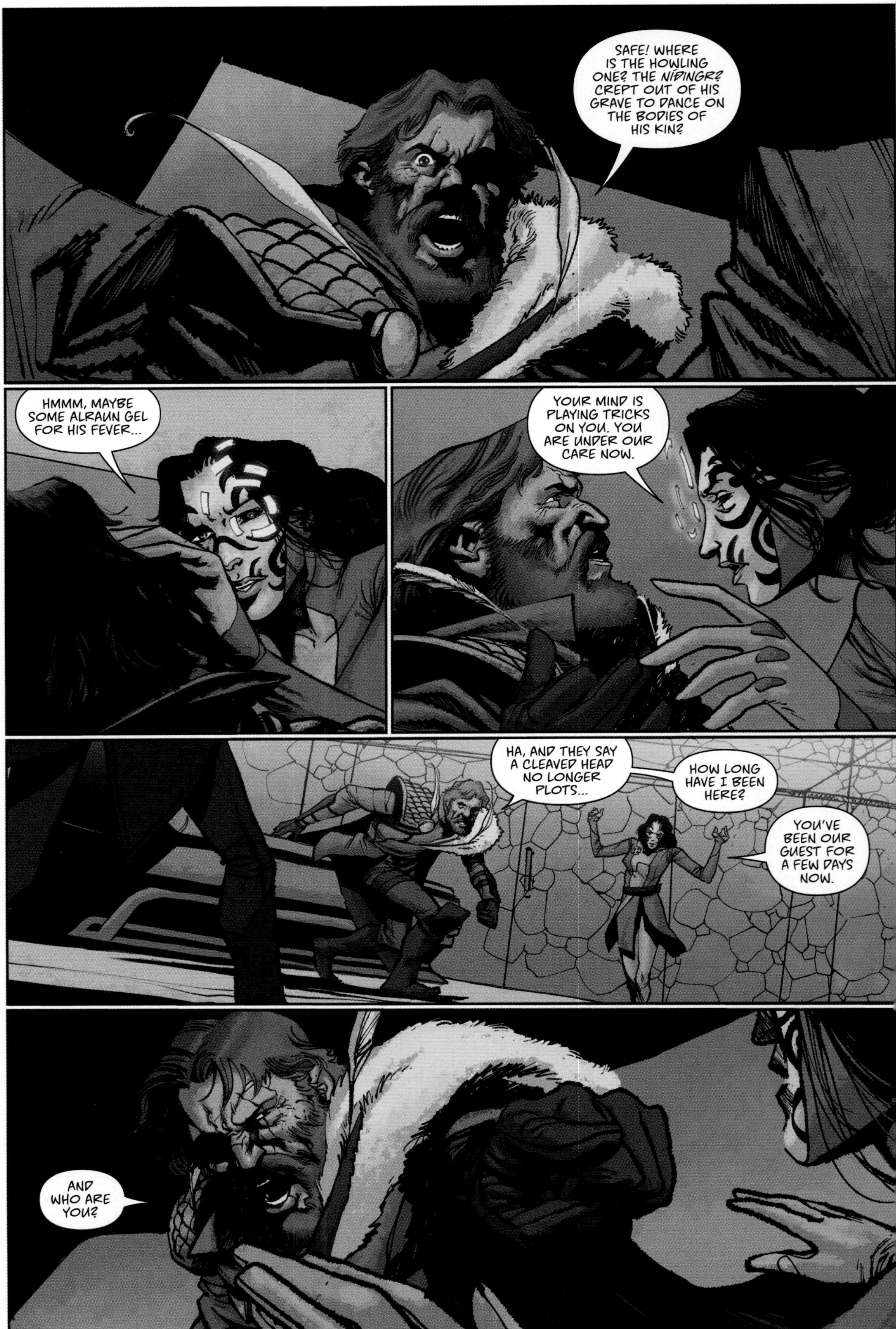

SAFE! WHERE IS THE HOWLING ONE? THE *NÍÐINGR*? CREPT OUT OF HIS GRAVE TO DANCE ON THE BODIES OF HIS KIN?
HMMM, MAYBE SOME ALRAUN GEL FOR HIS FEVER...
YOUR MIND IS PLAYING TRICKS ON YOU. YOU ARE UNDER OUR CARE NOW.
HA, AND THEY SAY A CLEAVED HEAD NO LONGER PLOTS...
HOW LONG HAVE I BEEN HERE?
YOU'VE BEEN OUR GUEST FOR A FEW DAYS NOW.
AND WHO ARE YOU?

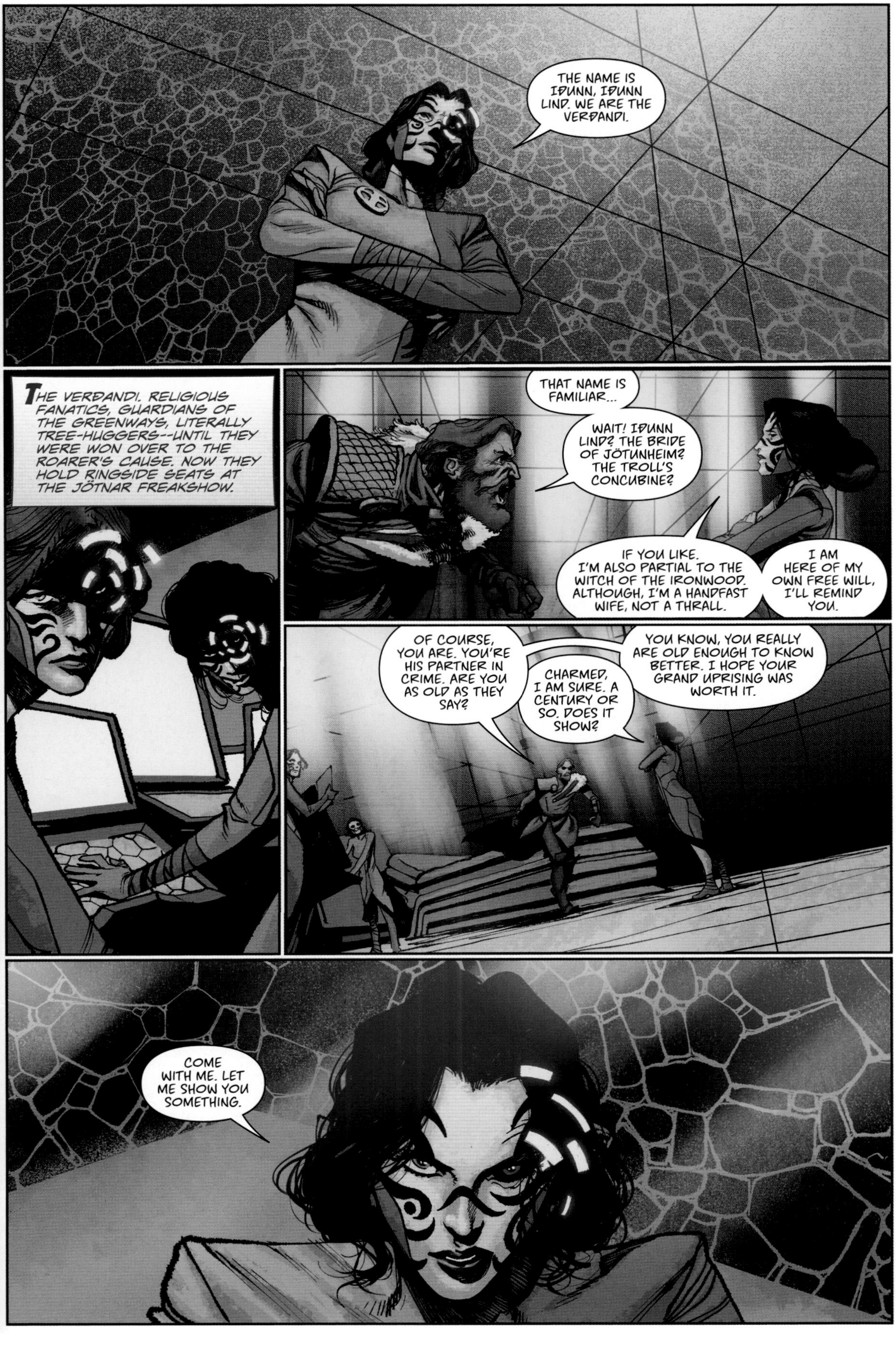
THE NAME IS IÐUNN, IÐUNN LIND. WE ARE THE VERÐANDI.
THE VERÐANDI. RELIGIOUS FANATICS, GUARDIANS OF THE GREENWAYS, LITERALLY TREE-HUGGERS--UNTIL THEY WERE WON OVER TO THE ROARER'S CAUSE. NOW THEY HOLD RINGSIDE SEATS AT THE JÖTNAR FREAKSHOW.
THAT NAME IS FAMILIAR...
WAIT! IÐUNN LIND? THE BRIDE OF JÖTUNHEIM? THE TROLL'S CONCUBINE?
IF YOU LIKE. I'M ALSO PARTIAL TO THE WITCH OF THE IRONWOOD. ALTHOUGH, I'M A HANDFAST WIFE, NOT A THRALL.
I AM HERE OF MY OWN FREE WILL, I'LL REMIND YOU.
OF COURSE, YOU ARE. YOU'RE HIS PARTNER IN CRIME. ARE YOU AS OLD AS THEY SAY?
CHARMED, I AM SURE. A CENTURY OR SO. DOES IT SHOW?
YOU KNOW, YOU REALLY ARE OLD ENOUGH TO KNOW BETTER. I HOPE YOUR GRAND UPRISING WAS WORTH IT.
COME WITH ME. LET ME SHOW YOU SOMETHING.

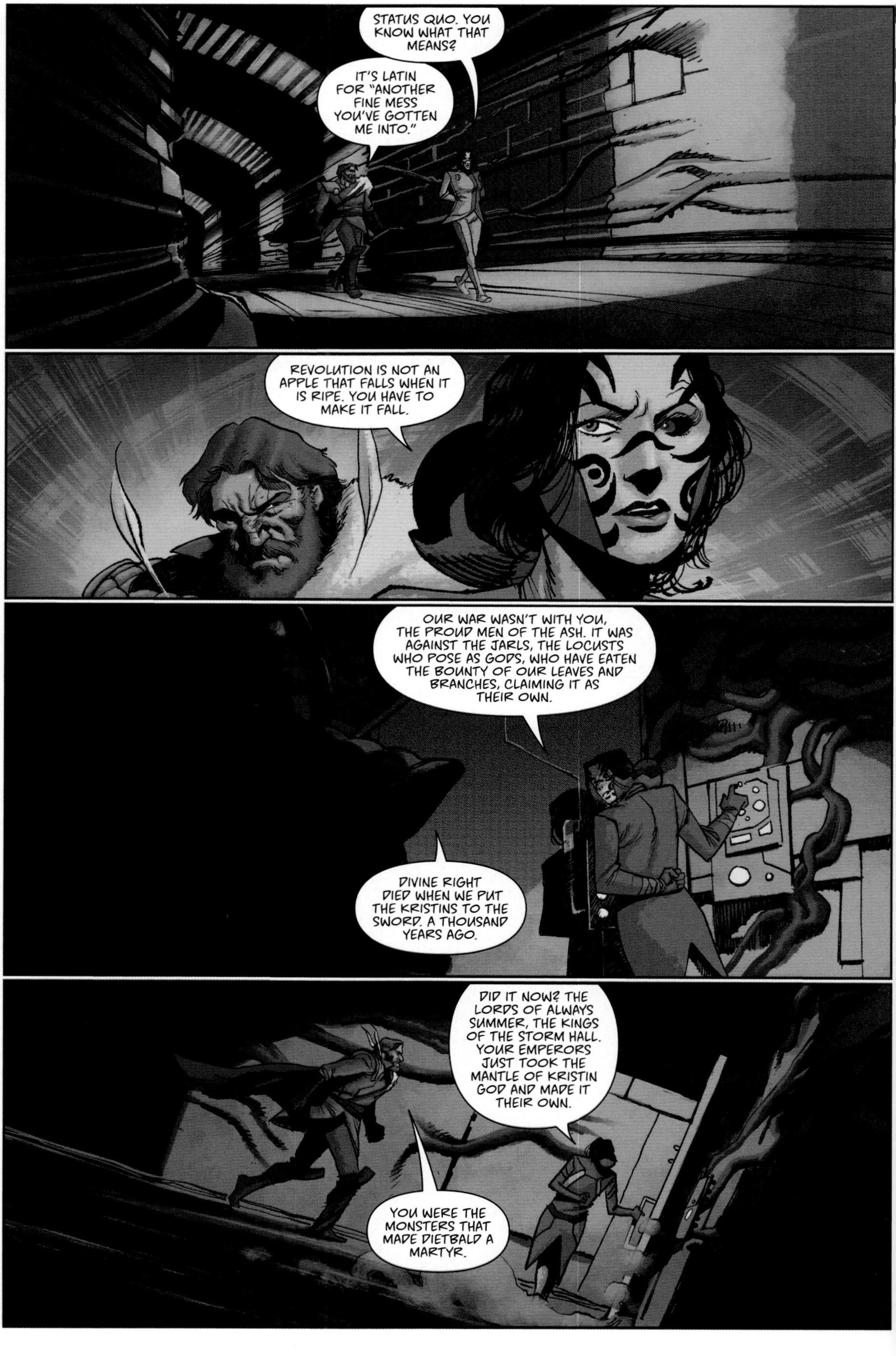
STATUS QUO. YOU KNOW WHAT THAT MEANS?
IT'S LATIN FOR "ANOTHER FINE MESS YOU'VE GOTTEN ME INTO."
REVOLUTION IS NOT AN APPLE THAT FALLS WHEN IT IS RIPE. YOU HAVE TO MAKE IT FALL.
OUR WAR WASN'T WITH YOU, THE PROUD MEN OF THE ASH. IT WAS AGAINST THE JARLS, THE LOCUSTS WHO POSE AS GODS, WHO HAVE EATEN THE BOUNTY OF OUR LEAVES AND BRANCHES, CLAIMING IT AS THEIR OWN.
DIVINE RIGHT DIED WHEN WE PUT THE KRISTINS TO THE SWORD. A THOUSAND YEARS AGO.
DID IT NOW? THE LORDS OF ALWAYS SUMMER, THE KINGS OF THE STORM HALL. YOUR EMPERORS JUST TOOK THE MANTLE OF KRISTIN GOD AND MADE IT THEIR OWN.
YOU WERE THE MONSTERS THAT MADE DIETBALD A MARTYR.

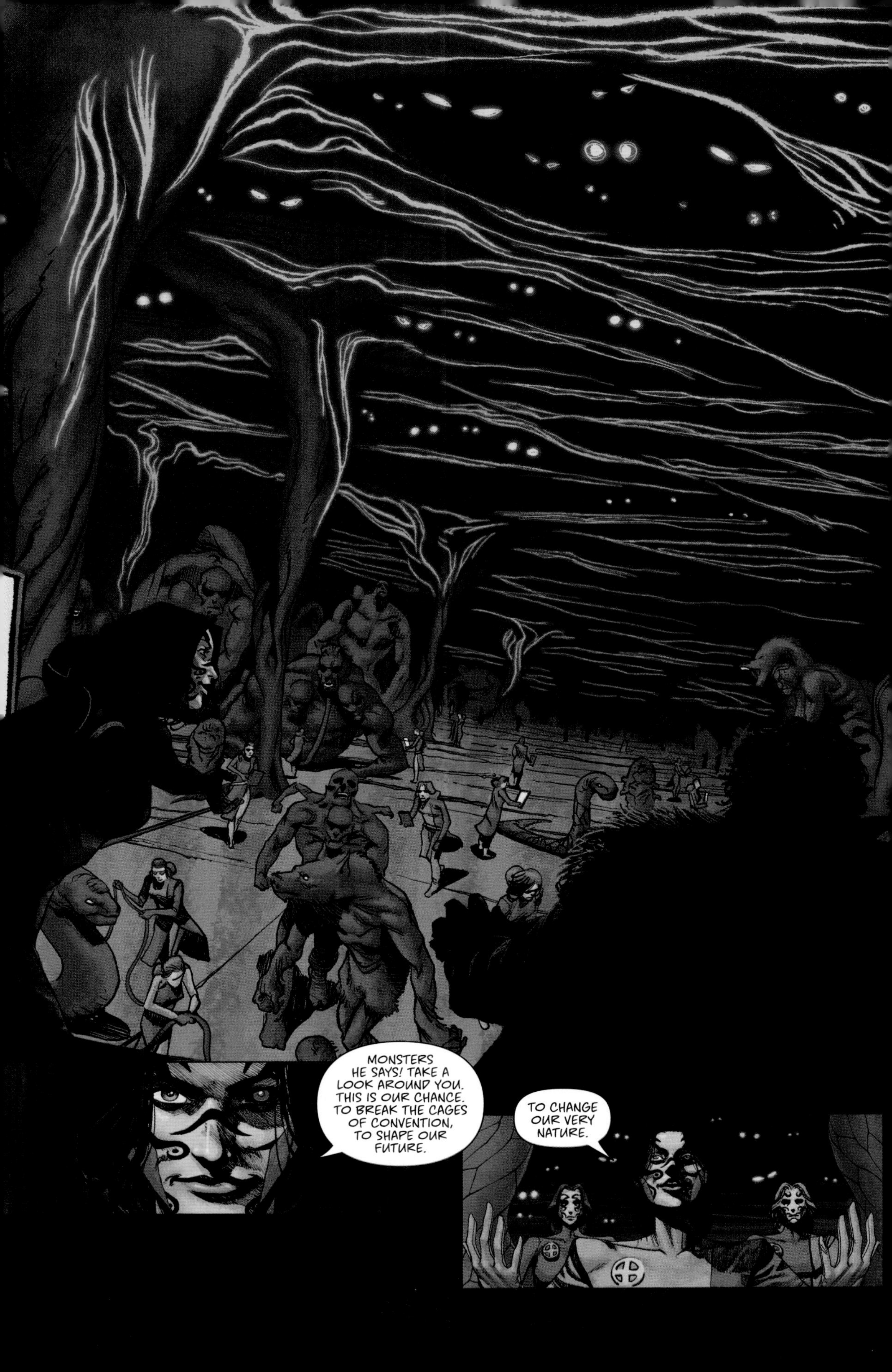
MONSTERS HE SAYS! TAKE A LOOK AROUND YOU. THIS IS OUR CHANCE. TO BREAK THE CAGES OF CONVENTION, TO SHAPE OUR FUTURE.
TO CHANGE OUR VERY NATURE.

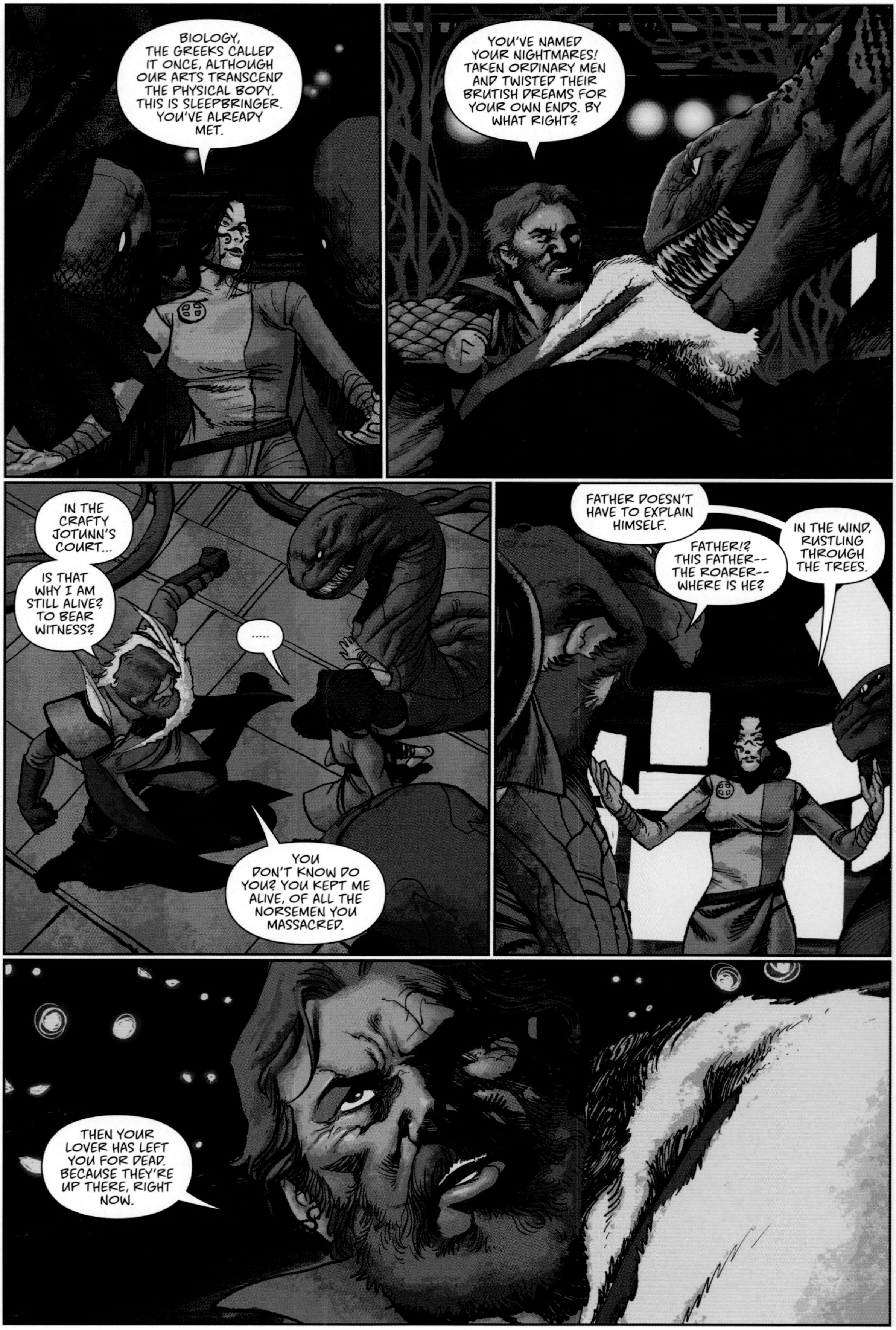
BIOLOGY, THE GREEKS CALLED IT ONCE, ALTHOUGH OUR ARTS TRANSCEND THE PHYSICAL BODY. THIS IS SLEEPBRINGER. YOU'VE ALREADY MET.
YOU'VE NAMED YOUR NIGHTMARES! TAKEN ORDINARY MEN AND TWISTED THEIR BRUTISH DREAMS FOR YOUR OWN ENDS. BY WHAT RIGHT?
IN THE CRAFTY JOTUNN'S COURT...
IS THAT WHY I AM STILL ALIVE? TO BEAR WITNESS?
.....
YOU DON'T KNOW DO YOU? YOU KEPT ME ALIVE, OF ALL THE NORSEMEN YOU MASSACRED.
FATHER DOESN'T HAVE TO EXPLAIN HIMSELF.
FATHER!? THIS FATHER-- THE ROARER-- WHERE IS HE?
IN THE WIND, RUSTLING THROUGH THE TREES.
THEN YOUR LOVER HAS LEFT YOU FOR DEAD. BECAUSE THEY'RE UP THERE, RIGHT NOW.

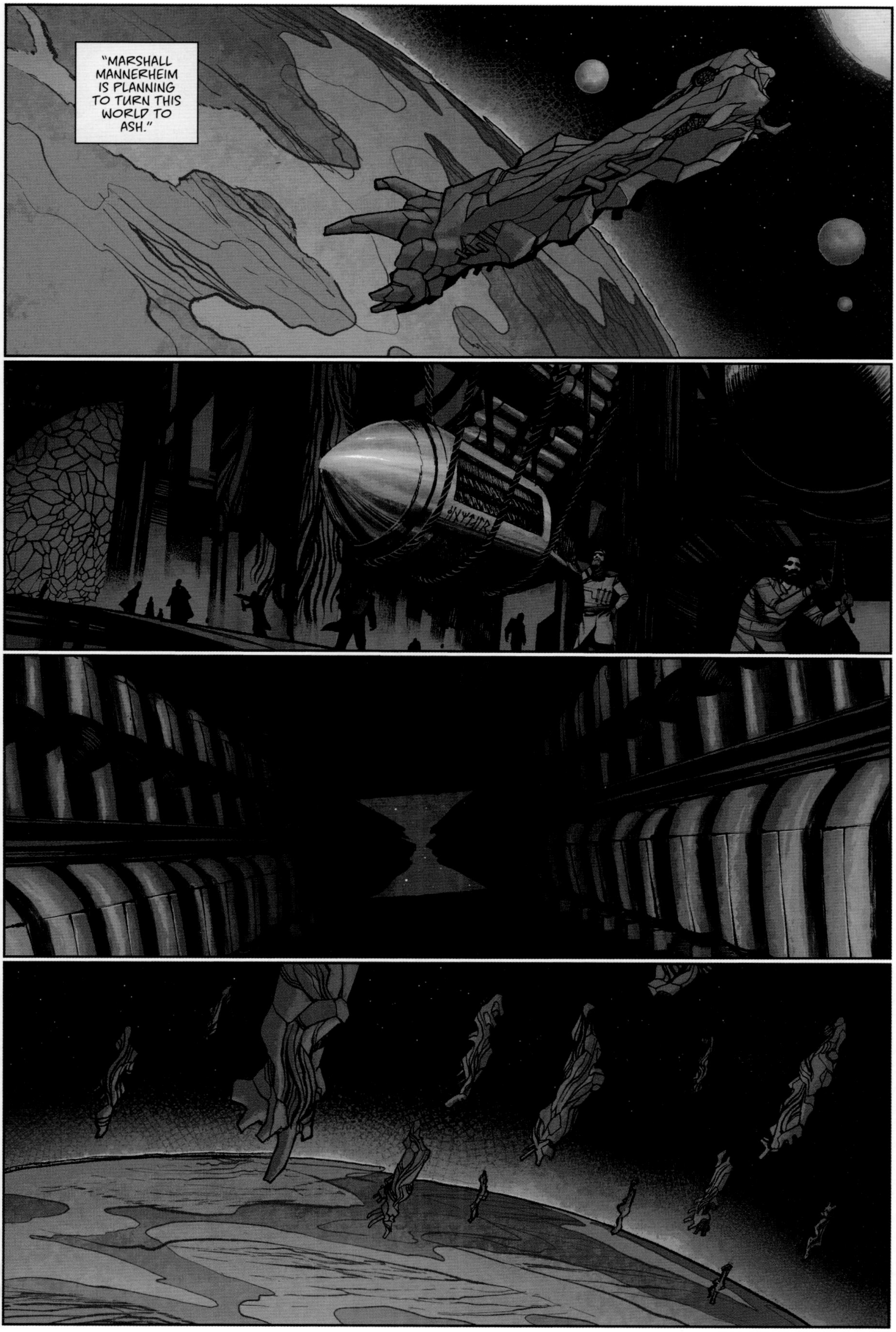
"MARSHALL MANNERHEIM IS PLANNING TO TURN THIS WORLD TO ASH."

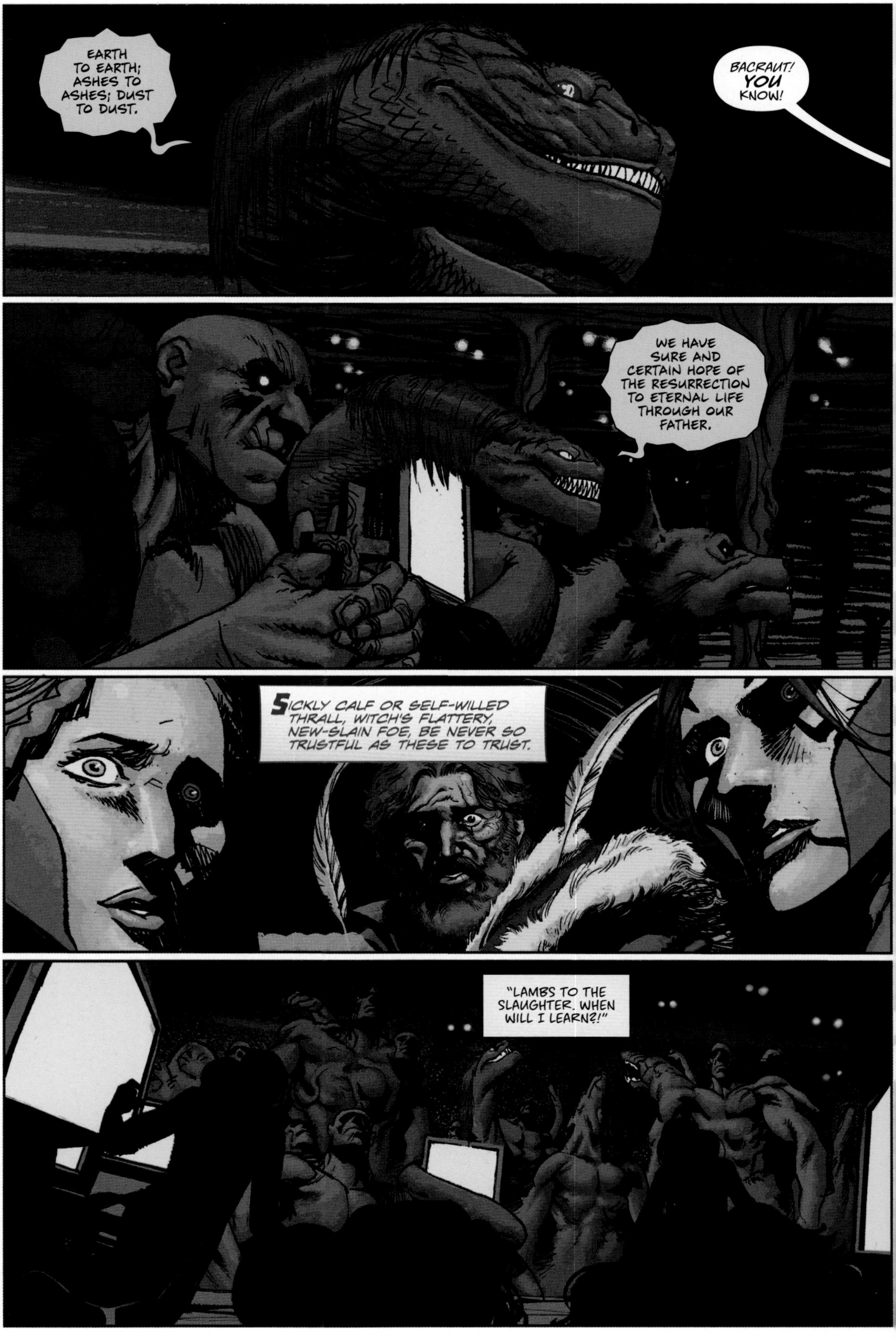
EARTH TO EARTH; ASHES TO ASHES; DUST TO DUST.
BACRAUT! YOU KNOW!
WE HAVE SURE AND CERTAIN HOPE OF THE RESURRECTION TO ETERNAL LIFE THROUGH OUR FATHER.
SICKLY CALF OR SELF-WILLED THRALL, WITCH'S FLATTERY, NEW-SLAIN FOE, BE NEVER SO TRUSTFUL AS THESE TO TRUST.
"LAMBS TO THE SLAUGHTER. WHEN WILL I LEARN?!"

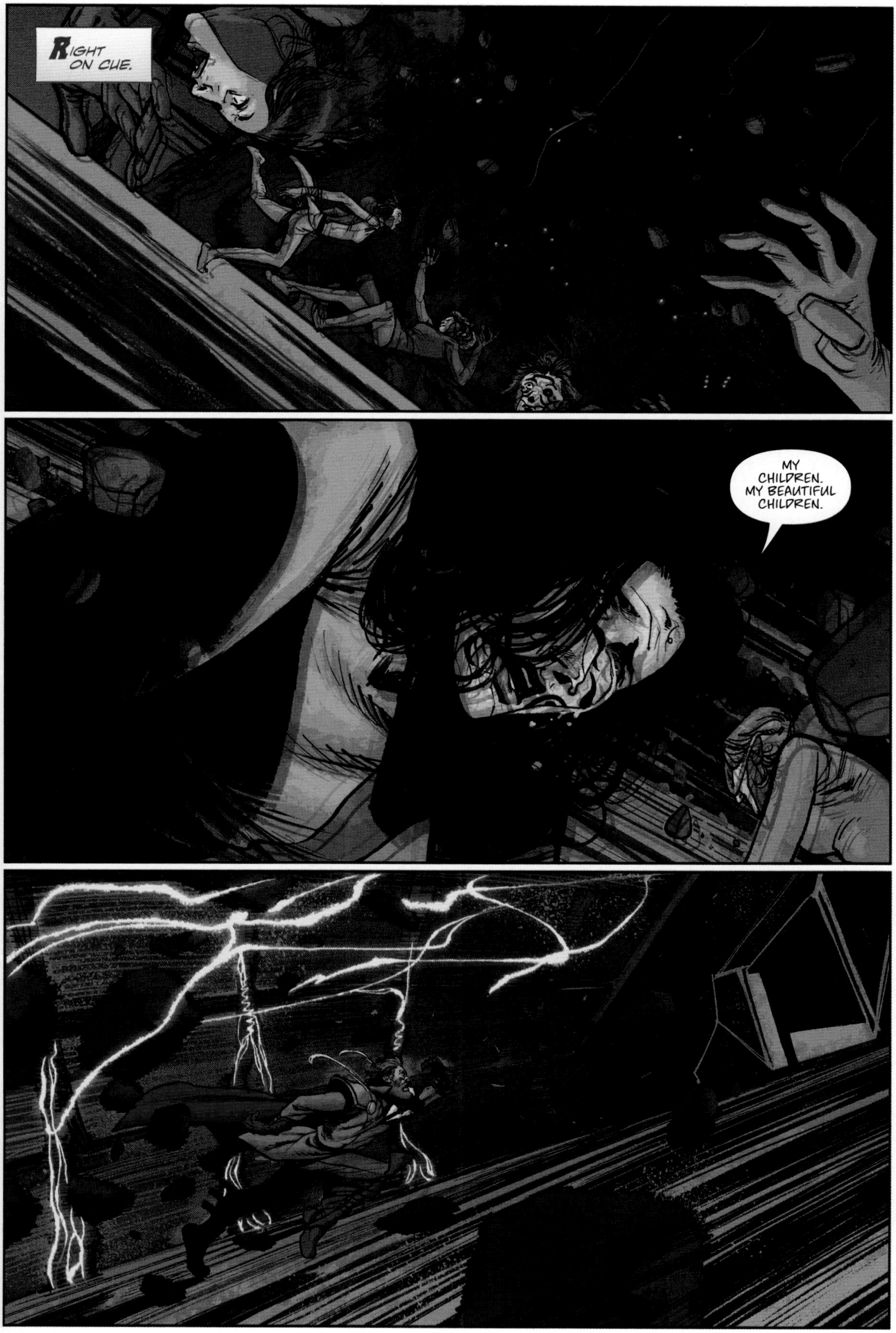
RIGHT ON CUE.
MY CHILDREN. MY BEAUTIFUL CHILDREN.

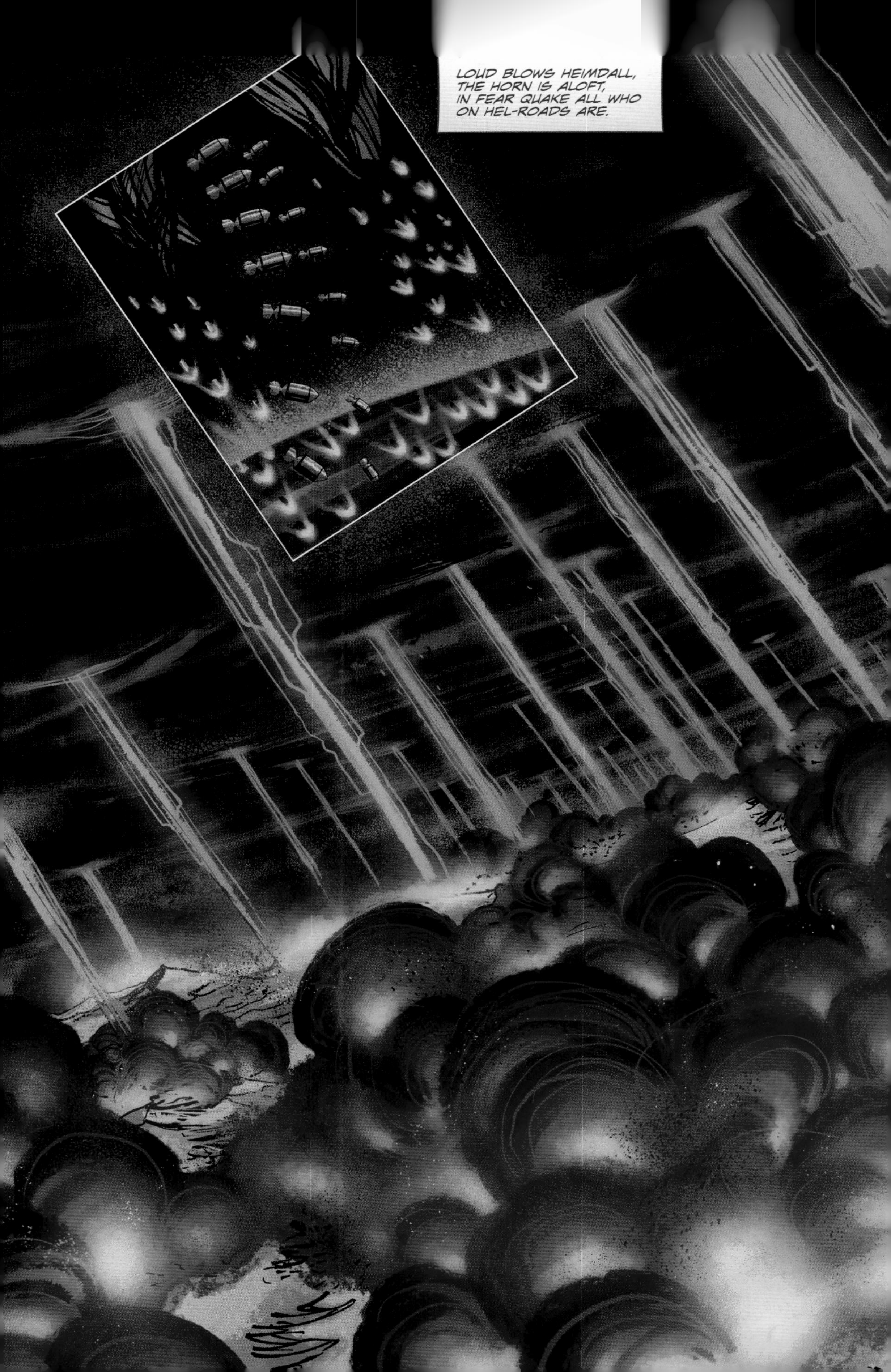
LOUD BLOWS HEIMDALL,
THE HORN IS ALOFT,
IN FEAR QUAKE ALL WHO
ON HEL-ROADS ARE.

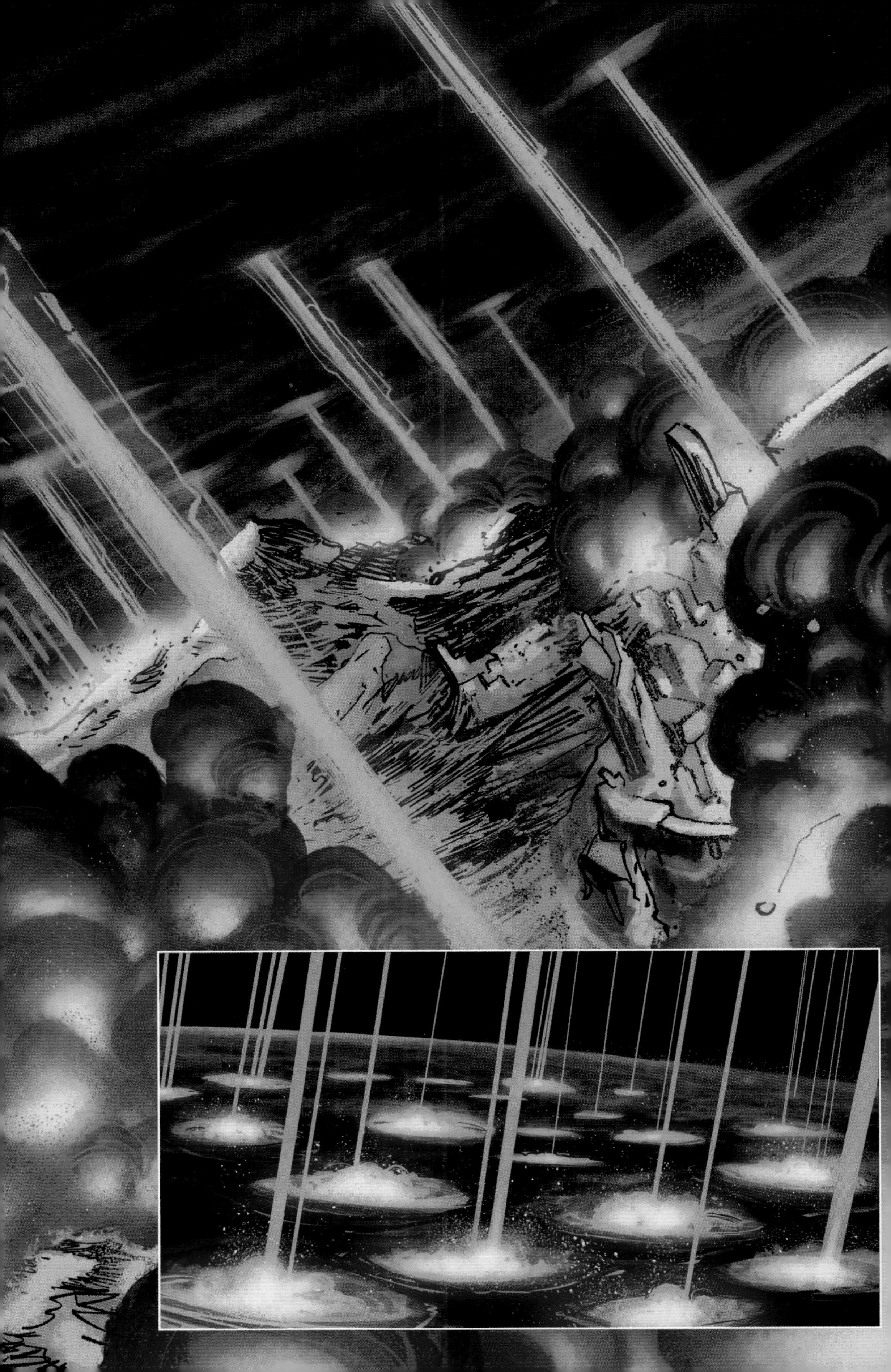

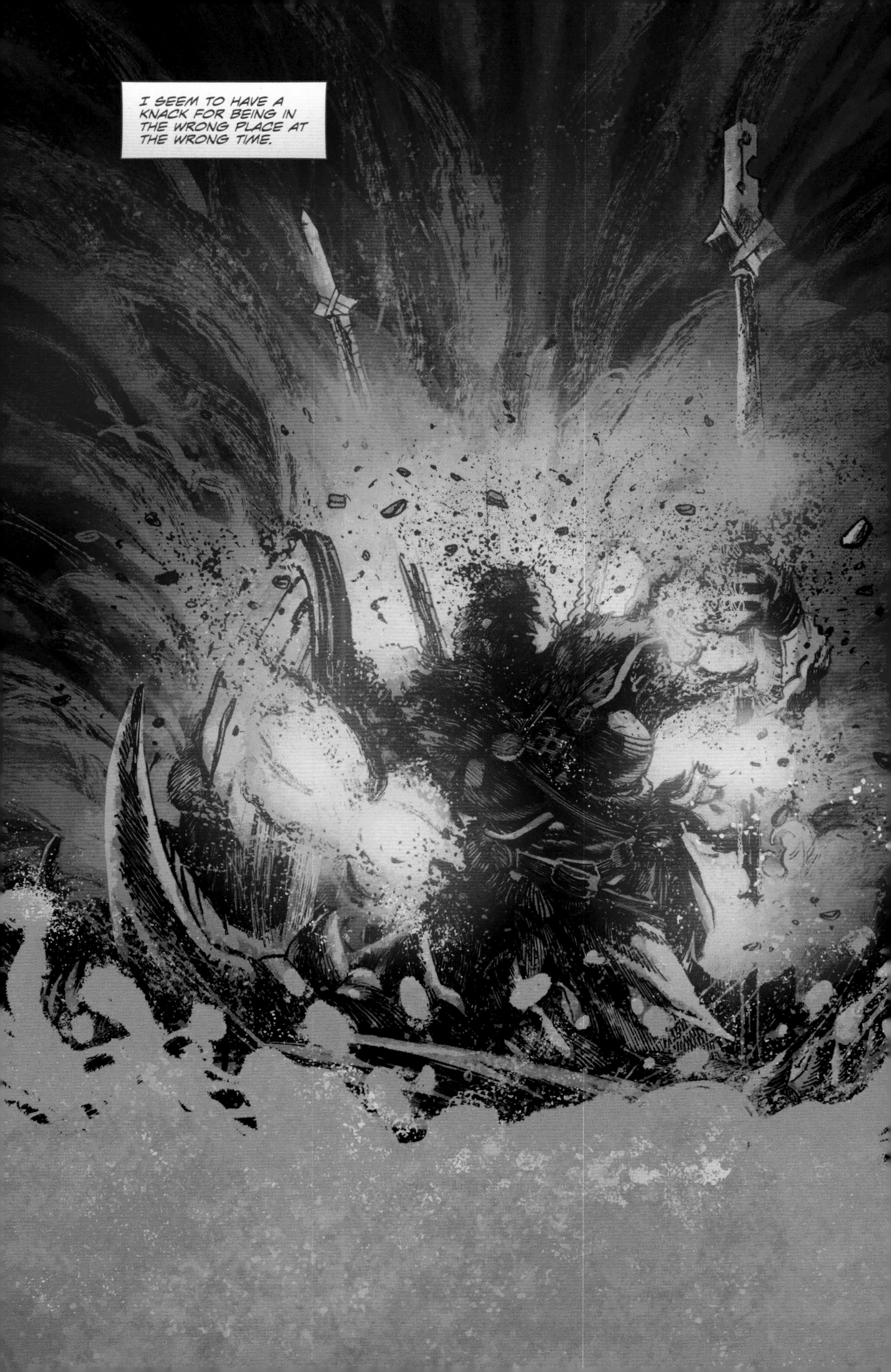
I SEEM TO HAVE A KNACK FOR BEING IN THE WRONG PLACE AT THE WRONG TIME.

SHARERS
OF OUR
GLORIOUS
PAST

BRÓðR, **MUST** WE PART AT LAST?
SHALL WE **NOT** THRO' GOOD AND ILL

CLEAVE TO ONE ANOTHER STILL?

THE NORNS' MYRIAD VOICES **CALL**,

"SONS, BE WELDED EACH AND ALL
INTO ONE IMPERIAL WHOLE,
ONE WITH THE NORTH, HEART AND SOUL!
ONE LIFE, ONE FLAG, ONÉ FLEET, ONE THRONE!"

NORSEMEN
HOLD
YOUR OWN

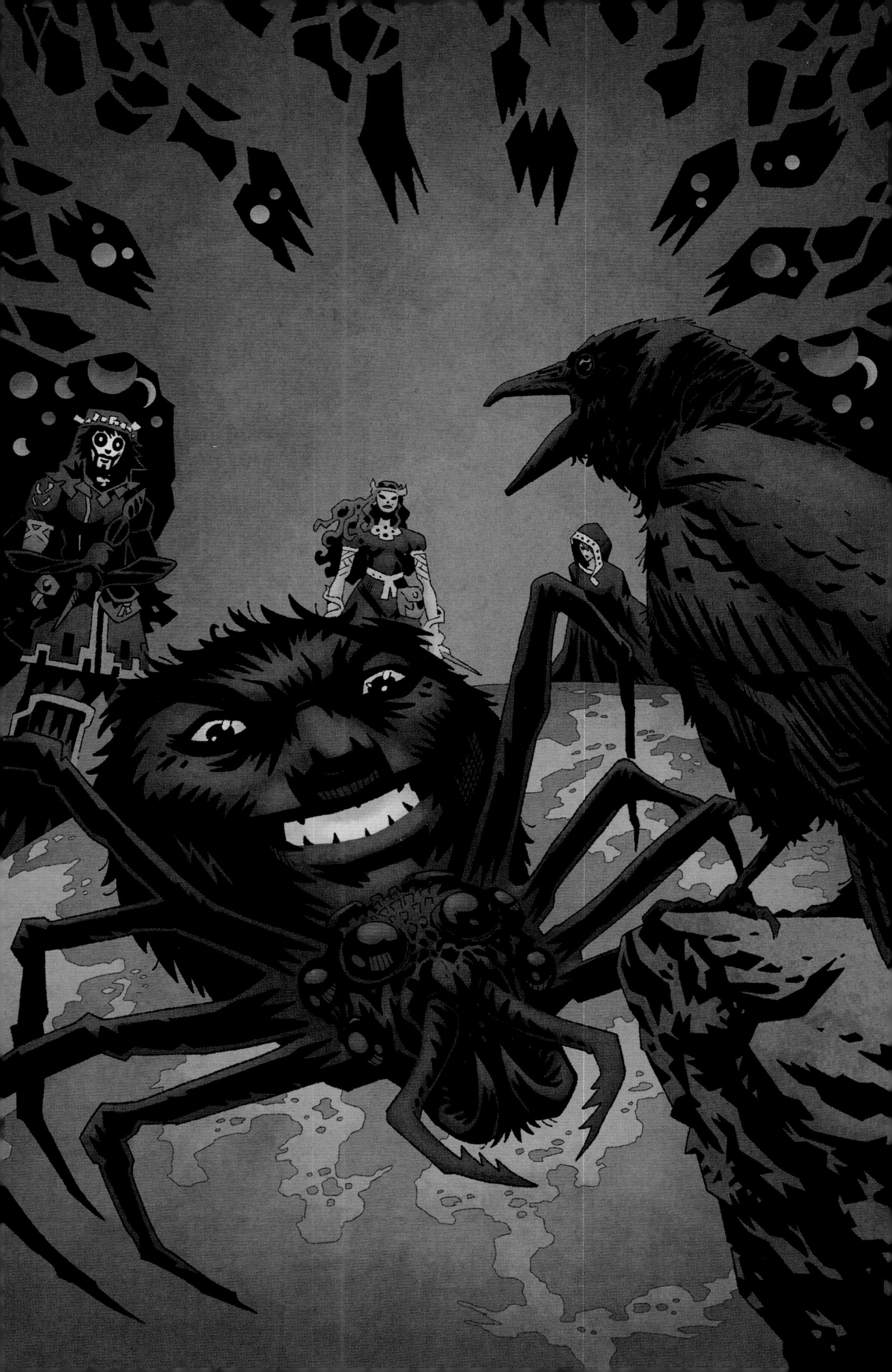

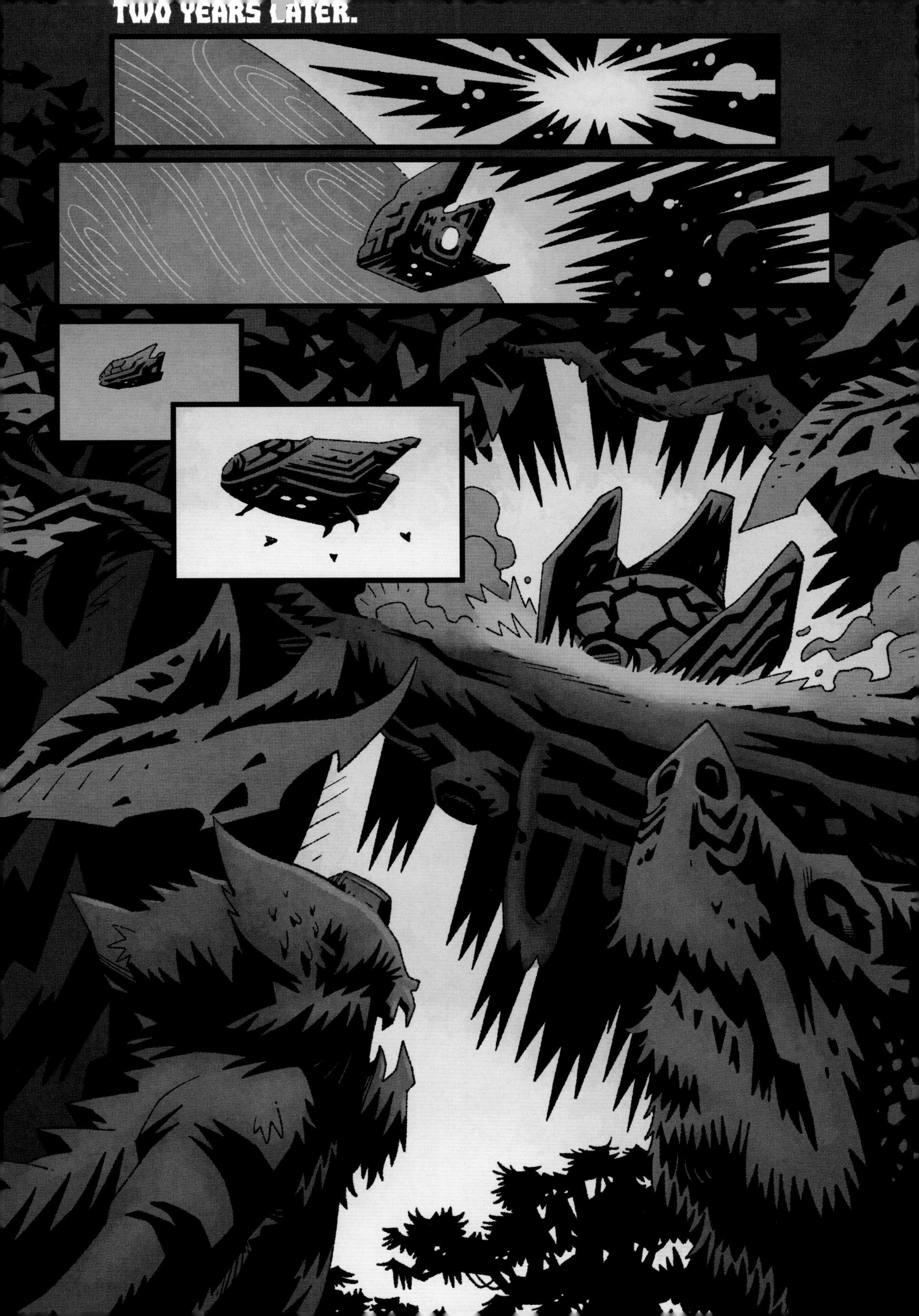
TWO YEARS LATER.

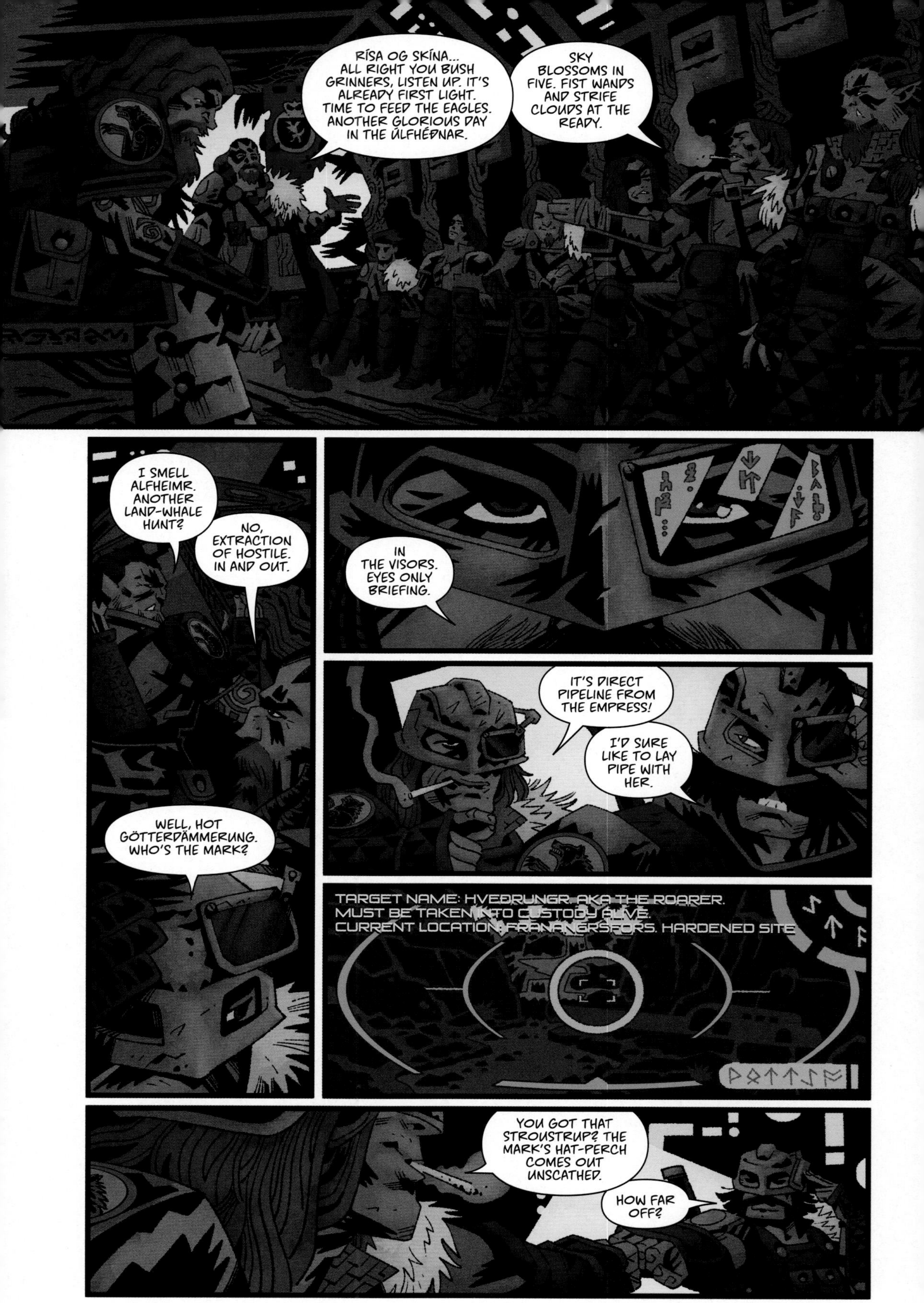
RÍSA OG SKÍNA... ALL RIGHT YOU BUSH GRINNERS, LISTEN UP. IT'S ALREADY FIRST LIGHT. TIME TO FEED THE EAGLES. ANOTHER GLORIOUS DAY IN THE ÚLFHÉÐNAR.
SKY BLOSSOMS IN FIVE. FIST WANDS AND STRIFE CLOUDS AT THE READY.
I SMELL ALFHEIMR. ANOTHER LAND-WHALE HUNT?
NO, EXTRACTION OF HOSTILE. IN AND OUT.
IN THE VISORS. EYES ONLY BRIEFING.
IT'S DIRECT PIPELINE FROM THE EMPRESS!
I'D SURE LIKE TO LAY PIPE WITH HER.
WELL, HOT GÖTTERDÄMMERUNG. WHO'S THE MARK?
TARGET NAME: HVEÐRUNGR. AKA THE ROARER.
MUST BE TAKEN INTO CUSTODY ALIVE.
CURRENT LOCATION: FRANANGRSFORS. HARDENED SITE
YOU GOT THAT STROUSTRUP? THE MARK'S HAT-PERCH COMES OUT UNSCATHED.
HOW FAR OFF?

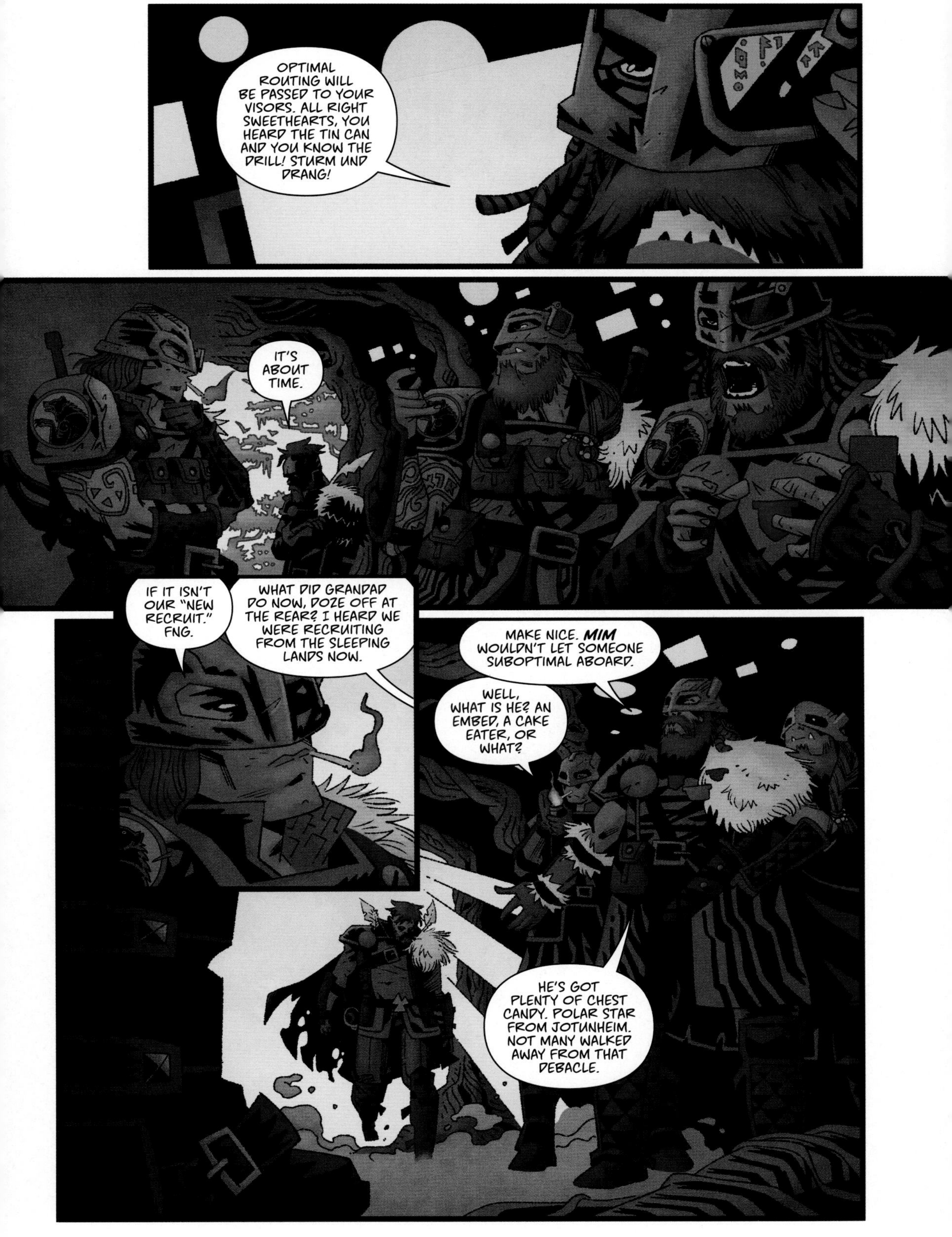
OPTIMAL ROUTING WILL BE PASSED TO YOUR VISORS. ALL RIGHT SWEETHEARTS, YOU HEARD THE TIN CAN AND YOU KNOW THE DRILL! STURM UND DRANG!
IT'S ABOUT TIME.
IF IT ISN'T OUR "NEW RECRUIT." FNG.
WHAT DID GRANDAD DO NOW, DOZE OFF AT THE REAR? I HEARD WE WERE RECRUITING FROM THE SLEEPING LANDS NOW.
MAKE NICE. MIM WOULDN'T LET SOMEONE SUBOPTIMAL ABOARD.
WELL, WHAT IS HE? AN EMBED, A CAKE EATER, OR WHAT?
HE'S GOT PLENTY OF CHEST CANDY. POLAR STAR FROM JOTUNHEIM. NOT MANY WALKED AWAY FROM THAT DEBACLE.

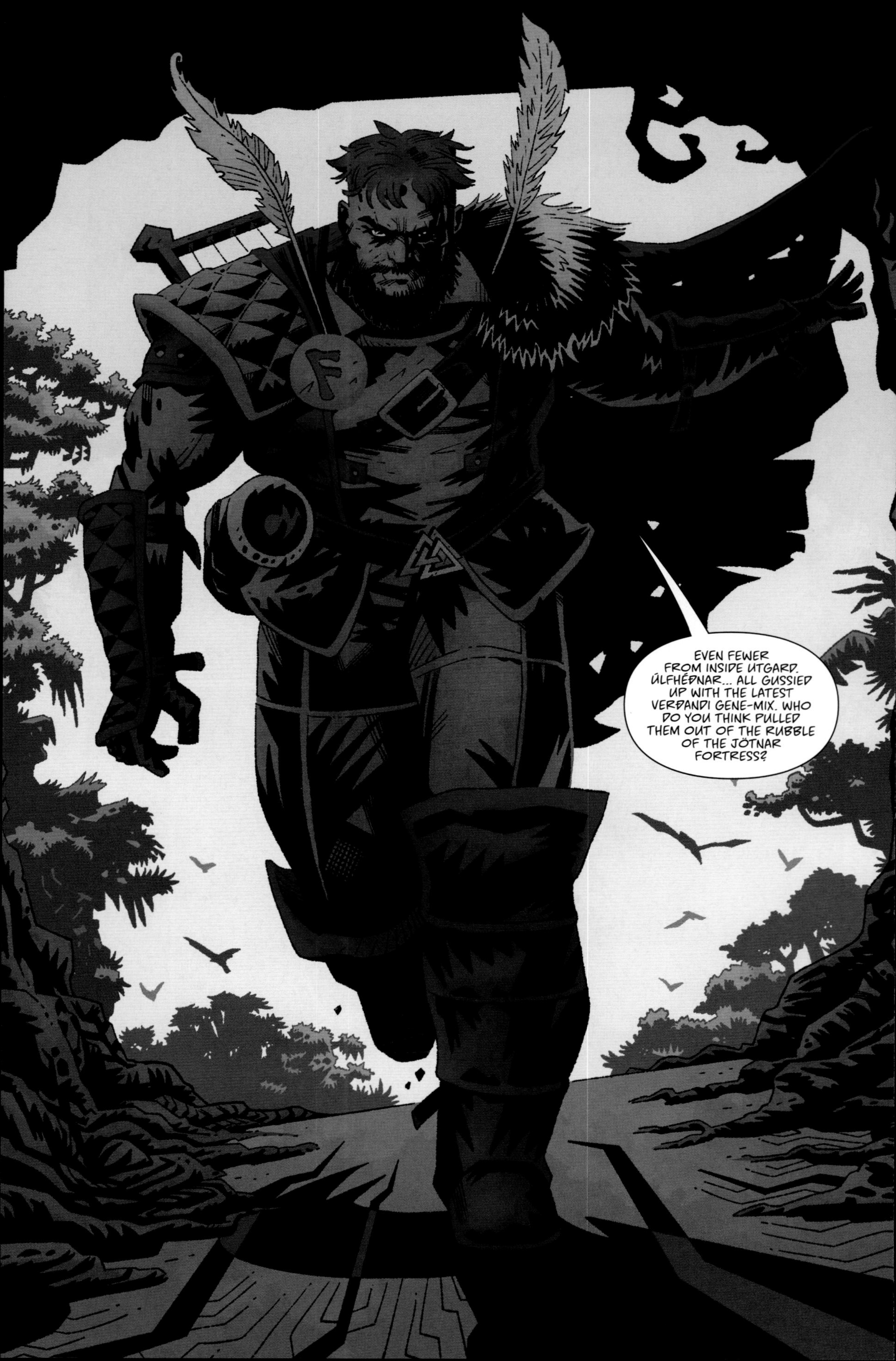
EVEN FEWER FROM INSIDE UTGARD. ÚLFHÉÐNAR... ALL GUSSIED UP WITH THE LATEST VERÐANDI GENE-MIX. WHO DO YOU THINK PULLED THEM OUT OF THE RUBBLE OF THE JÖTNAR FORTRESS?

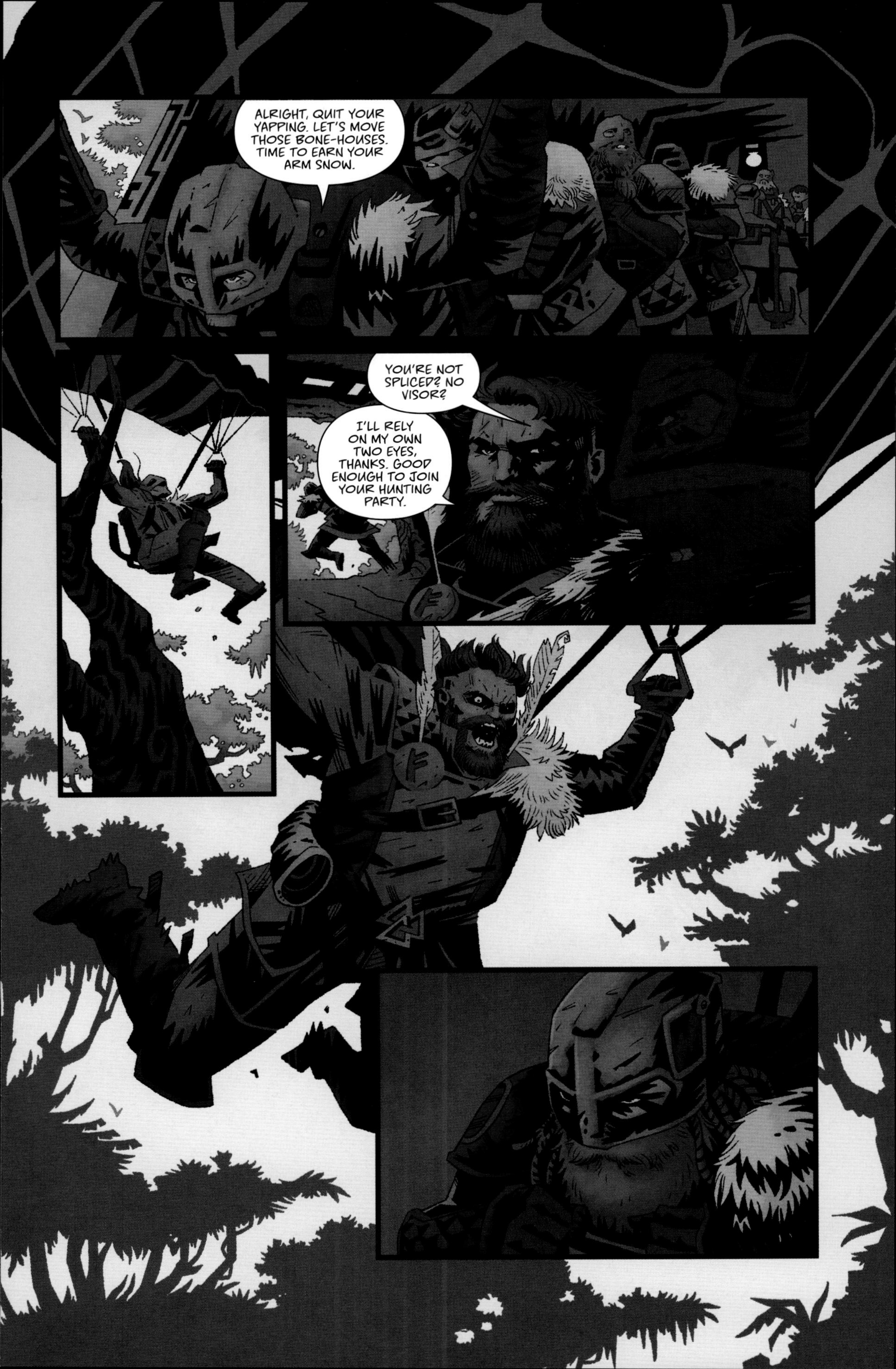
ALRIGHT, QUIT YOUR YAPPING. LET'S MOVE THOSE BONE-HOUSES. TIME TO EARN YOUR ARM SNOW.
YOU'RE NOT SPLICED? NO VISOR?
I'LL RELY ON MY OWN TWO EYES, THANKS. GOOD ENOUGH TO JOIN YOUR HUNTING PARTY.

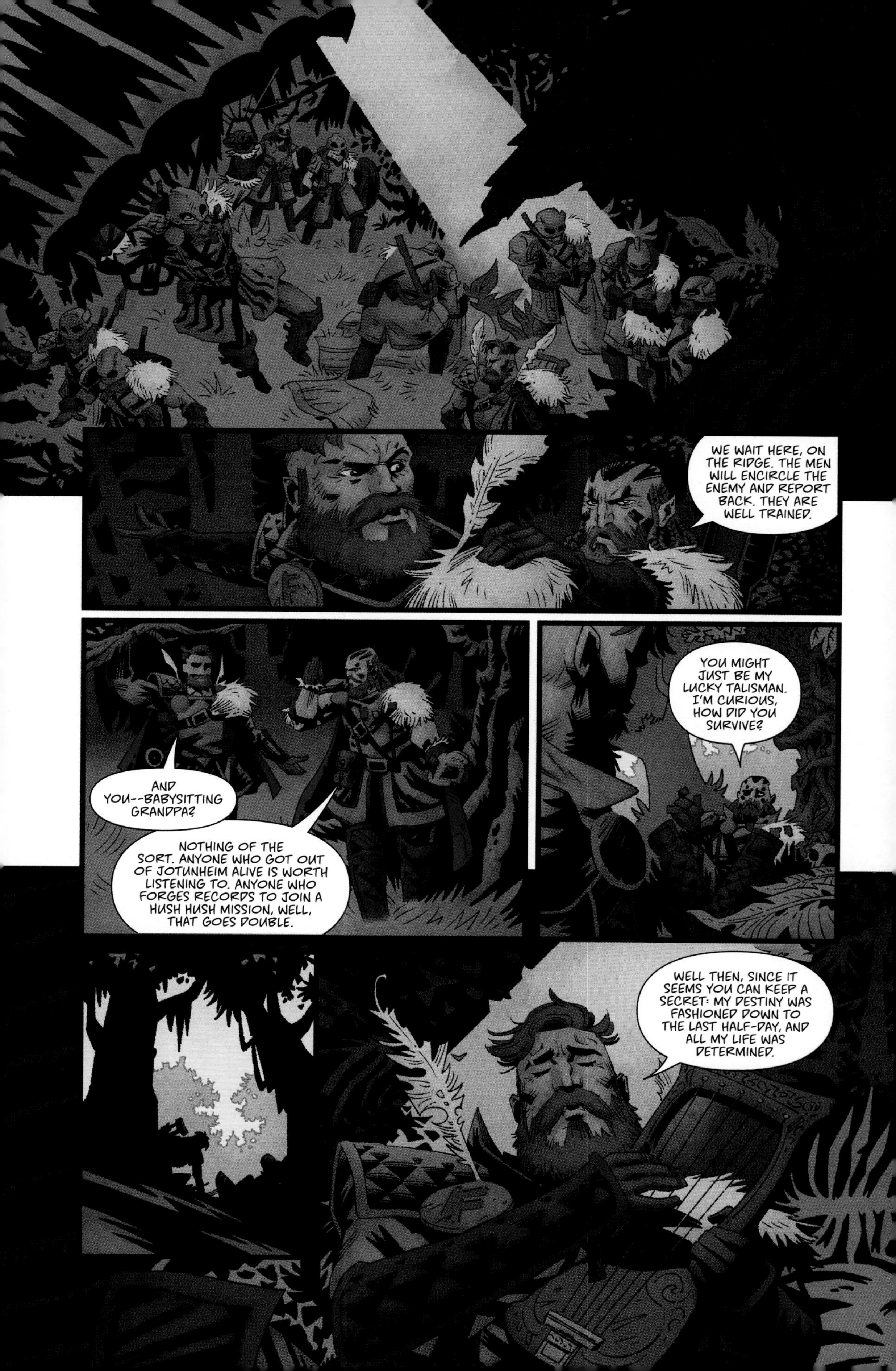
WE WAIT HERE, ON THE RIDGE. THE MEN WILL ENCIRCLE THE ENEMY AND REPORT BACK. THEY ARE WELL TRAINED.
AND YOU--BABYSITTING GRANDPA?
NOTHING OF THE SORT. ANYONE WHO GOT OUT OF JOTUNHEIM ALIVE IS WORTH LISTENING TO. ANYONE WHO FORGES RECORDS TO JOIN A HUSH HUSH MISSION, WELL, THAT GOES DOUBLE.
YOU MIGHT JUST BE MY LUCKY TALISMAN. I'M CURIOUS, HOW DID YOU SURVIVE?
WELL THEN, SINCE IT SEEMS YOU CAN KEEP A SECRET: MY DESTINY WAS FASHIONED DOWN TO THE LAST HALF-DAY, AND ALL MY LIFE WAS DETERMINED.

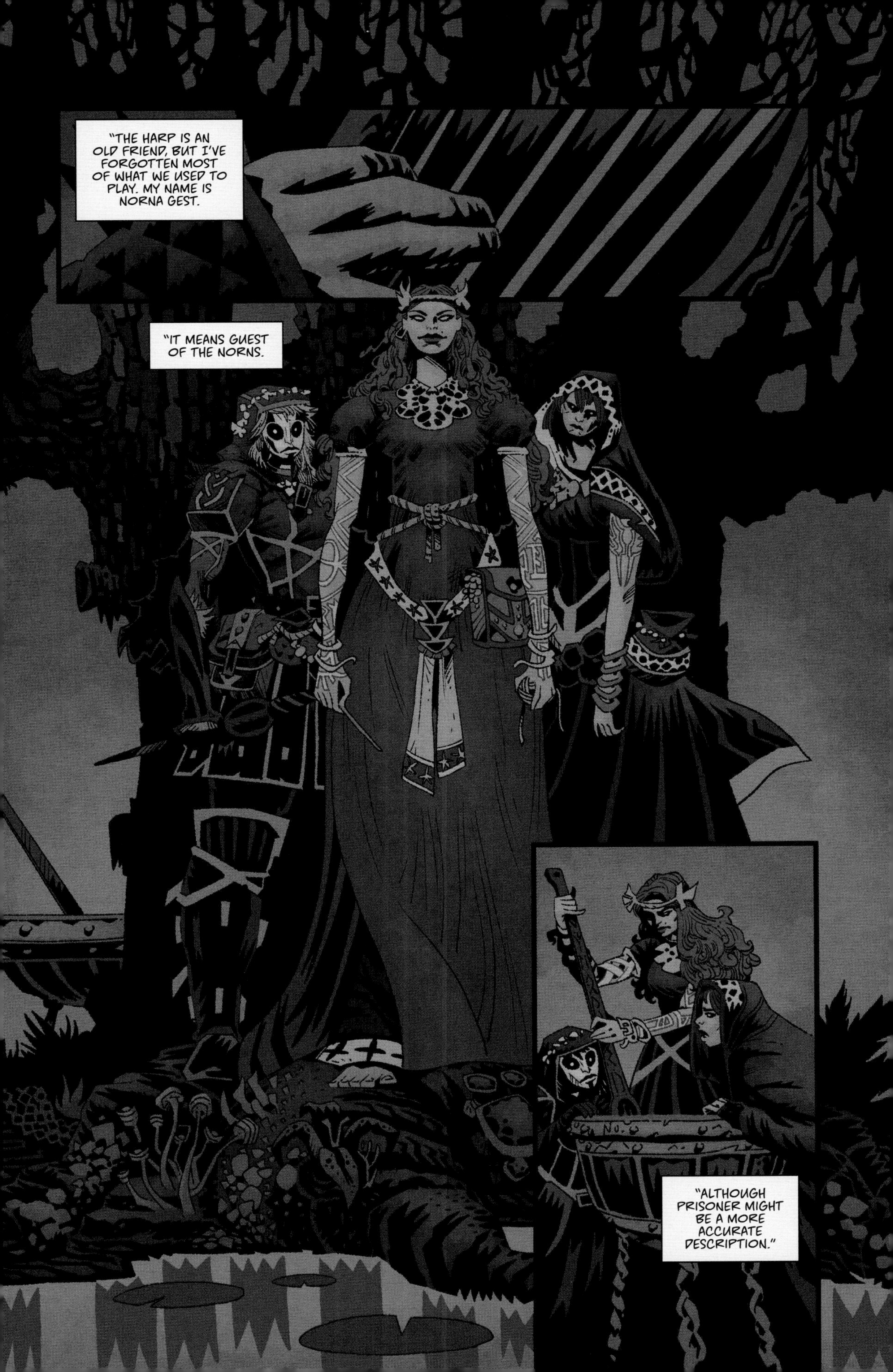
"THE HARP IS AN OLD FRIEND, BUT I'VE FORGOTTEN MOST OF WHAT WE USED TO PLAY. MY NAME IS NORNA GEST.
"IT MEANS GUEST OF THE NORNS.
"ALTHOUGH PRISONER MIGHT BE A MORE ACCURATE DESCRIPTION."

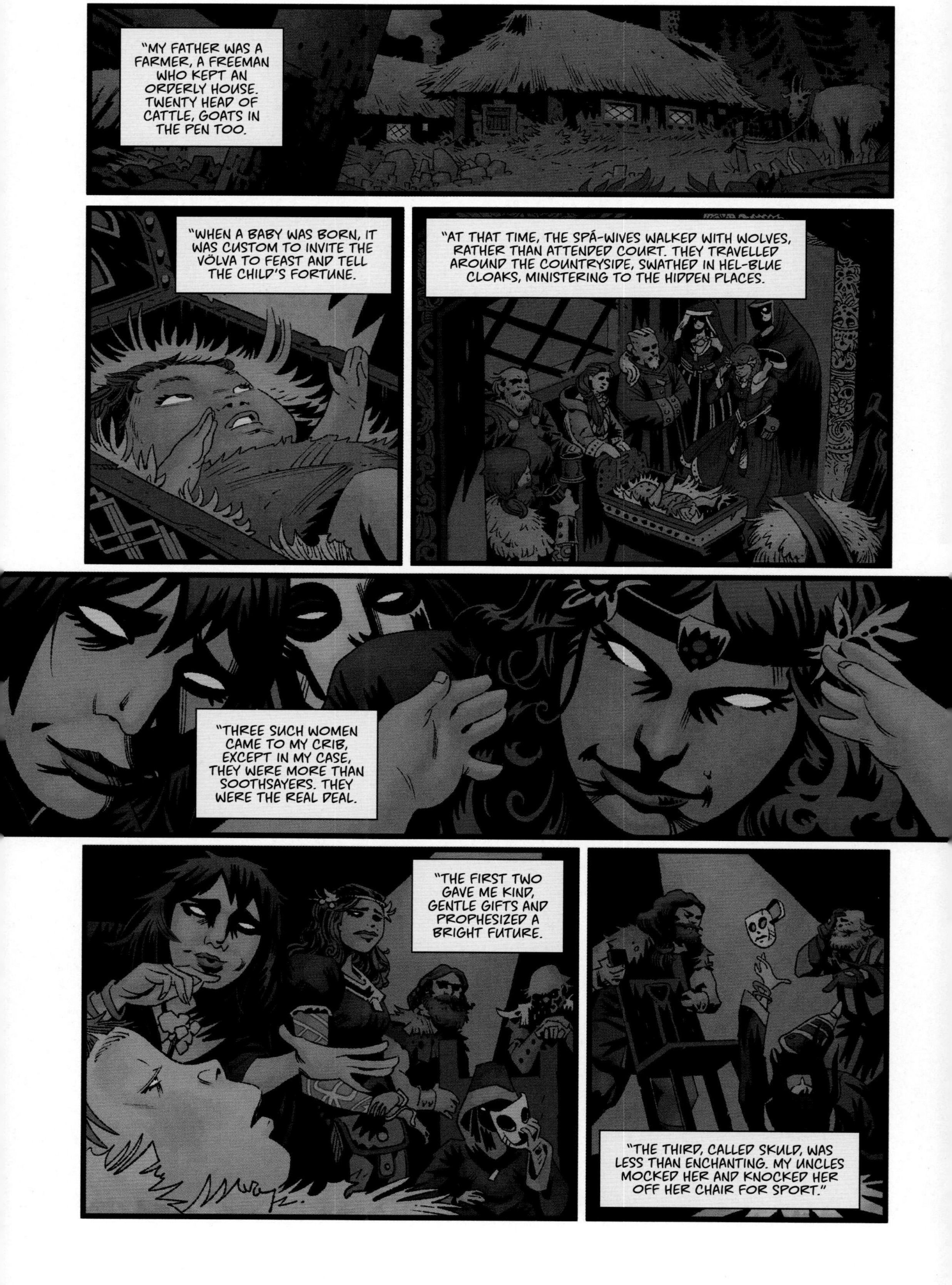
"MY FATHER WAS A FARMER, A FREEMAN WHO KEPT AN ORDERLY HOUSE. TWENTY HEAD OF CATTLE, GOATS IN THE PEN TOO.
"WHEN A BABY WAS BORN, IT WAS CUSTOM TO INVITE THE VÖLVA TO FEAST AND TELL THE CHILD'S FORTUNE.
"AT THAT TIME, THE SPÁ-WIVES WALKED WITH WOLVES, RATHER THAN ATTENDED COURT. THEY TRAVELLED AROUND THE COUNTRYSIDE, SWATHED IN HEL-BLUE CLOAKS, MINISTERING TO THE HIDDEN PLACES.
"THREE SUCH WOMEN CAME TO MY CRIB, EXCEPT IN MY CASE, THEY WERE MORE THAN SOOTHSAYERS. THEY WERE THE REAL DEAL.
"THE FIRST TWO GAVE ME KIND, GENTLE GIFTS AND PROPHESIZED A BRIGHT FUTURE.
"THE THIRD, CALLED SKULD, WAS LESS THAN ENCHANTING. MY UNCLES MOCKED HER AND KNOCKED HER OFF HER CHAIR FOR SPORT."

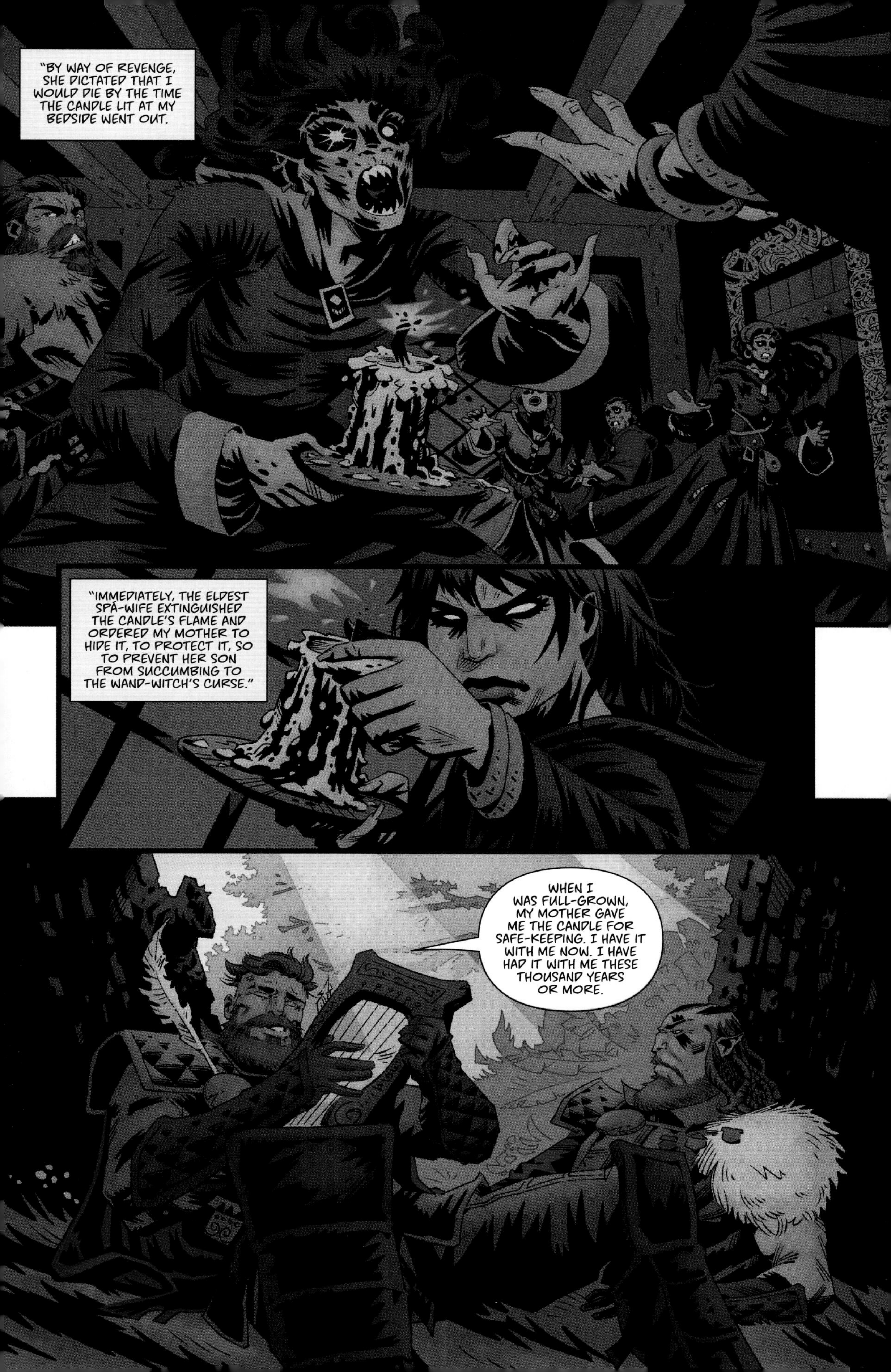
"BY WAY OF REVENGE, SHE DICTATED THAT I WOULD DIE BY THE TIME THE CANDLE LIT AT MY BEDSIDE WENT OUT.
"IMMEDIATELY, THE ELDEST SPÁ-WIFE EXTINGUISHED THE CANDLE'S FLAME AND ORDERED MY MOTHER TO HIDE IT, TO PROTECT IT, SO TO PREVENT HER SON FROM SUCCUMBING TO THE WAND-WITCH'S CURSE."
WHEN I WAS FULL-GROWN, MY MOTHER GAVE ME THE CANDLE FOR SAFE-KEEPING. I HAVE IT WITH ME NOW. I HAVE HAD IT WITH ME THESE THOUSAND YEARS OR MORE.

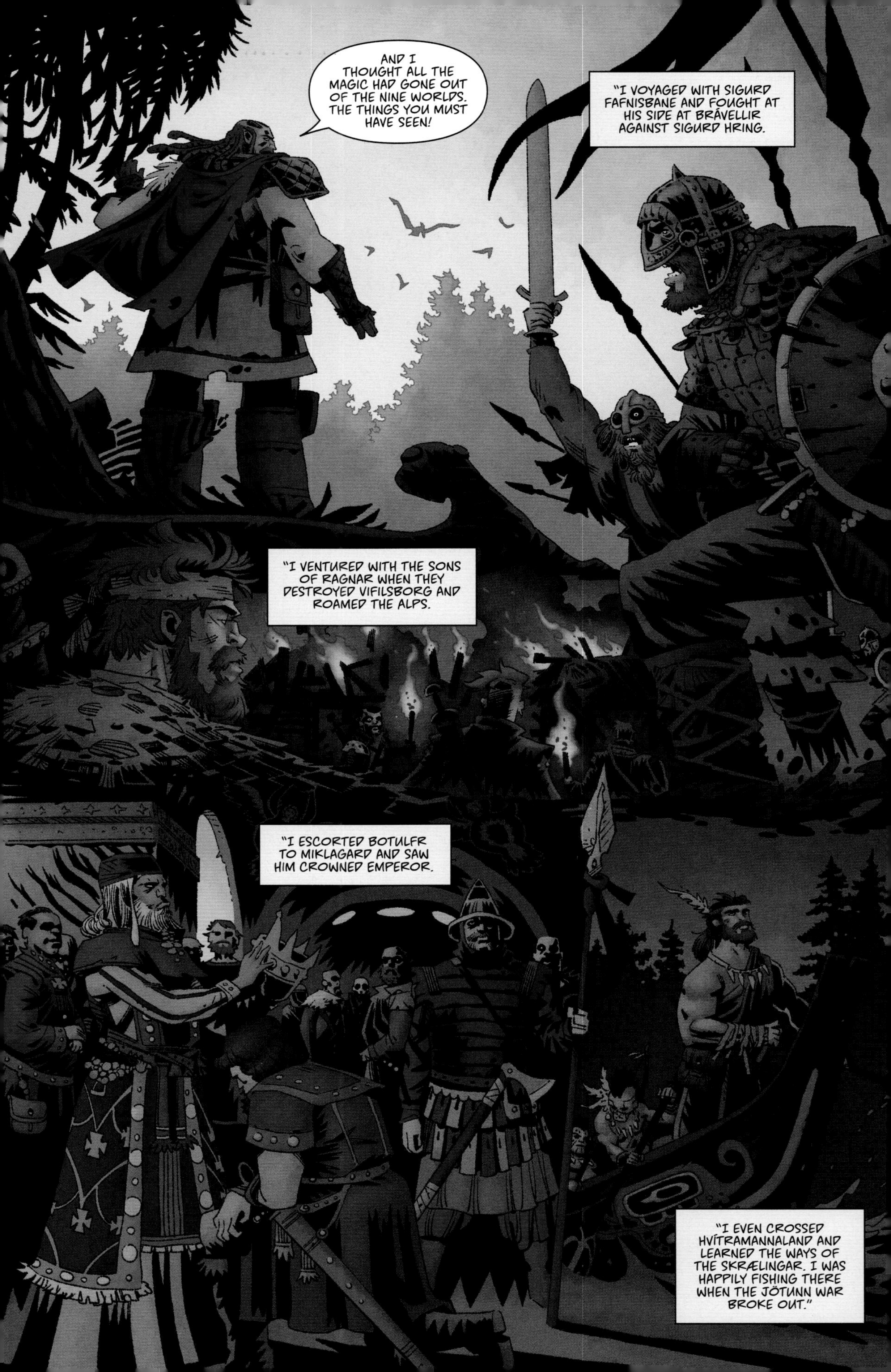

AND I THOUGHT ALL THE MAGIC HAD GONE OUT OF THE NINE WORLDS. THE THINGS YOU MUST HAVE SEEN!
"I VOYAGED WITH SIGURD FAFNISBANE AND FOUGHT AT HIS SIDE AT BRÁVELLIR AGAINST SIGURD HRING.
"I VENTURED WITH THE SONS OF RAGNAR WHEN THEY DESTROYED VIFILSBORG AND ROAMED THE ALPS.
"I ESCORTED BOTULFR TO MIKLAGARD AND SAW HIM CROWNED EMPEROR.
"I EVEN CROSSED HVÍTRAMANNALAND AND LEARNED THE WAYS OF THE SKRÆLINGAR. I WAS HAPPILY FISHING THERE WHEN THE JÖTUNN WAR BROKE OUT."

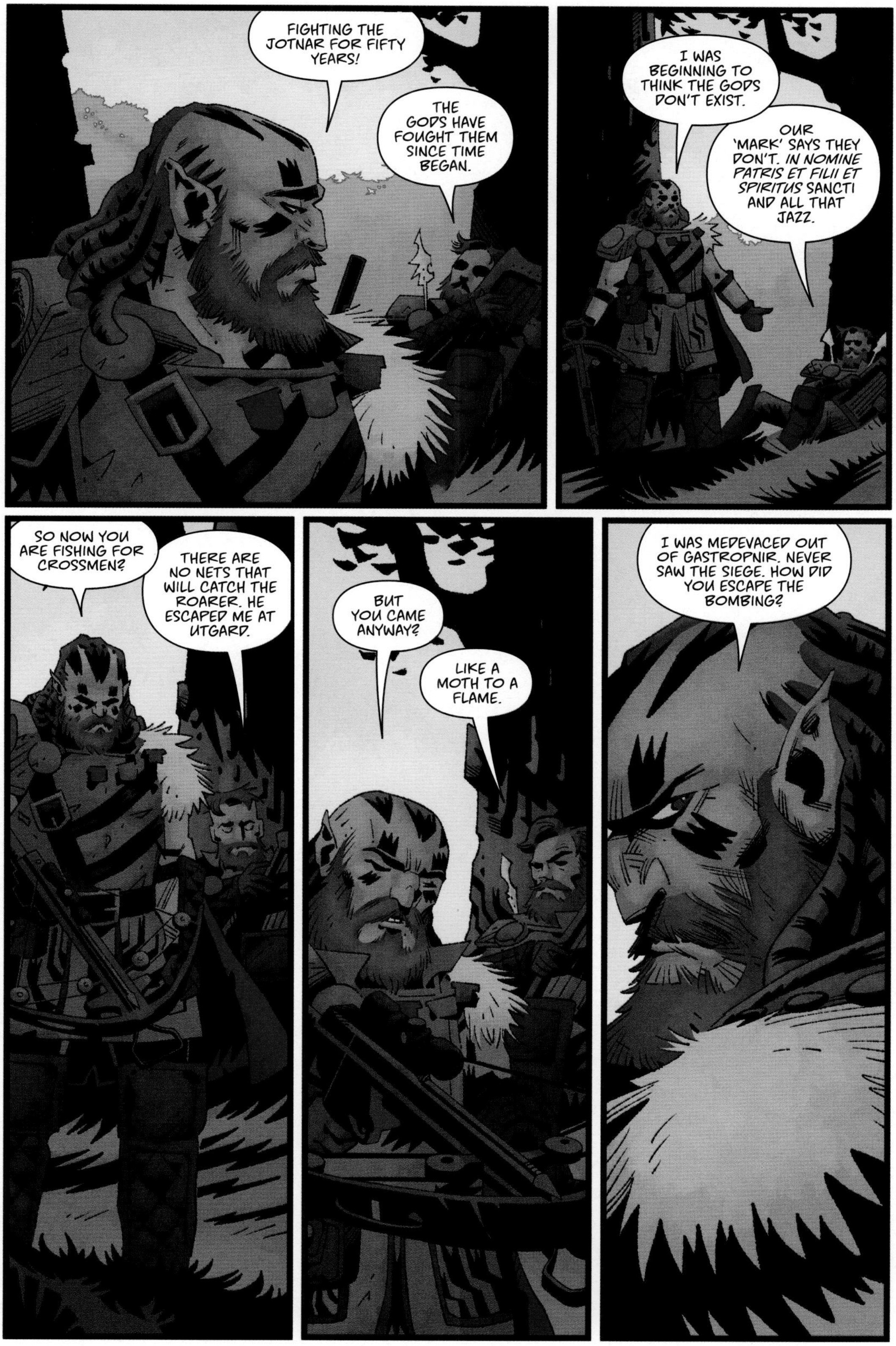
FIGHTING THE JOTNAR FOR FIFTY YEARS!
THE GODS HAVE FOUGHT THEM SINCE TIME BEGAN.
I WAS BEGINNING TO THINK THE GODS DON'T EXIST.
OUR 'MARK' SAYS THEY DON'T. *IN NOMINE PATRIS ET FILII ET SPIRITUS SANCTI* AND ALL THAT JAZZ.
SO NOW YOU ARE FISHING FOR CROSSMEN?
THERE ARE NO NETS THAT WILL CATCH THE ROARER. HE ESCAPED ME AT UTGARD.
BUT YOU CAME ANYWAY?
LIKE A MOTH TO A FLAME.
I WAS MEDEVACED OUT OF GASTROPNIR. NEVER SAW THE SIEGE. HOW DID YOU ESCAPE THE BOMBING?

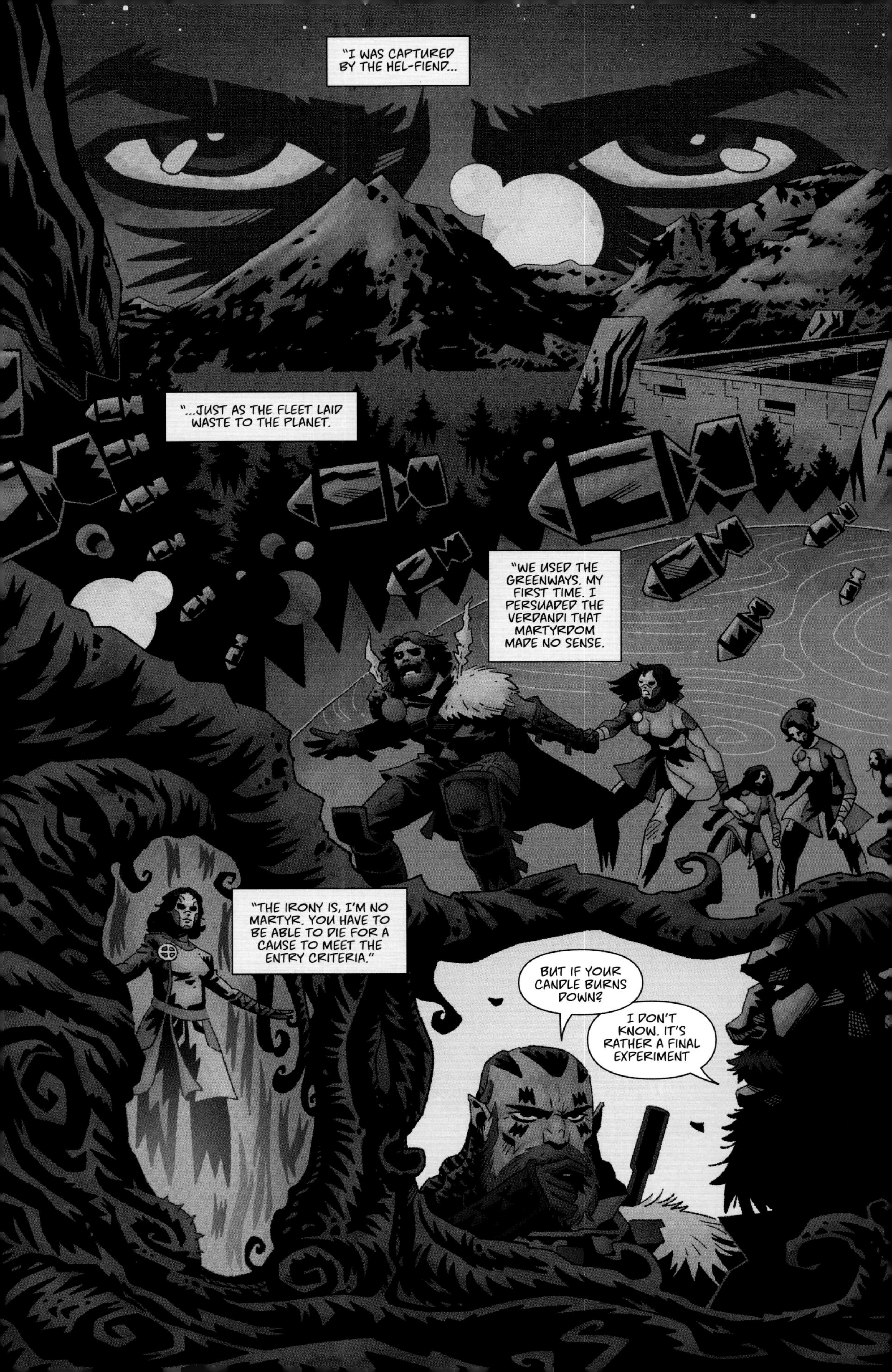
"I WAS CAPTURED BY THE HEL-FIEND...
"...JUST AS THE FLEET LAID WASTE TO THE PLANET.
"WE USED THE GREENWAYS. MY FIRST TIME. I PERSUADED THE VERDANDI THAT MARTYRDOM MADE NO SENSE.
"THE IRONY IS, I'M NO MARTYR. YOU HAVE TO BE ABLE TO DIE FOR A CAUSE TO MEET THE ENTRY CRITERIA."
BUT IF YOUR CANDLE BURNS DOWN?
I DON'T KNOW. IT'S RATHER A FINAL EXPERIMENT

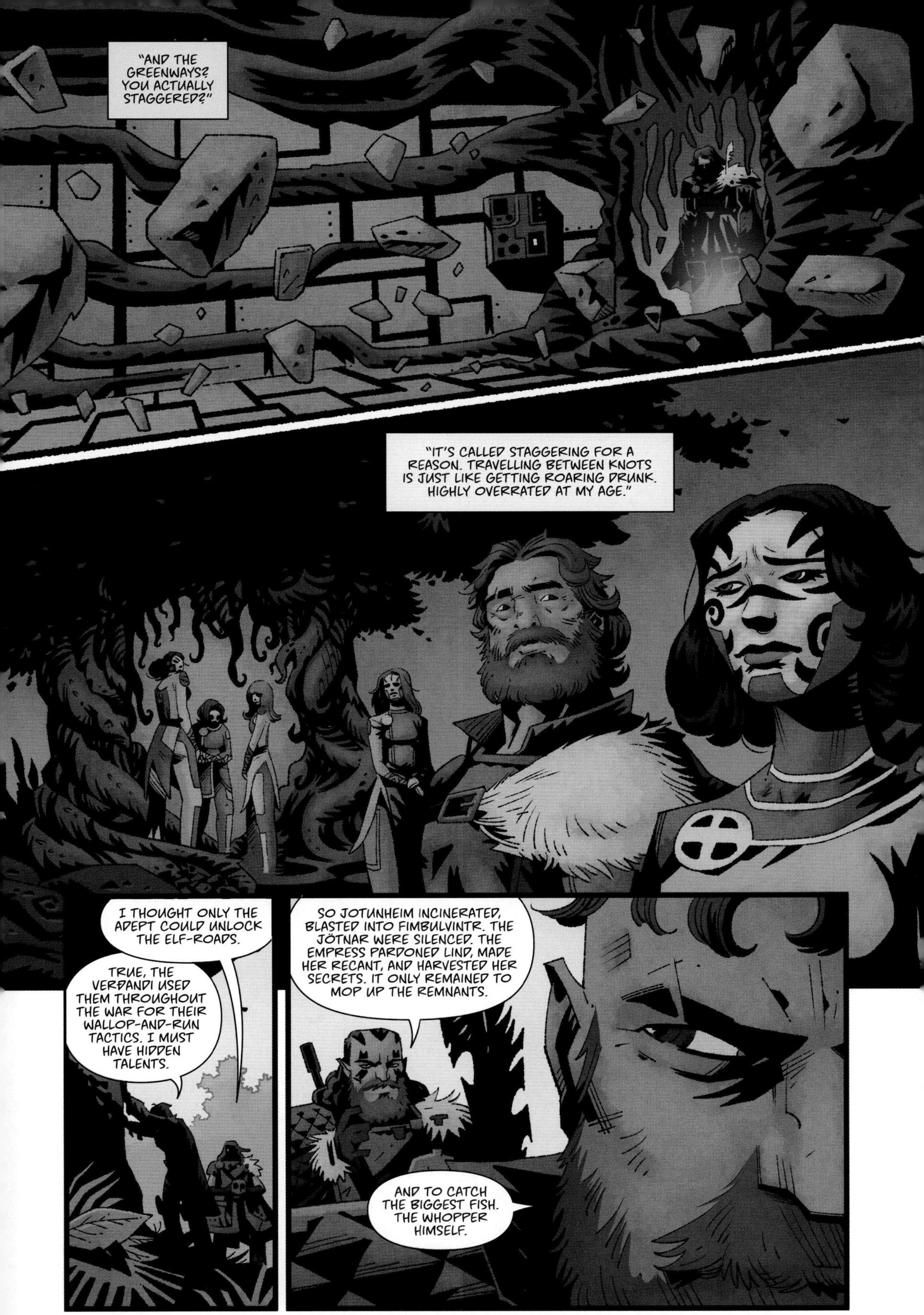
"AND THE GREENWAYS? YOU ACTUALLY STAGGERED?"
"IT'S CALLED STAGGERING FOR A REASON. TRAVELLING BETWEEN KNOTS IS JUST LIKE GETTING ROARING DRUNK. HIGHLY OVERRATED AT MY AGE."
I THOUGHT ONLY THE ADEPT COULD UNLOCK THE ELF-ROADS.
TRUE, THE VERDANDI USED THEM THROUGHOUT THE WAR FOR THEIR WALLOP-AND-RUN TACTICS. I MUST HAVE HIDDEN TALENTS.
SO JOTUNHEIM INCINERATED, BLASTED INTO FIMBULVINTR. THE JÖTNAR WERE SILENCED. THE EMPRESS PARDONED LIND, MADE HER RECANT, AND HARVESTED HER SECRETS. IT ONLY REMAINED TO MOP UP THE REMNANTS.
AND TO CATCH THE BIGGEST FISH. THE WHOPPER HIMSELF.

MAKE SURE HE STAYS DEAD.

WELL, YOUR HAMINGJA IS HOLDING. THE TARGET HAS BEEN SIGHTED. WHAT'LL YOU DO WHEN HE'S CAUGHT WITH HIS BEARD IN THE MAILBOX?

STAYS DEAD? ARE YOU RELATED?

WE WERE LIKE BRÓÐIR ONCE, BUT NO. THAT... ABOMINATION BRINGS NOTHING BUT BALE AND HATRED TO THE GODS.

YOU MAKE IT SOUND PERSONAL.

HONOUR MUST BE RESTORED, THE ROARER'S INSULTS AVENGED. IT IS MY RIGHT. IT IS MY DUTY.

REGARDLESS, I HAVE MY ORDERS. FROM THE EMPRESS. THE JÖTNAR MESSIAH COMES BACK ALIVE.

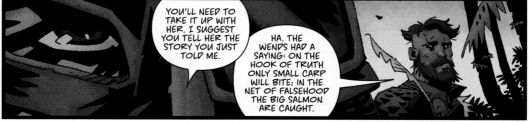

YOU'LL NEED TO TAKE IT UP WITH HER. I SUGGEST YOU TELL HER THE STORY YOU JUST TOLD ME.

HA. THE WENDS HAD A SAYING: ON THE HOOK OF TRUTH ONLY SMALL CARP WILL BITE; IN THE NET OF FALSEHOOD THE BIG SALMON ARE CAUGHT.

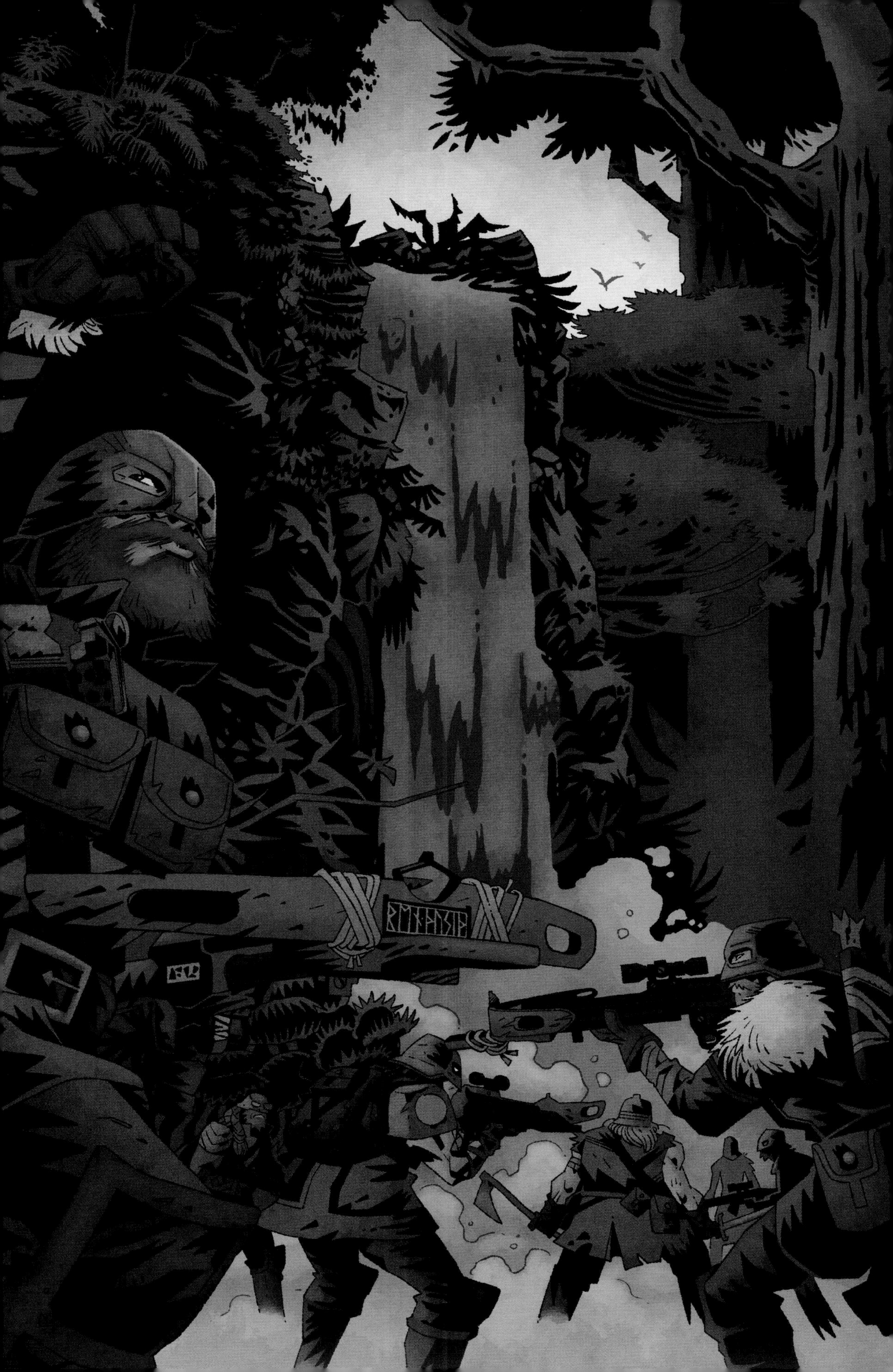

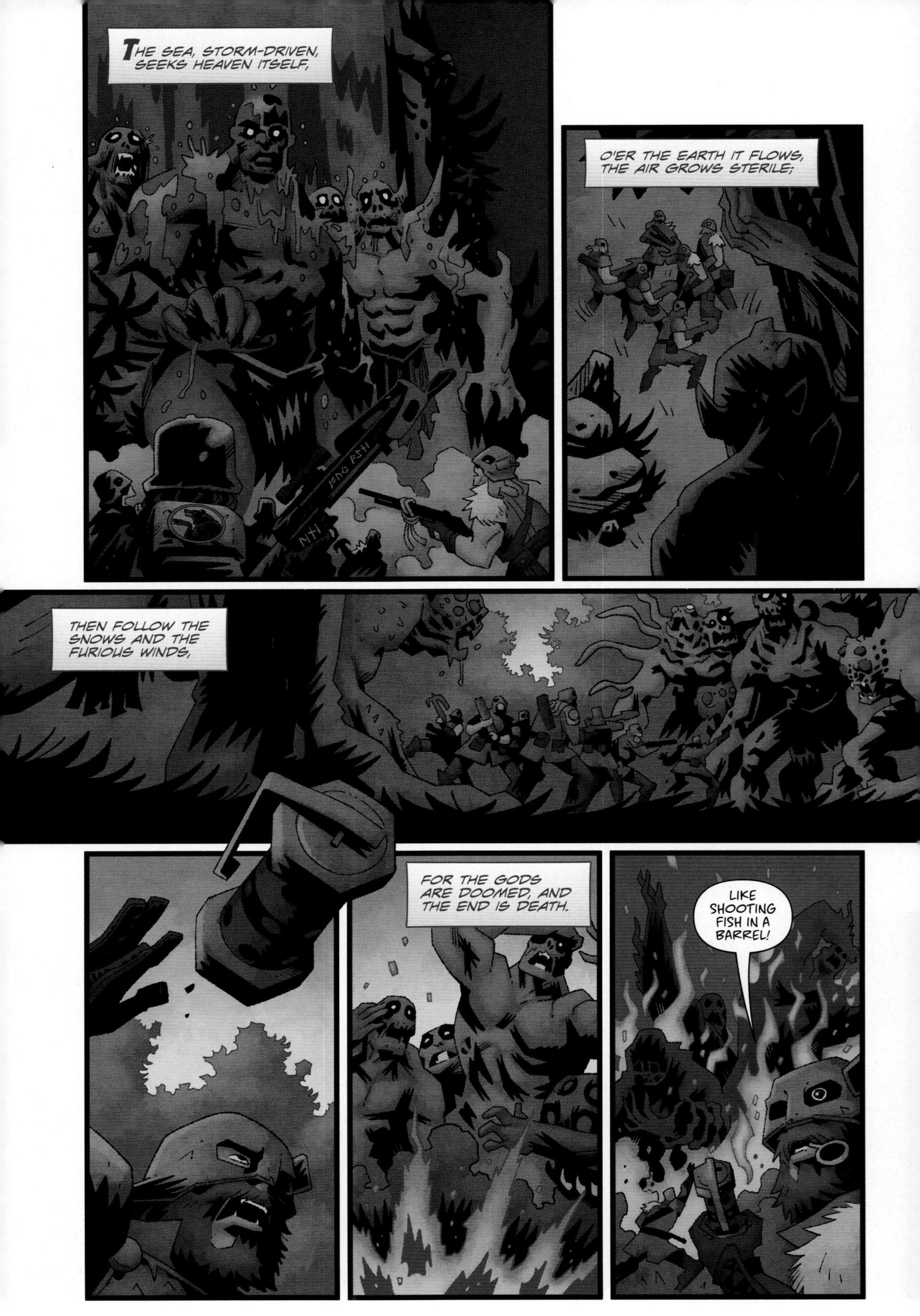
THE SEA, STORM-DRIVEN, SEEKS HEAVEN ITSELF,
O'ER THE EARTH IT FLOWS, THE AIR GROWS STERILE;
THEN FOLLOW THE SNOWS AND THE FURIOUS WINDS,
FOR THE GODS ARE DOOMED, AND THE END IS DEATH.
LIKE SHOOTING FISH IN A BARREL!

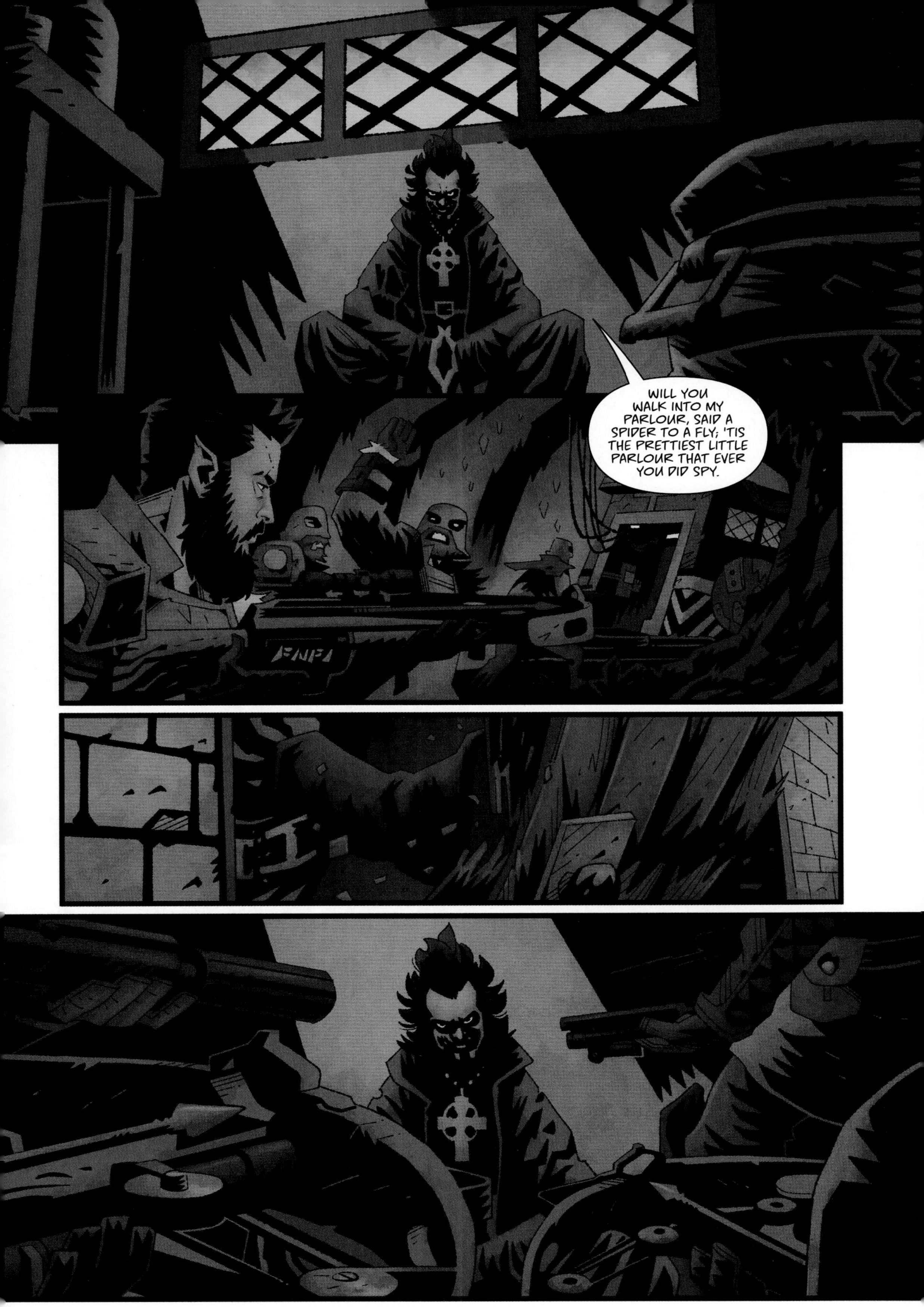
WILL YOU WALK INTO MY PARLOUR, SAID A SPIDER TO A FLY; 'TIS THE PRETTIEST LITTLE PARLOUR THAT EVER YOU DID SPY.
BNPD

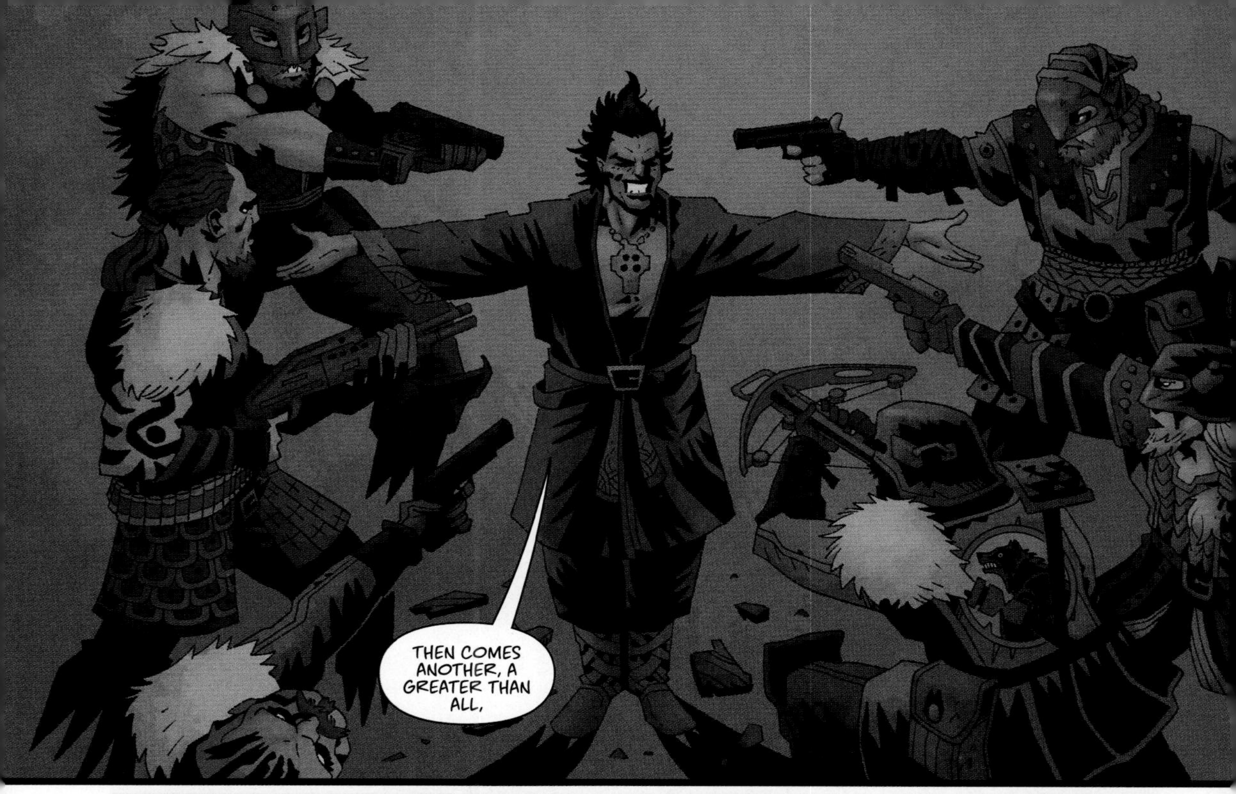
THEN COMES ANOTHER, A GREATER THAN ALL,

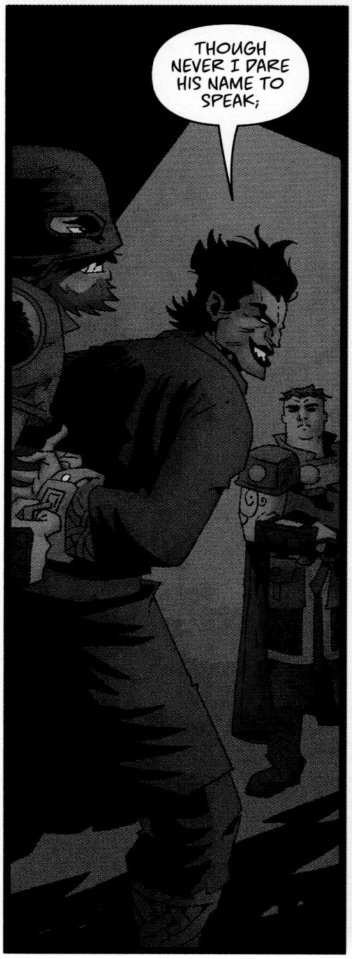
THOUGH NEVER I DARE HIS NAME TO SPEAK;

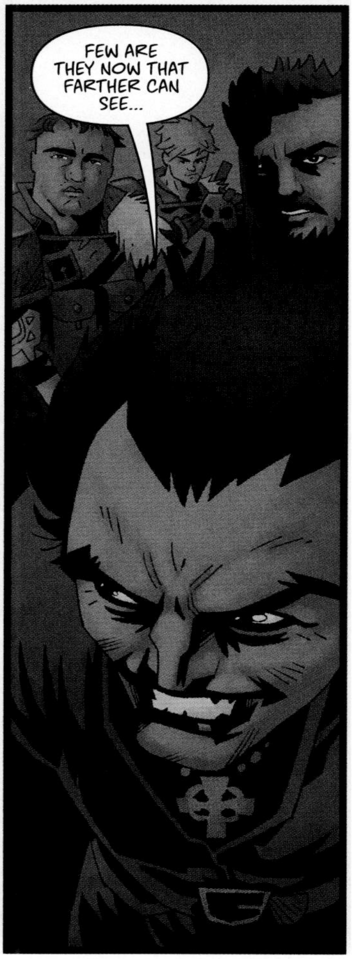
FEW ARE THEY NOW THAT FARTHER CAN SEE...

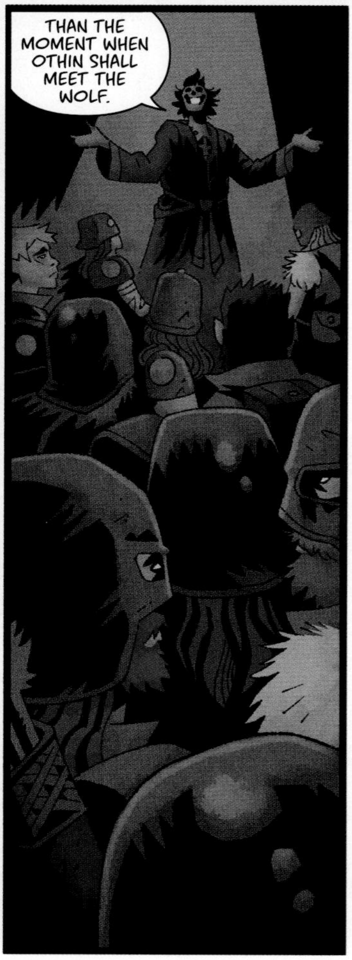
THAN THE MOMENT WHEN OTHIN SHALL MEET THE WOLF.

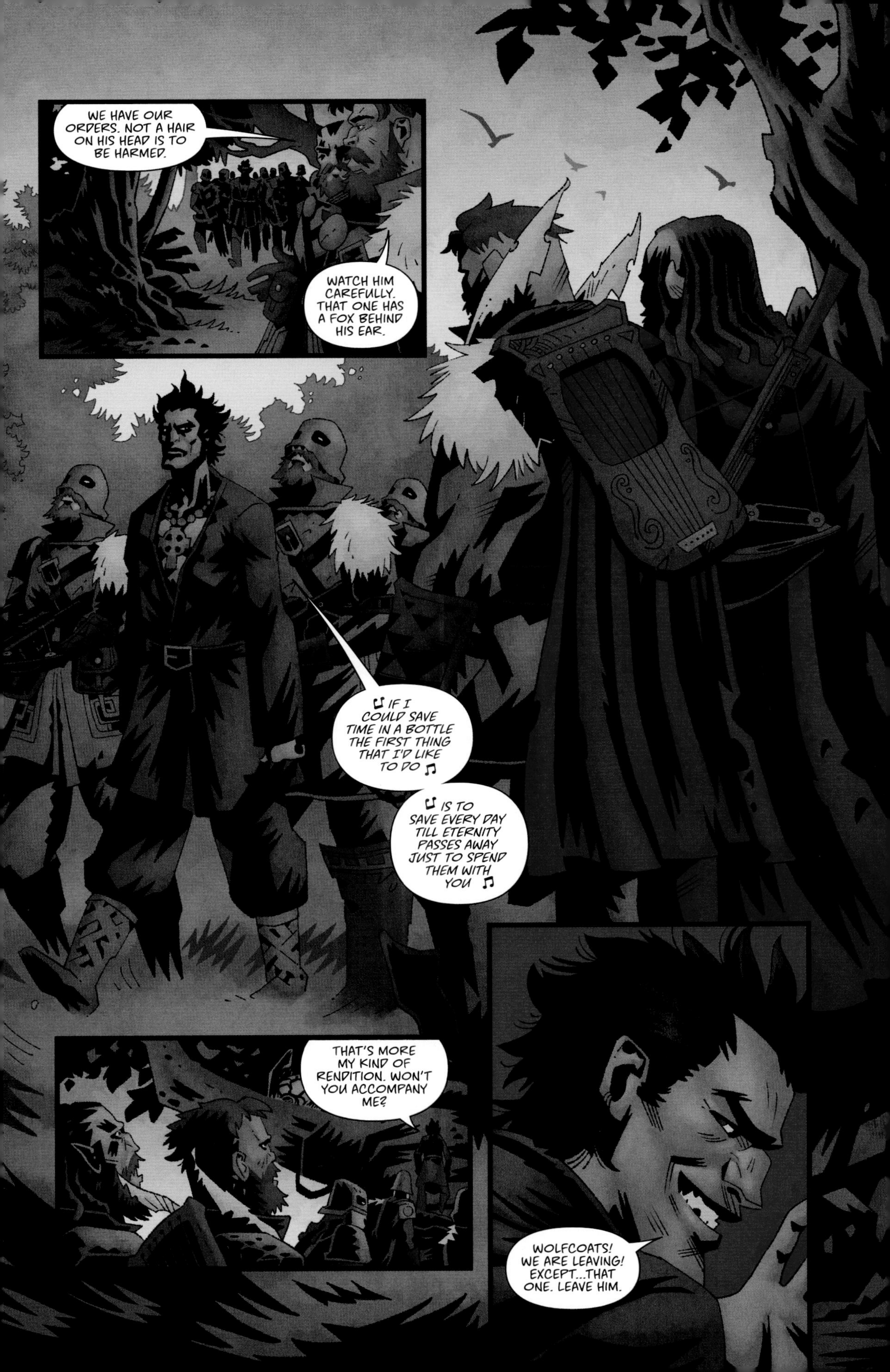
WE HAVE OUR ORDERS. NOT A HAIR ON HIS HEAD IS TO BE HARMED.
WATCH HIM CAREFULLY. THAT ONE HAS A FOX BEHIND HIS EAR.
♫ IF I COULD SAVE TIME IN A BOTTLE THE FIRST THING THAT I'D LIKE TO DO ♫
♫ IS TO SAVE EVERY DAY TILL ETERNITY PASSES AWAY JUST TO SPEND THEM WITH YOU ♫
THAT'S MORE MY KIND OF RENDITION. WON'T YOU ACCOMPANY ME?
WOLFCOATS! WE ARE LEAVING! EXCEPT...THAT ONE. LEAVE HIM.

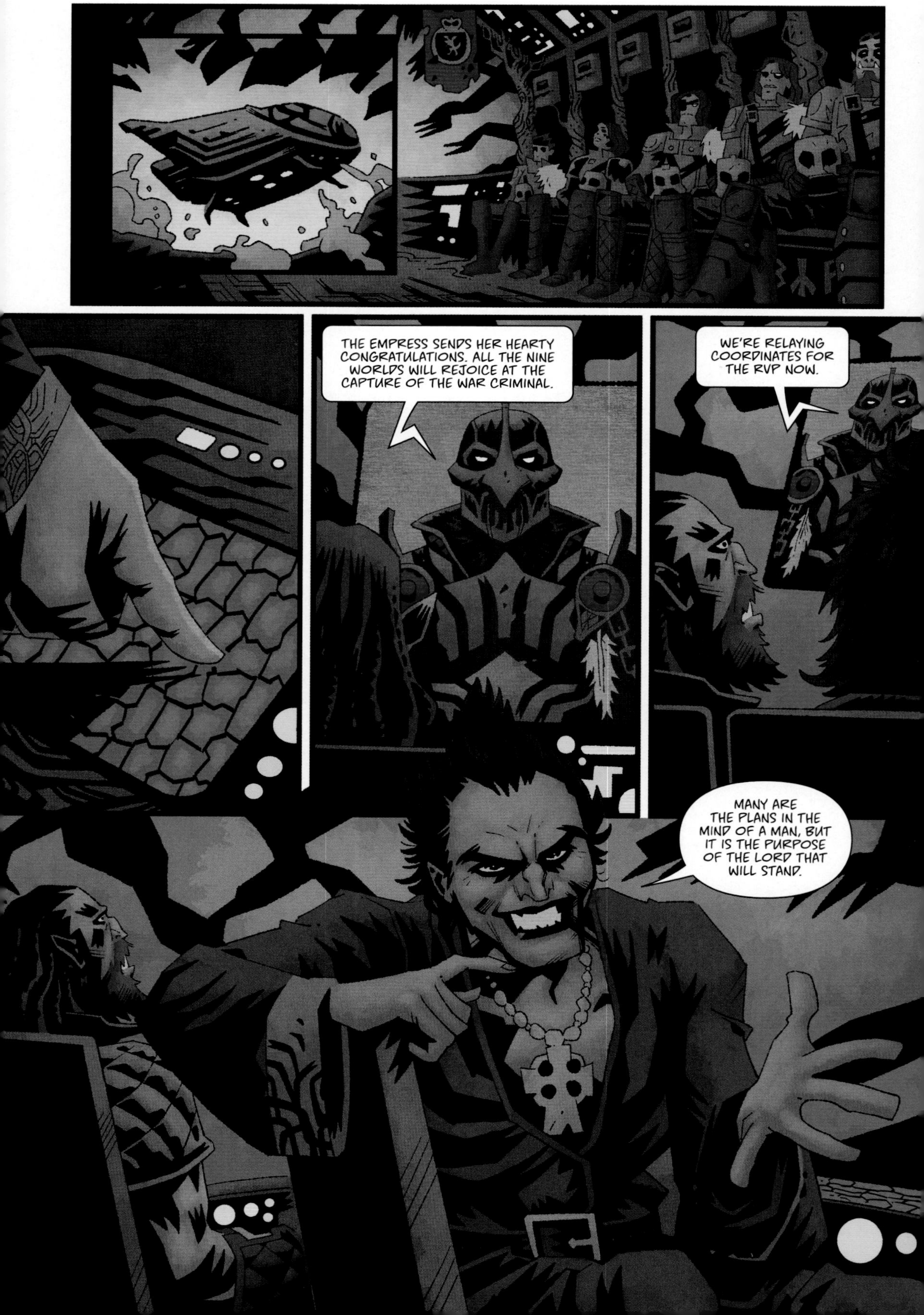
THE EMPRESS SENDS HER HEARTY CONGRATULATIONS. ALL THE NINE WORLDS WILL REJOICE AT THE CAPTURE OF THE WAR CRIMINAL.
WE'RE RELAYING COORDINATES FOR THE RVP NOW.
MANY ARE THE PLANS IN THE MIND OF A MAN, BUT IT IS THE PURPOSE OF THE LORD THAT WILL STAND.

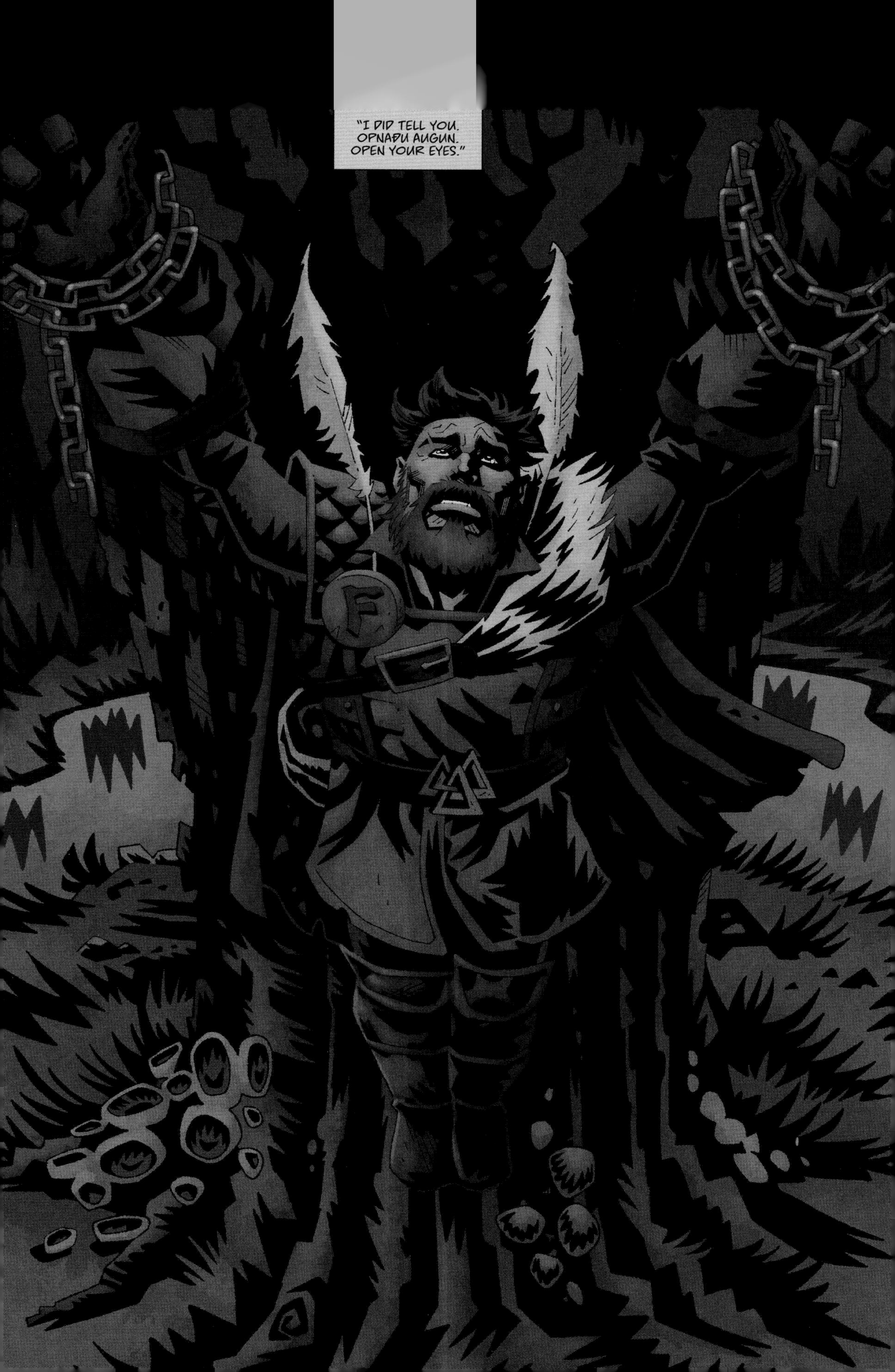
"I DID TELL YOU. OPNAÐU AUGUN. OPEN YOUR EYES."

"FAR VEL, MY ONLY FRIEND."

"MUCH HAVE I FARED, MUCH HAVE I FOUND, MUCH HAVE I GOT FROM THE GODS.

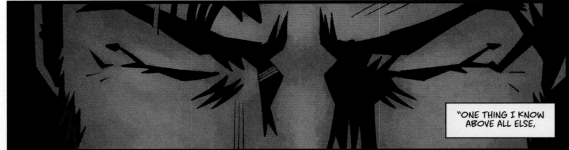

"ONE THING I KNOW ABOVE ALL ELSE,

"IT'S NOT OVER UNTIL THE FAT LADY SINGS..."

A GREAT TASK AWAITS YOU

YOU ARE TO **REVENGE** THE GRIEVOUS INJUSTICE THAT HAS BEEN DONE.
THE ROARER HAS **OVERTURNED** THE LAW OF RÍGR;
HE HAS **MOCKED** THE SACREDNESS OF THE IMPERIAL THRONE
IN A WAY **UNHEARD** OF IN WORLD HISTORY.

YOU KNOW FULL WELL THAT YOU ARE TO
***FIGHT** AGAINST A **CUNNING** AND **CRUEL** ENEMY.*
*WHEN YOU ENCOUNTER HIM, **KNOW THIS**:*
***NO QUARTER WILL BE GIVEN**.*
*THE FATHER OF MONSTERS IS **DEATH INCARNATE**.*

*SHOW THE OLD NORSE **VIRTUE**.*
*PRESENT YOURSELVES AS **GOD-FRIENDS** IN*
*THE CHEERFUL **ENDURANCE** OF SUFFERING.*
*MAY **HONOUR** AND **GLORY** FOLLOW YOUR*
***BANNER** AND **ARMS**.*

FAREWELL FELAGAR

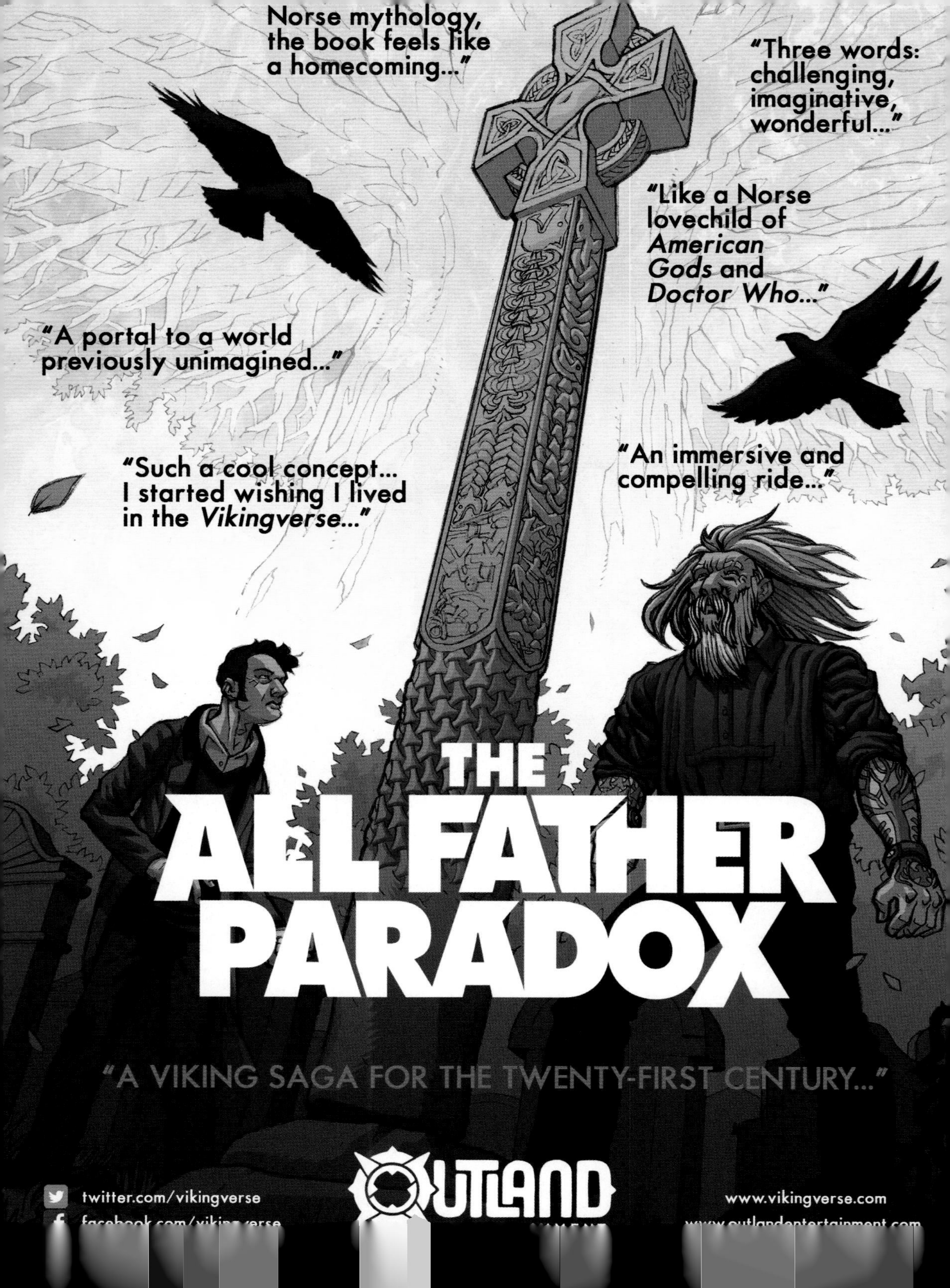

Norse mythology, the book feels like a homecoming..."
"Three words: challenging, imaginative, wonderful..."
"Like a Norse lovechild of *American Gods* and *Doctor Who*..."
"A portal to a world previously unimagined..."
"Such a cool concept... I started wishing I lived in the *Vikingverse*..."
"An immersive and compelling ride..."
THE ALL FATHER PARADOX
"A VIKING SAGA FOR THE TWENTY-FIRST CENTURY..."
OUTLAND
twitter.com/vikingverse
www.vikingverse.com

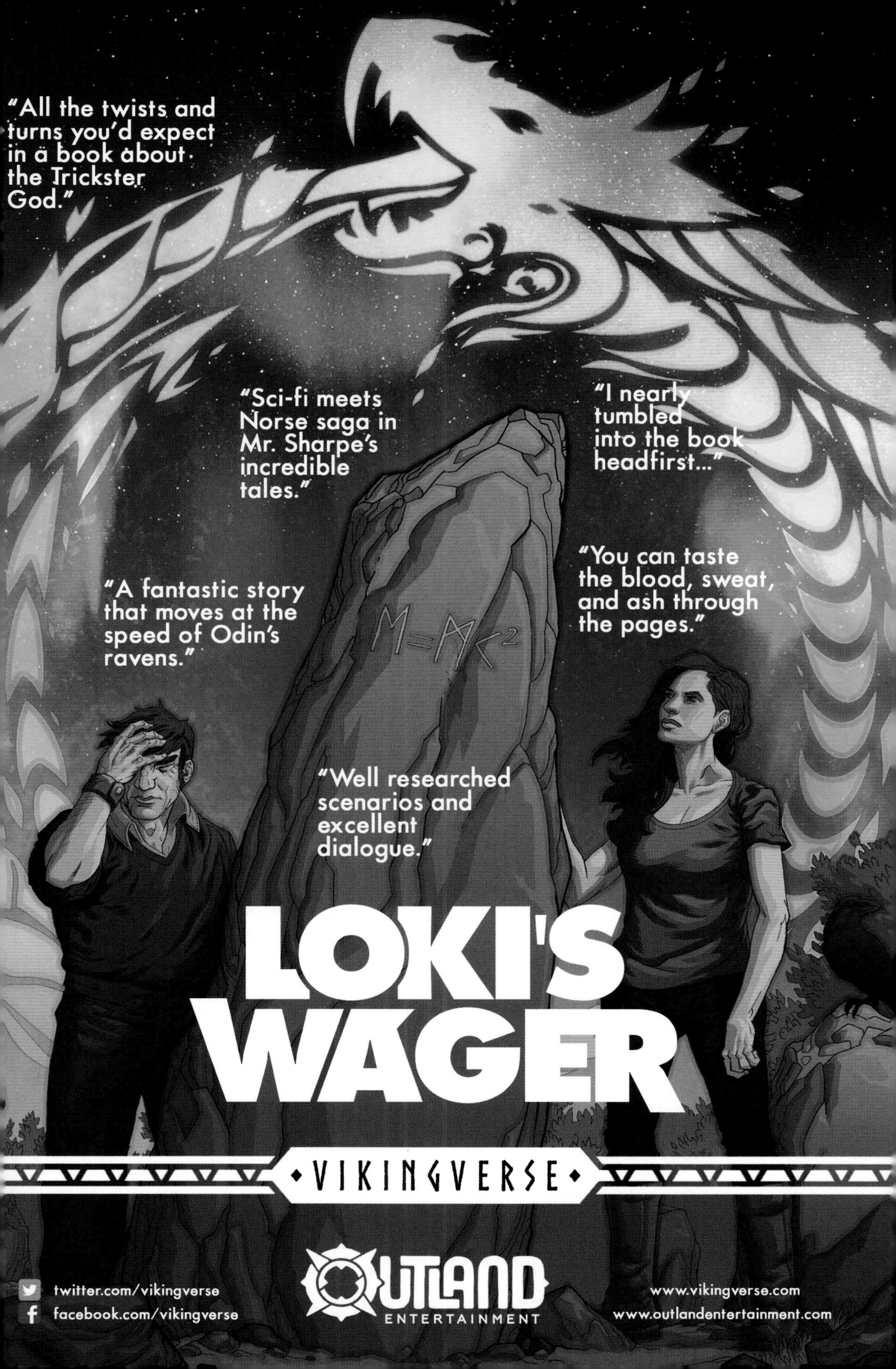
"All the twists and turns you'd expect in a book about the Trickster God."
"Sci-fi meets Norse saga in Mr. Sharpe's incredible tales."
"I nearly tumbled into the book headfirst..."
"You can taste the blood, sweat, and ash through the pages."
"A fantastic story that moves at the speed of Odin's ravens."
"Well researched scenarios and excellent dialogue."
LOKI'S WAGER
VIKINGVERSE
OUTLAND ENTERTAINMENT
twitter.com/vikingverse
facebook.com/vikingverse
www.vikingverse.com
www.outlandentertainment.com

VIKINGVERSE
PRESENTS

"Loved this book! It will have you speaking like the silver tongued Loki in no time."

"A delightful, funny, and outrageously clever guide"

OLD NORSE FOR MODERN TIMES

IAN STUART SHARPE
DR. ARNGRÍMUR VÍDALÍN
JOSH GILLINGHAM

"If *Latin for All Occasions* was right up your toga, you'll appreciate its spiritual successor, *Old Norse for Modern Times*"

"I keep finding it in other parts of the house instead of next to my computer where I've left it."

twitter.com/vikingverse
facebook.com/vikingverse

OUTLAND
ENTERTAINMENT

www.vikingverse.com
www.outlandentertainment.com

BRINGS STORIES TO LIFE